PULPIT, PRESS, AND POLITICS

Methodists and the Market for Books in Upper Canada

SCOTT MCLAREN

Pulpit, Press, and Politics

Methodists and the Market for Books in Upper Canada

UNIVERSITY OF TORONTO PRESS
Toronto Buffalo London

Toronto Buffalo London
utorontopress.com

ISBN 978-1-4426-4923-1

Studies in Book and Print Culture

Library and Archives Canada Cataloguing in Publication

Title: Pulpit, press, and politics : Methodists and the market for books in Upper Canada / Scott McLaren.
Names: McLaren, Scott, 1970– author.
Series: Studies in book and print culture.
Description: Series statement: Studies in book and print culture | Includes bibliographical references and index.
Identifiers: Canadiana 20190094036 | ISBN 9781442649231 (hardcover)
Subjects: LCSH: Methodist Book Concern. | LCSH: Books and reading – Religious aspects – Christianity. | LCSH: Methodist Church – Publishing. | LCSH: Methodist Church – Canada. | LCSH: Publishers and publishing – Canada – History. | LCSH: Books and reading – Canada – History. | LCSH: Books and reading – Canada – Sociological aspects.
Classification: LCC BX8385.M4 M35 2019 | DDC 070.509768/55—dc23

This book has been published with the assistance of the York University Libraries' Research & Awards Committee.

University of Toronto Press acknowledges the financial assistance to its publishing program of the Canada Council for the Arts and the Ontario Arts Council, an agency of the Government of Ontario.

Canada Council for the Arts
Conseil des Arts du Canada

Funded by the Government of Canada
Financé par le gouvernement du Canada

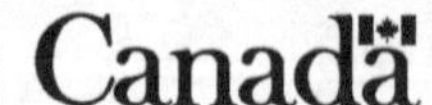

For Maura Matesic

Contents

Acknowledgments

One of the first things book historians attempt to teach their students is that the romantic picture we hold in our minds of the solitary author toiling away in towering isolation – a sort of literary Byronic hero – is a myth. Books are never the effort of one person alone. And that is certainly true in the present instance. I am grateful to all those who have urged me along this path in countless large and small ways over the past several years. Among my friends and colleagues at York University, the University of Toronto, and the Canadian Society of Church History, I wish to thank especially Janet Friskney, Matthew Kaufman, Cynthia Archer, Joy Kirchner, Bernie Lightman, Von Totanes, Greta Golick, Jeannine DeLombard, Jamie Robertson, Stuart Barnard, Robynne Healey, Mark McGowan, Stuart Macdonald, Lucille Marr, Bruce Douville, Patti Kmeic, and Denis McKim. Todd Webb deserves a very special mention for the myriad hours we spent bantering about Wesleyans, Methodists, and all varieties of religion in nineteenth-century Canada. I am also inexpressibly thankful to Leslie Howsam and Patricia Fleming for the innumerable ways that they have supported my scholarship over the past decade or more. Their remarkable graciousness has made them something more than mere mentors. They are each models of what every scholar should be.

I am grateful for the support I have received from a variety of organizations and committees over the years. Among them I would like to thank the Research and Awards Committee at York University Libraries for providing both time and funding when they were most needed. I am also very thankful to the American Antiquarian Society and the family of Stephen Botein for allowing me to spend an uninterrupted month poring over their wonderful collections relating to early Upper Canada. Archivists at both the United Methodist Archives and History Centre at Drew University and the United Church Archives of Canada were also unfailing in their support. I am especially grateful in this respect to Julia Holland and Alex Thomson.

This book would not be what it is without the sure and steady support of my editor at the University of Toronto Press, Mark Thompson. Mark guided me through every stage of the process with an expert hand. I also wish to acknowledge the extraordinarily helpful comments made by my anonymous peer reviewers and the members of the University of Toronto Press's Manuscript Review Committee. Their generous insights were invaluable.

Finally, and most importantly, I wish to thank my wife and partner in life, Maura Matesic. She has sustained and nurtured this book every step of the way. It simply would not have been written without her.

PULPIT, PRESS, AND POLITICS

Methodists and the Market for Books in Upper Canada

Introduction

"Reading the Most Useful Books"

John Wesley never tired of urging his followers to "Read the most useful Books and that regularly and constantly." Wesley, who established Methodism as a renewal movement in the Church of England in the middle decades of the eighteenth century, was much more than a voracious reader himself. He was also one of England's most successful booksellers. At a time before subscription, public, and even Sunday school libraries, Wesley supplied his followers with affordable access to cheap books by authoring, editing, and publishing relentlessly throughout the course of his long lifetime. In the process, he earned a degree of prominence and commercial success that few, perhaps only Samuel Johnson and Daniel Defoe, could rival. By the time Wesley died, in 1791, his bookselling activities alone were bringing in as much as £10,000 a year – a sum equivalent to the enormous annual income enjoyed by Jane Austen's dashing young worthy Mr Darcy in *Pride and Prejudice*.[1]

Pulpit, Press, and Politics is about books and ownership: not merely how people come to acquire books as possessions – although it is certainly about that – but also, and perhaps more importantly, how books make claims on the identities of those who own them. Of course, the words books contain have the potential to affect the way readers perceive the world and their place in it. Indeed, books would hardly be worth reading otherwise. But, like other commodities, books can also function as cultural status objects in their own right. As such, the acquisition of a book can be understood to be something more than a straightforward commercial transaction. Purchasing a book can also serve as a profound symbolic act with the power to inform the identity of the new owner before it is even opened. *Pulpit, Press, and Politics* seeks to understand how this kind of transformation – between the book as commodity and the book as cultural status object – played out in a particular historical and transnational context among Methodists in North America. More specifically, it will consider how the cultural production of denominational books and periodicals contributed to the growth and expansion of the Methodist Book Concern and its unrivalled market in the United States and Upper Canada; how the religious identities of Methodist readers on both sides of the border separating the United States from British North America were influenced and shaped by that market; and ultimately, how that market's extraordinary durability – and flexibility – contributed to the emergence of a distinct form of Canadian Methodism and Canadian Methodist publishing that was neither American nor British in its cultural outlook.

I

Religion is a particularly fertile context in which to study the book. The relationship between religion and the recorded word – carved, written, printed, or rendered digitally – is both profound and ancient. Indeed, for thousands of years, it was universally believed that religion had given birth to the book. In Wesley's own time, Daniel Defoe argued that the origin of all written culture could be traced to the encounter between Moses and God on Mount Sinai. "But God," wrote Defoe, "from Heaven giving Laws to Men, gave not an oral, but a written Law, and it was from him, that Letters were cloathed [*sic*] with Sounds ... It was his own doing, and from him alone it deriv'd. Here I place the true Original of Writing, and indeed of all Literature." Defoe was hardly alone in his view. For almost as long as there has been writing, there have been myths to describe its divine beginnings. In Mesopotamia, the Sumerians believed the god Enlil, who wove the universe into being, was also the originator of writing. The Egyptians attributed the origin of writing to the god Thoth, who was responsible for holding all things in existence. Similarly, early Greeks held that Hermes, the messenger of the gods, had fashioned their alphabet.[2]

What makes Methodism so well suited to a study of this kind is not merely that the practices historians of the book are so keen to explore are typically exaggerated in religious contexts – as Harold Bloom rightly notes, religious readers of the Bible interrogate Scripture with a deep sense of urgency that the mere word "reading" falls far short of capturing – but also the historical reality that Methodists organized their religious lives around the written word in ways that were intensive even by the standards of other religious groups and evangelical denominations. Indeed, from the very start, John Wesley's Methodism was inextricably bound up with books. When Wesley recognized a need to define and defend his followers against the calumnies hurled against them by detractors – that they were closet papists, that they were seditious Jacobites, that they were witches in league with the Devil – he used the press to explain how Methodism had emerged as an organic movement without a political or ecclesiastical agenda. He also assigned Methodism not one but three separate beginnings.[3]

Wesley located the first "rise" of Methodism, to borrow his own term, at Oxford, where he and some like-minded friends, including his brother Charles, decided to practise a strict and decidedly ascetic form of Christianity while distributing to the poor bibles, hymnbooks, and other books, including the seventeenth-century anonymous classic, *The Whole Duty of Man*. The second "rise" of Methodism occurred in England's new colony of Georgia, or more precisely, in the middle of a ferocious transatlantic storm that scared a young John Wesley out of his wits during the crossing. As Wesley listened below decks to the heavens pour forth their wrath and the mast of the ship shatter apart under the lashing of a relentless wind, he was stunned to witness the impossible calm that prevailed among the ship's Moravian Christians as they quietly passed the time singing hymns together. Chastened and humbled by the experience, Wesley translated some of these same hymns from German and had them published at Charleston in what came to be recognized as one of the first hymnbooks printed in North America. Later, partly in response to having his romantic attentions disastrously spurned by a young woman in the colony, Wesley returned to London where he once again had a profound spiritual experience that was rooted in religious book culture. This Wesley framed as the third "rise" of Methodism, when he famously felt his "heart strangely warmed" while listening to one of Martin Luther's commentaries on Romans as it was read aloud. That remarkable experience gave birth to what Wesley called "experimental religion" – religion that had as much to do with the heart as it did with the head. But, of course, Wesley never forgot that the hearts of his followers could never be rightly ordered without clear and well-informed heads. And that meant for him that they must always and everywhere have ready and inexpensive access to the right books.[4]

When Wesley published his dictionary of "hard words" in 1753, he described a Methodist simply as "one that lives according to the method laid down in the bible [*sic*]." The Bible, though undoubtedly the first among all books for Wesley, was only the beginning. When Wesley formed his first congregations, and later began establishing preaching houses, he made sure that the bookshelves found at the back of each of his chapels groaned under the weight of good books that he not only wrote himself, but also edited, abridged, and in some cases outright plagiarized. And if the latter made him guilty of breaking the laws of man – or or at least the Statute of Anne, the first copyright law passed by Parliament, in 1710 – he no doubt consoled himself with the knowledge that he remained obedient to a Higher Lawgiver. After all, one could hardly be a Christian without books: "It cannot be that the people should grow in grace," Wesley insisted, "unless they give themselves to reading." His preachers he instructed to "recommend reading to all the people, frequently and earnestly," while urging them to "take care that every Society is supplied with Books." As for the preachers themselves, they were required to spend at least five hours a day in study. For those who found that disagreeable, Wesley was adamant: "Contract a taste for it by use, or return to your trade."[5]

It would be easy for statements like these to give the wrong impression. Apart from John Wesley himself and a small handful of others, Methodism was hardly regarded as a movement of intellectuals. On the contrary, because early Methodism proved particularly appealing to tradespeople and other members of the working class, and because its preachers rarely possessed much in the way of formal education, Methodists routinely found themselves accused of being "ignorant enthusiasts" who preached a faith they did not understand. Wesley spent a good part of his life attempting to blunt such criticisms by selling inexpensive books written in plain language to Methodists in London, across the British countryside, and anywhere else his itinerant preachers ventured. In America, members of the Methodist Episcopal Church carried on in that same spirit when they became the first religious body in the United States to establish their own denominational publishing house in 1789. By the middle of the nineteenth century, Methodism had grown to become America's leading religious denomination and its denominational publisher, the Methodist Book Concern, one of the largest publishing houses in the world.[6]

This shared triumph of church and publisher was no accident. From the beginning, Methodist preachers in North America worked hard to persuade their congregations that the success of the one depended on and drove the progress of the other. More than just a business, the Methodist Book Concern was, in the words of one layman, "the focus where all the scattered energies of the Church were collected, and the radiating point from which a thousand salutary influences proceeded to cheer and bless our widespread congregations."[7] Later, in the 1790s, when American preachers crossed the US border into Upper Canada, they brought with them more than a contagious religious faith. They also brought saddlebags full of books. In the space of just a few short years, these itinerants blazed new preaching circuits across the colonial wilderness to the furthest reaches of white settlement; organized powerful revivals that led to dizzying rates of Methodist expansion; and opened a new transnational market for the Methodist Book Concern that supplied denominational readers, particularly those outside Upper Canada's few urban areas, with unprecedented access to improving books and tracts.

II

The first contribution that this book hopes to make is to the literature of book history. This study explores how the Methodist Book Concern made claims on the identities of its customers on both sides of the border in ways that were as successful as they were pioneering for the time. The Methodist Book Concern did not approach the market in the same way that other publishers did. Unlike commercial publishers, making money was not its sole or even primary aim. And yet, the Concern almost never gave away its wares at no cost as many other religious and non-denominational publishers did. The Methodist Book Concern's methods of distribution were also decidedly circumscribed by the fact that the vast majority of its sales took place in largely denominational settings through the mediation of preachers rather than among a wider reading public through third-party booksellers. As quixotic as this may have seemed, it worked. At a time when all along the Eastern Seaboard other publishers were spiralling down into bankruptcy, the Methodist Book Concern was growing at an unparalleled rate.[8]

Historians have advanced a number of arguments to account for the success that religious publishers, including the Methodist Book Concern, achieved in America's early national period. Nathan Hatch contends that at the heart of American evangelicalism was a powerful "democratic urge to multiply authors and readers" that transformed the pulpit and the press into mutually reinforcing means for driving the evangelical project. Methodists set themselves at the forefront of what Hatch calls a "democratic religious press" when they aggressively deployed preachers as commissioned booksellers across Methodism's far-flung preaching circuits. Hatch's narrative has been extremely influential, but it has not gone unchallenged. David Paul Nord, in particular, has suggested that Hatch's "linking of publishing and religion to the market revolutions ... does not tell the whole story about either." Nord argues, instead, that many evangelicals viewed the market as a "wily and dangerous foe" and for that reason sought ways to subvert it by giving books away "regardless of ability or even desire to pay."[9]

These approaches undoubtedly go a long way to account for the success of some religious publishers – particularly large non-denominational publishers such as the American Tract Society and the American Sunday School Union. But the Methodist Book Concern's unmatched success in the market is more complicated than either Hatch's democratic emphasis or Nord's anti-capitalist narrative implies. Although the Concern certainly had a religious mission that transcended mere commercial ends, American Methodists showed almost no interest either in approaching their market on nationalist terms or in giving books away for free. In that way, the Methodist Book Concern bore a striking similarity to the British and Foreign Bible Society, which also maintained a strong aversion to giving away bibles at no cost. Unlike the British and Foreign Bible Society, however, the Methodist Book Concern was unmistakably denominational in its mission and outlook. Its market was meant to be coterminous not with the boundaries of Christianity or even the United States, but with those of the Methodist Episcopal Church. That basic premise, together with the pressure John Wesley exerted after the Revolutionary War on his overseas followers to account for book proceeds at an institutional level, yielded an approach to the market that was to pay dividends for many decades to come.[10]

Shortly after its establishment, and in the face of growing competition from other publishers and printers, the Concern's book agents began to use titles pages, prefaces, catalogues, advertisements, and the pages of denominational periodicals to link the purchase of its books with loyalty to the Methodist Episcopal Church as a whole. The book agents did this by loudly and consistently proclaiming that all profits from the sale of the Concern's wares would be directed wholly back into Methodism's wider charitable activities. Those who chose to purchase books produced on rival presses were thus made guilty of more than failing to support the denominational publisher. They were also condemned for robbing the Church itself. The persistent use of this rhetoric forged an increasingly robust relationship between the choices readers made in the market and their religious identities as Methodists. Those who found themselves at the helm of the denominational publisher as the years passed were under no illusion on this point: protecting the Methodist Book Concern's interests was paramount not just because Methodists needed books to read, but also because profits earned from selling books were essential for supplementing the salaries of preachers and underwriting the whole of the Church's wider economy.[11]

In Upper Canada, things were decidedly more problematic. While in the United States the relationship between a burgeoning denominational print culture and Methodism's economic prospects proved to be an easy one, in British North America too great an emphasis on linkages between publisher and church had the potential to subvert the Methodist interests. Much of this had to do with the War of 1812 and the rising anti-American sentiment that followed that conflict north of the border. Because Methodism had spread to Upper Canada from the United States and had remained under the oversight of American Methodist bishops even after the war, the denomination began to be viewed with growing suspicion by outsiders. Everyone from Lieutenant Governor Francis Gore and Commander Isaac Brock to rank-and-file Orangemen condemned Methodists "as disloyal because of their American origin." John Strachan, an Anglican clergyman who would eventually become Methodism's chief critic in Upper Canada, observed simply that the denomination's "close connections with American Conferences" caused it to be "tainted by religious dissent and republicanism."[12]

Those who actually read the Methodist Book Concern's books and periodicals knew that the problem was even thornier. It wasn't just the contents of the books that had the potential to complicate the religious and political loyalties of readers. It was the market itself. Because Canadian Methodists, like Methodists across North America, were taught to interpret their participation in the Concern's market as an act of denominational solidarity, every purchase they made inevitably affirmed their membership in what was ultimately a foreign church. Yet, because these books were so inexpensive, so readily available, and so important for financially sustaining Methodism's corps of preachers and other charitable undertakings, Canadians could not easily sever the Concern's access to its market in British North America without incurring major financial losses in the process. As a result, the Methodist Book Concern's market strategies for framing books as religious status objects came under far more pressure in Upper Canada than they ever did in the United States. It is that fact that makes the Canadian context a particularly revealing setting in which to examine how aspects of a book's cultural production could be reinterpreted – and even subverted – by booksellers and readers loath to forego the material and economic benefits ongoing participation in that market would otherwise continue to yield.

III

The second contribution that this book hopes to make relates to three specific questions in Canadian religious historiography that have proven resistant to the analyses of previous scholars who have tended to focus their narratives on polity rather than print culture. First, why did Canadian Methodists adamantly refuse to declare themselves unilaterally independent of the Methodist Episcopal Church when the latter declined to grant them independence until almost an entire generation after the War of 1812? Second, after years of opposition to their advances, what prompted Canadian Methodists abruptly to change course, in 1833, and propose an ecclesiastical union with British Wesleyans? Third, why did British Wesleyan missionaries, despite their superior social status and their place at the head of Methodism's governance structures, fail to exercise a more enduring cultural influence on Canadian Methodism after the ecclesiastical unions of 1833 and 1847? An answer to all three questions can be found in the way the Methodist Book Concern's market continued to operate – and how its wares were variously interpreted as both denominational status objects and straightforward commodities – throughout the first half of the nineteenth century.

By the time the War of 1812 had run its course, Methodism in Upper Canada was undeniably on its knees. Under the direction of only a tiny handful of American preachers while the conflict lasted, the flock became all but permanently scattered. When the preachers finally got around to counting heads, those who remained discovered that the war had reduced their numbers by half. An unmistakable shift in the colony's political complexion was also taking place. Many people who had suffered the loss of family, the destruction of property, or simply been forced to live under the constant threat of invasion had come to resent the Americans. As if that were not enough, British Wesleyans took the opportunity of Methodism's wartime decline to answer a call from Montreal to establish rival altars across both Upper and Lower Canada in an effort to displace their American cousins from British North America altogether.

Why the Methodists in Upper Canada refused to initiate unilateral secession under these difficult circumstances is a question that has been passed over in silence by recent scholars. Those who have written about the development of Canadian Methodism after the War of 1812 have instead tended to argue that, whatever the formal ecclesiastical arrangements may have been, American Methodist influence in British North America entered a period of slow and steady decline as a growing number of Canadian-born preachers joined the ministry. And yet, the political advantages that Canadian Methodists would have reaped by making a dramatic and clean break with the Methodist Episcopal Church in the United States would have been far more immediate and consequential. Not only would that have put a complete stop to exasperating and persistent claims on the part of detractors that the province's Methodists were guilty of perfidy for remaining part of an American church, but by acting on their own initiative, they also would have earned the right to proclaim from the rooftops their courage for heroically throwing off the yoke of a republican episcopacy. That did not happen. Instead, the Canadians continued to bide their time and beg the General Conference of the Methodist Episcopal Church at every opportunity to recognize the legitimacy of their request for independence. This tenacity suggests that the bonds uniting Canadian and American Methodists remained almost as strong after the War of 1812 as they had been before it – bonds that the postwar revival of the Methodist Book Concern's market in Upper Canada played no small part in reinforcing.[13]

Methodism in North America was more than a single polity, more than a set of common beliefs, and more than a corps of preachers shared across a geopolitical border. Methodism in North America was also a functioning economy, an economy that depended for a huge proportion of its revenues on the ongoing workings of the Methodist Book Concern's sprawling market for books and periodicals. As Methodism grew, and with it the Concern, those revenues became steadily larger and increasingly important. Moreover, because the sale of the Methodist Book Concern's wares was everywhere framed as an act of denominational solidarity rather than a straightforward economic transaction – one that supplemented the salaries of itinerant preachers, provided for widows and orphans, underwrote the costs of missions to Natives, and most importantly, paid yearly dividends to the annual Methodist conferences across North America in recognition of the undivided support they provided to the publisher – Methodists in the United States and in Upper Canada alike came to believe that they had a vested financial interest in the denominational publisher and its assets. Thus, the Methodist Book Concern, or at least a portion of it, belonged to Canadian Methodists every bit as much as it belonged to American Methodists. Canadians were only too aware that any unilateral declaration of independence would jeopardize their place in that transnational economy, compromise their religious identities, and thus throw into question their status as more than mere commercial participants in the Concern's denominational market. Not only would they lose their entitlement to annual dividends and other financial supports, but they would also lose their capital interest in the Concern itself. The benefits of independence in Upper Canada simply did not outweigh these potential losses. And so, the Canadians waited.

After the General Conference in the United States reluctantly and belatedly granted the Canadians their independence in 1828, the latter continued to participate in the Methodist Book Concern's market as though nothing had changed. The Canadians continued to receive the same discounts on books and periodicals, their preachers continued to sell the Concern's wares along their preaching circuits, revenues continued to support missions to Natives in Upper Canada, and annual dividends continued to be paid. As a result, Canadians continued to believe that they possessed partial ownership over the Concern itself. At the General Conference in 1832, Canadian Methodists thus submitted a formal petition to have that partial ownership recompensed in the form of a single and very sizeable financial payment that would allow them to bolster their own publishing activities in Canada. The Canadians expected a favourable outcome – so favourable that it would have put them on a sound financial footing for years to come. At that very delicate moment, however, the British Wesleyans decided to return to Upper Canada in defiance of an earlier agreement to remain east of the Ottawa River. The timing of that move, at least as far as Canadian interests south of the border were concerned, could not have been worse.

Historians have struggled to account for the fact that, despite resisting Wesleyan advances in the colony for decades, Canadian Methodists suddenly and unexpectedly reversed course at this critical moment by abruptly proposing a union with the British Wesleyans. Elizabeth Cooper argues that the Canadians had little choice because they were simply financially ill-equipped to compete with their wealthier cousins from across the Atlantic. More recently, Todd Webb has suggested that demographic shifts in Upper Canada's population rendered continued opposition impracticable. Yet, according to the testimony of Canadian Methodists themselves, they had never been stronger: "The circulation and influence of the *Christian Guardian* (then the leading newspaper in Upper Canada) increased daily; the number and power of the Methodist Church grew more and more every year; so that the greedy few felt that their prey was in great danger of being lost." In addition to all that growth, prosperity, and influence, between 1828 and 1832 the financial support Canadians continued to receive from the Americans, despite their independence, had more than doubled. Add to all that the fact that the Canadians stood on the verge of receiving a financial payment large enough to buy every printer operating in Upper Canada a new press, and it seems very doubtful that the decision to propose a union with the Wesleyans came from a place of weakness.[14]

What the Canadians really wanted was the best of both worlds. On the one hand, with a large financial payment from the Methodist Book Concern all but secured, their financial difficulties would be at an end. On the other, a union with the British Wesleyans would open the way to unprecedented political advancement in the province together with the possibility of additional financial support from overseas. Alas, events in Canada moved so quickly that they soon overtook events in the United States. As the Canadians and the British Wesleyans began to lay formal plans for an ecclesiastical union in Britain and in Upper Canada, American Methodists attending the General Conference unexpectedly refused to authorize the payment without first consulting each of its annual conferences over the course of the next year. Delegates attending those scattered conferences voted overwhelmingly in favour of the Canadian claim – that is, until the Americans caught word of the imminent union between the Canadians and the Wesleyans. After that, every vote went against the Canadians.

As American Methodists no doubt suspected, once the Canadians had formalized their union with the British Wesleyans, in 1833, they largely ceased to patronize the Methodist Book Concern. Despite these dramatically altered circumstances, however, Canadian Methodists continued their campaign to have their claim against the Concern recognized at the General Conference of the Methodist Episcopal Church in 1836. Although American Methodists remained unmoved, the Canadian delegates did not come away completely empty-handed. In place of a large financial payment – their original desideratum – the Canadians secured tremendously favourable discounts on the Methodist Book Concern's books and periodicals with the understanding that whatever common religious identity they had once shared with the Americans – and that had been represented by the Concern's transnational market – was forever at an end.

This settlement set the Methodist Book Concern's market in Upper Canada on a new footing by irretrievably altering the cultural status of its books and periodicals. For the first time since Methodist preaching began north of the border, the Methodist Book Concern's offerings were no longer encumbered by an unwelcome rhetoric tying their purchase to membership in a foreign church. Instead, these books and periodicals would be treated by Canadian Methodists like any other commodity – desirable if they were well made, easy to procure, and inexpensive, and undesirable if they were not. Because the discounts Canadians were now entitled to on the Concern's books were so steep, and because the offerings of the Wesleyan Book Room in London had always been and remained relatively expensive, the Canadian Methodists were only too happy to revert to an all but exclusive reliance on the Concern to supply their market.

The Methodist Book Concern's reinvigorated market in Canada had a pronounced effect on Wesleyan fortunes. In addition to galvanizing friendly relations between American and Canadian Methodists while at the same time permanently irritating Wesleyan sensibilities – the latter would have much preferred the Canadians to rely on London for their supply of books – it also opened a way for Canadians to begin experimenting with reasserting their own preferences. Canadian Methodists began by retaking control of the Methodist Book Room in Toronto and later the denominational newspaper. When the British Wesleyans found themselves unable to rein in what they saw as the renewed editorial excesses of that newspaper, they dissolved the union. For the next seven years, while the union remained in abeyance, Canadian Methodists strengthened their commercial relationship with the Methodist Book Concern and found new ways to interpret its books and periodicals as straightforward commodities that in no way compromised their political loyalties. By the time that the union was eventually restored, in 1847, although the terms themselves were largely the same as they had been in 1833, the cultural landscape was not: indeed, the cultural landscape had been altered permanently.

Goldwin French vaguely attributes the failure of the Wesleyans to exert a more decisive cultural influence on Canadian Methodists after reunion to a wide variety of causes, including "internal problems of the Wesleyan Conference, the caliber of its representative in Canada, the reactions of the Canadian Methodists, and the provincial environment." The list is almost too long to be instructive. What French does not note, however, is that, although the British Wesleyans reassumed their positions at the head of the Canada Conference, they never again secured control over the province's market for Methodist books. The resulting undiminished Canadian dependency on the Methodist Book Concern both helped to blunt Wesleyan influence in Upper Canada and opened a way for American Methodists to exercise their own surprisingly protracted, if indirect, influence over religious developments north of the border. Although this influence undoubtedly discomfited some, the tenacious hold of the Methodist Book Concern on its Canadian market ultimately proved to be more durable than any of the assorted ecclesiastical mergers and unions that Canadian Methodists attempted – and often abandoned – throughout the first half of the nineteenth century. *Pulpit, Press, and Politics* will attempt to account for this market's extraordinary durability, the protracted impact it had on Methodist religious identity, and ultimately, how it set Methodist publishing in Canada on a unique course that would see it evolve to become one of the chief pillars of Canadian literary culture.[15]

Chapter One

"What a Boon Were These Publications": Buying and Selling Methodist Books in Early Upper Canada

Shortly after his twenty-first birthday, as the snows slowly receded across the countryside in the spring of 1799, Nathan Bangs crossed the border from New York into Upper Canada in search of two things. The first was a job. The second was God. Employment proved the easier quarry. A tall man with a square jaw, Bangs was scrupulous about fashion and never appeared in public without ruffles at his neck and his long dark hair pulled neatly back behind his head in a cue. A natural at parlour games, dancing, and witty conversation, Bangs had long since become accustomed to idling away his time in the pleasant company of young ladies. In the absence of such affable diversions, his solid New England education meant that he could lose himself almost as happily in a good book. Bangs knew he could afford to be easygoing. After all, even without his many social charms, he could always fall back on a distinguished pedigree that linked his prosperous family to the original Plymouth settlers themselves. Here, then, was a young man who had every reason to be pleased with himself.

But Bangs was not pleased with himself. On the contrary: when he crossed the border into Upper Canada, he was in the midst of a full-blown religious crisis. Ever since he had first heard a Methodist preacher call a crowd of curious onlookers to repentance four or five years earlier, Nathan Bangs had found his family's long-standing Episcopalianism increasingly hollow. He had even begun to feel that his immortal soul was in jeopardy. It was a feeling he knew his father would not understand. Bangs had never forgotten his father's stubborn refusal to hear Jesse Lee preach when that legendary Methodist itinerant had descended on Bangs's boyhood hometown to deliver a fiery sermon from the steps of the local courthouse. Jesse Lee was a celebrity of sorts, regarded by many as the most prominent preacher in New

England, but Bangs's father had forbidden his family from attending – because such men were "uneducated" and therefore beneath the notice of decent citizens who wished to retain their standing as respectable members of the community.[1]

When he grew into adolescence and took a teaching job in a neighbouring settlement, Nathan Bangs finally had an opportunity to hear one of these disruptive evangelists – and to see firsthand how right his father had been about them. Secretly pierced to the heart by the impassioned pleas of the preacher, Bangs could not help but notice that those who showed even the slightest evidence of having fallen under the Methodist spell were derided by the majority as religious fanatics. Rather than become an object of public scorn himself, Bangs joined in the ridicule before slinking away from the gathering filled with quiet remorse. No sooner had the preacher moved on to the next settlement than Bangs was struck down by illness and confined to his bed. With the hours stretching out before him, the young man upbraided himself for cowardice and accounted his infirmity the just punishment of an angry God. "Such was the weight of my guilt," he later recalled, "that I felt I should sink into perdition."[2]

Divine punishment or not, Bangs soon recovered and tried to forget the whole affair. Yet, he could not shake the words of that preacher. For the next four years until he migrated to Upper Canada, his conscience tormented him. After settling just outside the colony's former capital of Newark (now Niagara-on-the-Lake), Bangs sought relief among both Anglicans and Calvinists. Unfortunately, however, he found the local clergyman, Robert Addison, particularly disappointing. "Though in holy orders," Bangs complained, "he was a card-player and a drunkard, and performed the liturgical service with indecent haste, following it with a brief, rapid, and vapid prelection [*sic*]." While Addison left him cold, the rigid determinism peddled by zealous Calvinists only heightened Bangs's religious anxieties. Finding it impossible to believe himself numbered among the spiritual elect, he wandered the lonely forests at night in a vain attempt to assuage his agonies "in a flood of tears."[3]

Nathan Bangs continued to vacillate hopelessly between these denominational extremes until James Coleman arrived in town later that same year. A short man with piercing black eyes, Coleman was a veteran itinerant, having preached Methodism along the Niagara circuit for more than four years. Yet, although Bangs was irresistibly attracted to the consolations Coleman offered in his rousing sermons, he found himself equally repelled by the preacher's obvious lack of social grace. However much the two might agree on theological matters, Bangs simply could not yield to a man who not only possessed so little in the way of social standing, but who also lacked, as his Episcopalian father would have been quick to point out, even the barest rudiments of any real learning.[4]

Things suddenly changed the following summer when a new preacher, Joseph Sawyer, replaced Coleman on the Niagara circuit. If not a learned man when measured against the likes of Addison, Sawyer was no rustic, and he made a lasting impression on Nathan Bangs. Decades later, Bangs would describe this companionable preacher as "exhibiting at once the urbanities of the Christian gentleman, and the meekness and quietness of the submissive disciple of Jesus." At last, here was an itinerant who could meet Bangs's minimum standard for social respectability. But it was not in Sawyer's urbanity alone that Bangs justified his change of heart. Sawyer was, as Bangs was no doubt delighted to discover, more than just a peripatetic preacher. He was also a travelling bookseller.[5]

From about the time Joseph Sawyer appeared in Niagara onward, all Methodist preachers in North America were obliged by the American General Conference to work as commissioned salesman on behalf of the Methodist Book Concern to ensure that each "circuit be duly supplied with books." Clearly designed to protect the Concern's denominational interests in an increasingly competitive post-Revolutionary market for books in the United States, this new policy nevertheless had a profound impact on readers in the more sparsely populated settlements of Upper Canada. Although Addison, that reputedly dissolute clergyman, possessed what was believed to be the largest private library in the colony, books were not easy to come by even in Niagara. Bangs often complained about the paucity of reading material and rejoiced when he stumbled upon a family that was willing to lend him the odd volume from their own tiny collection of books. Addison, meanwhile, sequestered among the many books that crowded the rectory shelves, quietly reaped the social benefits his library afforded as the more respected settlers in the community admired him, despite his supposedly uninspiring pulpit oratory, as a man of sober study and learning. The moment Bangs yielded to Sawyer, however, he gained access to something almost as good as Addison's library. Suddenly, Bangs was both a member in a new faith community and a participant in a growing transnational market for books that extended as far as into the wilderness as the Gospel itself. Bangs did not need his father to tell him what must have been only too obvious: Sawyer's dual role as itinerant preacher and travelling bookseller had the potential to open a way for Methodists everywhere to achieve a degree of social respectability that continued to elude them on both sides of the border.[6]

Joseph Sawyer and his fellow preachers carried an interesting and eclectic selection of titles with them into the backwoods. As one might expect, these included the Bible, the Methodist hymnbook, as well as Methodism's standard polity documents: the *Minutes of Conference* and *The Doctrine and Discipline of the Methodist Episcopal Church*. Standard works by British Methodists were also staples, especially the writings of John Fletcher, a variety of authorized biographies of John Wesley, as well as Wesley's sermons and editions of his *Journals*. Wesley's diverse interests and his preoccupation with the uncanny would have made the *Journals* particularly good reading. In addition to the usual narratives about conversions and revivals, Wesley also described at some length his own dreams, the sightings of ghosts, demonic possessions, and even the spontaneous combustion of corpses. Wesley was undoubtedly fascinated by all of this on an emotional level, and he believed that these kinds of stories were a necessary antidote to the materialism of the Enlightenment, since they provided his readers with empirical evidence of an otherwise unseen world. Whatever the epistemological stakes may have been for Wesley in the eighteenth century, however, there can be little doubt that these hair-raising accounts also kept more than one itinerant nervously awake at night as he made his way quietly along the remote preaching circuits that cut through Upper Canada's immense and lonely forests.[7]

Some of the most popular titles with readers across North America were undoubtedly traditional fire-and-brimstone warnings to sinners. Indeed, the Methodist Book Concern almost never issued a catalogue that did not include all three of Joseph Alleine's *Admonition to Unconverted Sinners*, Richard Baxter's *Call to the Unconverted*, and William Law's *Serious Call to a Devout and Holy Life*. These books were calculated to fill readers with fear and trembling – and that is exactly what they did. "Dost thou hear the creation groaning under thee, and hell groaning for thee, and yet think thy case good enough?" warned Alleine in a typical passage, and "Dost thou laugh at hell and destruction, or canst thou drink the envenomed cup of the Almighty's fury, as it were but a common potion?" These words, taken to heart, would have echoed through the minds of preachers and readers alike as they laboured with few distractions and less entertainment in their solitary cabins and shelters. Indeed, even the urbane Samuel Johnson was brought to the brink of a nervous breakdown when, as a young man, he first read William Law's *Serious Call to a Holy Life* – and was ever after so dogged by a sense of his own sinfulness that he never ceased to look over his shoulder with dread at the inevitable approach of death and final judgment.[8]

An eager convert, Nathan Bangs applied himself with unyielding diligence to the books that Joseph Sawyer and other preachers peddled when they visited the community every other week. Observing the young man's determination, Sawyer encouraged Bangs to consider the life of a preacher. At first he demurred, but Bangs's reading steadily bolstered his confidence until he finally worked up the courage to join Sawyer as that preacher made his way around the Niagara circuit. Nineteenth-century denominational historians would later recall these seemingly obscure events unfolding in a colonial backwater as nothing short of providential. In August 1801, Bangs was licensed to preach, and soon he became one of Upper Canada's leading Methodist itinerants before the War of 1812, carving out new preaching circuits in the remote western reaches of the colony and selling the books and tracts of the Methodist Book Concern wherever he went.[9]

Many years later, after returning to the United States, Nathan Bangs took charge of the Methodist Book Concern as senior book agent in New York, expanded its catalogue of offerings, added its first printing presses, founded a denominational newspaper, and wrote the first official history of Methodism in America. It was not without justice, then, that his nineteenth-century biographer, Abel Stevens, referred to him as the "principal founder of the American literature of Methodism." Yet, for Methodists like Bangs, books were never an end in themselves. Everything that happened at the Concern was aimed squarely at improving Methodism's ministerial requirements, raising the educational standards of the laity, and ultimately achieving a higher degree of social respectability in North America. Denominational efforts in this direction could hardly have been more successful. By the middle decades of the nineteenth century, the Methodist Book Concern had grown to become one of the largest publishers in the world and Methodism the dominant religious denomination in both the United States and Canada. In the process, the relationship between denominational publisher and church became both inescapable and mutually reinforcing.[10]

I

The circulation of books in Upper Canada played a vitally important role in the battle for denominational converts during the early decades of the province's history – a period that largely coincides with that rapid expansion of evangelicalism in North America known as the Second Great Awakening. Yet, historians of religion have paid remarkably little attention to this important dimension of religious culture. Nancy Christie, for example, although noting that those recruited as Methodist preachers typically came from uneducated, humble backgrounds, adds nothing about the requirement placed on them by the American General Conference to improve their minds daily by study. Similarly, although George Rawlyk writes extensively about Nathan Bangs as a key religious figure in early Upper Canada, he quietly passes over the role that books played in Bangs's turbulent spiritual life and eventful itinerancy. To the limited extent that those few historians of the book have written about the role print played in religious developments in Upper Canada, they have tended to focus almost exclusively on the distribution work of British philanthropic organizations.[11]

This chapter, by contrast, will argue that it was American preachers, and American Methodist preachers in particular, who provided Upper Canadians – especially those living outside Kingston, York, and Niagara – with the bulk of their religious reading material during these early years of the province's history. Indeed, by the time organizations like the British and Foreign Bible Society began to develop a reliable infrastructure of volunteers to assist in the distribution of bibles, in the late 1820s, Methodist preachers, over the course of an entire generation, had already built a durable and remunerative market for the New York Methodist Book Concern's books and periodicals that extended across the entire colony.

To understand what gave rise to the determined and systematic book distribution activities of Methodist preachers in early Upper Canada, one must look back to John Wesley and the relationship he had with his American followers. Wesley, who in the mid-eighteenth century established Methodism as a renewal movement in the Church of England, insisted that his followers, whatever their geopolitical context, be known as a reading people. From his own earliest days distributing books while at Oxford, Wesley worked almost as tirelessly to put books in the hands of readers as he did to save their lost souls from the wrath to come. For Wesley, spiritual progress could hardly be divorced from reading. "It cannot be that the people should grow in grace unless they give themselves to reading," an aged Wesley remarked to a preacher just months before his death. "Press this upon them with your might," he urged, "and you will soon see the fruit of your labours."[12]

Both to protect his followers from improper and dangerous reading material and to exonerate them from the calumnies directed against them by other clergymen and those belonging to the professional classes, John Wesley took it upon himself to write and edit, and publish and distribute, countless books and tracts with the help of his travelling preachers and through the little bookstores that operated in his preaching houses. At the centre of this remarkable publishing enterprise was Wesley's distribution warehouse – known simply as the Book Room – in London. So central was the Book Room to Wesley's vision that he even insisted that his American followers refrain from printing anything on their own initiative and, instead, at very great inconvenience, import all their reading material from London. Wesley's efforts to maintain close oversight of his movement's printed discourse on both sides of the Atlantic caused problems almost from the beginning. The resulting difficulties, however, provided American Methodists with the germ or an idea that evolved to become a remarkably durable strategy for insulating their denominational market from the offerings of competitors – at the very moment that the market became deluged by a glut of cheap books after the close of the Revolutionary War.

The decades preceding the Revolutionary War witnessed not only the arrival of the first Methodist preachers to America, but also important changes in the way books were produced and distributed in the colonies. The first printers to ply their trade in North America were mostly immigrants who imported their presses, types, and even paper from overseas. The first book printed in British North America, *The Bay Psalm Book*, was produced by Massachusetts printer Stephen Day in 1640. But when the British Parliament passed the Licensing Act in 1662, the London Stationers' Company became the patent owner of bibles, psalters, and the majority of most other titles. As a result, printers in America constrained their output and survived by producing mostly handbills, government documents, local almanacs, and on rare occasions, schoolbooks. The vast majority of books sold in America – sermons, hymnals, poetry, histories, manuals – were imported from London by general merchants.[13]

Beginning around 1740, however, the number of printers operating in the colonies increased dramatically – a change closely connected with the rise of the colonial newspaper. These printers forged relationships with their London counterparts and soon displaced general merchants as North America's largest importers of British books. When a large market for cheap reprints emerged in Scotland and Ireland, around the middle of the eighteenth century, colonial booksellers, eager to increase their margins, made a point of importing these cheaper books for their American customers. By the 1760s, when it became clear that the American market for books was increasingly lucrative, a number of printers operating in Scotland and Ireland pulled up stakes and emigrated to the colonies in the hope of establishing bookselling businesses of their own. As events turned out, they were highly successful. That success did not escape the notice of the first Methodist preacher to plant his feet on American soil that same decade.[14]

In 1768, a small but growing body of Methodists in New York wrote to ask Wesley to send help. They needed preachers. Wesley raised the matter at the Leeds Conference in August 1769. "Who is willing to go?" he asked. No one responded. He had to ask twice more before two volunteers, Richard Boardman and Joseph Pilmore, reluctantly raised their hands. A collection of £50 was taken up to speed them on their way and to serve, in Wesley's words, as "a token of our brotherly love." Yet, despite the obvious difficulty Wesley had in prodding Boardman and Pilmore to cross the Atlantic, there was a third preacher who was more eager than all the rest, but who did not offer himself in Conference. Without any financial support or public endorsement, Robert Williams, a Welshman who cut his teeth as a Methodist preacher in Ireland, quietly set about making preparations to embark for America. The young preacher had at least one very good reason for not bothering to raise his hand when Wesley called for volunteers: Wesley didn't much like him. While admitting Williams possessed a rare pulpit oratory to hold thousands "quiet and attentive," Wesley found the younger man's cheeky attitude towards the Church of England all but intolerable. But, no doubt reminding himself of his own pledge that Methodism was open to all regardless of religious inclination, Wesley permitted himself to be practical rather than principled in the matter.[15]

Shortly after Robert Williams learned that he would have the unenthusiastic company of Richard Boardman and Joseph Pilmore in America, he made an abrupt and chaotic departure. "He hurried down to the town near to which the ship lay," wrote that famous American preacher Jesse Lee, "sold his horse to pay his debts, and taking his saddle-bags on his arm, set off for the ship, with a loaf of bread and a bottle of milk, and no money to pay his passage." Williams's haste delivered him to the American shore sometime in August 1769 – some two months before the slightly more dignified Boardman and Pilmore would eventually arrive.[16]

Wesley's concerns about how Williams might conduct himself overseas were borne out almost immediately. One of the first things Williams did when he landed was to settle on a way to make Wesley – or at least Wesley's hymnbook – pay his way. Preachers in Britain were forbidden from publishing anything without Wesley's approval; Robert Williams, however, seems to have thought the same restriction ought not to apply in America. And he can hardly be blamed for that. After all, as soon as he set foot on American soil, Williams found himself all but surrounded by British books and advertisements for British books printed not in Britain, but by Scottish and Irish immigrants on American presses. The financial success that these printers and publishers achieved in America's burgeoning reprint market rested on their common conviction that the colonies were, like Scotland and Ireland, beyond the jurisdiction of the London Stationers' Company. It was an infectious idea. As Williams reached into his pocket and pulled out one of his only remaining possessions – a battered copy of the best-selling Methodist hymnbook – the circumstances must have seemed almost providential.[17]

Using Robert Williams's own hymnbook for copy, John Dunlap in Philadelphia soon placed three hundred inexpensive duodecimo copies of Wesley's *Hymns for the Nativity of Our Lord* in Williams's hands. Stuffing his saddlebags with as many as he could carry, Williams sold them wherever he went. When his inventory became depleted, he printed a cheap edition of Wesley's sermons in New York with the help of a leading local Methodist whose name was Philip Embury. The next time he was passing through Philadelphia, Williams ordered more hymnbooks from Dunlap. Wesley's sanctioned preachers, meanwhile, Boardman and Pilmore, didn't lift a finger to stop him. They didn't even report him to Wesley. It wasn't until a young Francis Asbury finally arrived in America, in October 1771, that Wesley had any chance at all of finding out what Williams was doing. At first, Williams's ministry impressed Asbury. "Brother Williams," he enthused in his journal, "gives a flaming account of the work. Many people seem to be ripe for the Gospel and ready to receive us."[18]

Asbury's enthusiasm was dampened, however, when he learned that Williams was doing more than just preaching. And he wasted no time writing to Wesley about it. Then, in the autumn of 1772, Asbury received a letter from Wesley appointing him general assistant in place of Richard Boardman and charging him to ensure that, "Mr Williams might not print any more books without my consent." This sudden promotion was almost certainly a reward for, among other demonstrations of loyalty, tattling on Robert Williams. Although the benefits to himself were not to be doubted, Asbury seems to have been sincere in his censure of Williams. When Williams died in September 1775, Asbury remarked darkly, "Perhaps brother Williams was in danger of being entangled in worldly business, and might thereby have injured the cause of God.

So he was taken away from the evil to come." Those familiar with Williams's ministry would have had no difficulty interpreting the phrase "worldly business" as a veiled reference to Williams's unsanctioned publishing endeavours.[19]

Despite Francis Asbury's loyalty, Wesley was not quite ready to leave everything in the hands of a man quite so young and untested. In the spring of 1773, veteran preacher and Church of England clergyman Thomas Rankin was dispatched to restore order and make certain that others would not be tempted to follow Williams's bad example. Rankin was a hard man with a reputation for dealing quickly with problems. In less time than it would have taken him to cross the Atlantic, he had called all the preachers in America back to Philadelphia, where they met together in June of that same year. Acting on orders from Wesley, Rankin affirmed the subordination of Methodist preachers to Church of England clergymen, forbade those preachers from administering the sacraments, and made it perfectly clear that Wesley's rule against publishing applied every bit as much in America as it did in Britain. "No preacher," the minutes read, "shall be permitted to reprint our books, without the approbation of Mr Wesley, and the consent of the brethren." As for Williams, the practical Wesley allowed that he would be permitted to "sell what he has, but reprint no more."[20]

David Hempton has noted, "One of the most striking features of Methodism is the extent to which Wesley tried to secure control over the discourse of the movement by remorselessly selecting, editing, publishing and disseminating print." Wesley was deeply committed to maintaining that control on both sides of the Atlantic. Indeed, his preachers were specifically enjoined in the minutes of conferences to "sing no hymns of your own composing," to publish no tracts without first obtaining approval, to print nothing until Wesley had first revised it, and in general, to avoid what Wesley called "that evil disease the *scribendi cacoethes*" or "itch for writing" that threatened to infect some of his preachers and assistants.[21]

What is perhaps most remarkable, in view of these formal constraints, is that Thomas Rankin cited none of Wesley's fundamental editorial concerns when he set out to explain why Methodists must not follow the example set by Robert Williams and other Scottish and Irish immigrant printers in America. Instead, Rankin said, the rule was merely in place to ensure fairness, "so that the profits arising therefrom, might be divided among the preachers, or applied to some charitable purpose." Wesley's preachers in America proved themselves to be remarkably tractable on this point in the short term, and no further unauthorized editions of Wesley's works were printed on American presses at the behest of Methodist preachers until the darkest days of the Revolutionary War. Nevertheless, Rankin's carefully crafted language eventually provided Methodists in North America with just the opening they needed to begin assuming control over their own printing and publishing activities.[22]

By the end of the 1770s, Methodism in America was in a state of serious disarray. Since the outbreak of hostilities, Methodist preachers had come under heavy persecution as suspected Loyalists. As a result, all of the preachers Wesley had dispatched overseas, with the single exception of Francis Asbury, fled the continent. The appearance of Wesley's disconcerting anti-revolutionary tract, *A Calm Address to Our American Colonies* – partly plagiarized from Samuel Johnson's *Taxation No Tyranny* – hardly helped. Controversial on both sides of the Atlantic, in America the *Calm Address* was nothing short of dangerous, and it no doubt contributed to the frustration of Wesley's overseas followers. Indeed, despite Asbury's continued presence in America and his intense loyalty to Methodism's founder, before long Wesley's authority outside Britain was hanging by a thread.[23]

In 1779, Francis Asbury narrowly prevented a body of southern Methodist preachers from arrogating to themselves the sacramental powers of ordained clergymen – a move that would have certainly invited Wesley's profoundest censure. The following year, John Dickins, a rising star in the Methodist fold who would go on to become a key figure in American Methodist publishing, called for the formal separation of Methodism from the Church of England in the full knowledge that John Wesley would oppose such a move. With so many ready to set aside Wesley's authority in relatively weighty matters, it is not surprising that Asbury came to the conclusion that printing a few Methodist books amounted to no great trespass under the circumstances. "May I print any of your books? We are in great want," Asbury pleaded in a letter written to Wesley in the waning weeks of the summer of 1780, adding by way of explanation that the last shipment received from London "was huddled and improper." A reply would have been a long time coming, and Asbury didn't bother to wait. "We have come to the conclusion to print the four volumes of Mr Wesley's Sermons," he wrote in his journal a month later.[24]

The extraordinary circumstances under which these books were printed might have been taken by some to mean that no binding precedent about printing Methodist books in America had been set. At least that seems to have been Wesley's view. When regular lines of communication were restored after the Revolutionary War, it became clear that Wesley had every expectation that his followers on the far side of the Atlantic would resume their unwavering patronage of his London Book Room. But a different sentiment now prevailed in America. After the cessation of hostilities, everyone knew that the London Stationers' Company could no longer even pretend to hold sway over publishing in the new republic. American Methodists slowly evolved a similar view about Wesley's Book Room. When Wesley dispatched Rankin to put a stop to Williams's publishing activities more than a decade earlier, Rankin had argued that such restrictions were necessary in order to ensure that "the profits arising therefrom, might be divided among the preachers, or applied to some charitable purpose." With that language at the forefront of their minds, American Methodists passed a new resolution requiring that profits arising from the sale of all books – those printed locally as well as those imported from London – be used to make up deficiencies in the salaries of the preachers. The result was that Wesley and his lieutenants could no longer complain about an unfair distribution of profits. This also set books published by the London Book Room and those published on American presses on an equal footing for the first time. Wesley, who remained as committed as ever to controlling the discourse of the movement, was not appeased. [25]

Over the next several years, it became increasingly clear that Wesley's endorsement of a truly independent Methodism in the United States was not quite as unqualified as many had hoped. In 1784, Wesley had reluctantly sanctioned the establishment of an independent church under the joint superintendence of Francis Asbury and Thomas Coke, but he seems to have been surprised when Americans made attempts to accommodate Methodism to the realities of their new environment. It was around this time that John Dickins, who had attempted to push back against Wesley's authority during the Revolutionary War, began to play an increasingly important role in Methodist affairs. Born and educated in London, Dickins travelled to America as a tutor before joining the Methodists on the eve of the war in 1774. In spite of his British birth, Dickins's sympathies were wholly with the disgruntled colonists. Dickins's remarkable talent for rhetoric became apparent when the time came to bestow a new name on the movement that had once been known by Wesley simply as "circuit number 50" in his transatlantic renewal movement within England's established church. Dickins suggested the Methodist Episcopal Church – a shrewd formulation that signalled both Methodism's independence from the Church of England and that, in three simple words, seized upon the same sacramental prerogatives that he and his southern coreligionists had been demanding for years.[26]

Tensions between Wesley and his American followers finally came to a head in 1787. That year, in an effort to reassert his authority, Wesley attempted to blunt Francis Asbury's influence by installing Richard Whatcoat in his place – a candidate who promised to be far more deferential. But the Americans, who had already come to regard Asbury as a kind of evangelical hero, flatly refused. Wesley, they contended, was simply too far removed from the situation on the ground to know what was best. Some Methodists even went so far as to suggest Wesley could expect no duty of obedience from those who had joined the ranks of the preachers after the establishment the independent Methodist Episcopal Church in 1784.[27]

With John Wesley's influence thus diminished, and no doubt recalling the good that had resulted from Robert Williams's unauthorized reprinting activities a decade or so earlier, John Dickins, at the urging of the preachers, began the work of reviving Methodist printing in America. In the spring, he issued a thoroughly revised edition of Wesley's familiar *Minutes of Several Conversations* under the distinctly American title *Form of Discipline*. It was a landmark document that further diminished Wesley's authority by excluding his name from the list of preachers, styling Asbury a bishop against Wesley's thunderous but futile opposition, and unambiguously placing the right to decide what would be printed in the hands of American preachers. Importantly, it also anticipated any criticism Wesley might make on the grounds of financial fairness by codifying the principle that "the profits of the books, after all the necessary expences [*sic*] are defrayed, shall be applied, according to the discretion of the conference, towards the college, the preachers' fund, the deficiencies of the preachers, the distant missions, or the debts of our churches." That itself did not put an end of the importation of books and periodicals from Wesley's London Book Room, but Americans now placed their overseas orders by choice rather than by compulsion. "From that time," observed Jesse Lee, "we began to print more of our own books in the United States than we had ever done before."[28]

In May 1789, Methodist preachers meeting together in New York made Dickins's role official by appointing him the first book steward of the newly established Methodist Book Concern – the first denominational publishing house in America. With the full weight of the preachers' authority now behind him, and even Wesley's own reluctant agreement, John Dickins turned his full attention towards ensuring the Concern's survival. It would not be easy. Three serious threats to its existence emerged almost immediately. First, America's booming postwar market for books meant that Methodist converts had no need to patronize the Methodist Book Concern to fill their shelves with the right books. Rival editions of Methodist hymnbooks, works by John Wesley, and other staples of Methodist spirituality were pouring forth from the presses of competing publishers in Philadelphia, Baltimore, and New York. Second, in 1790 the US Congress passed a Federal Copyright Act that effectively threw the whole of the Methodist canon, with the exception of a tiny proportion of literature actually authored by American Methodists, into the public domain. Third, financial pressure on the Concern to succeed was increased that same year when Asbury's controversial Bishops Council invested the Preachers' Fund in the book business in exchange for the right to draw dividends arising from the sale of the Concern's books. But, with fewer than a dozen books in print at that time, there was no guarantee that the Concern would even survive, much less turn a profit.[29]

Competition in the market, internal financial demands, and the lack of a distribution infrastructure all drove the book business into an early debt. Under these pressures, Dickins began to evolve a truly remarkable market strategy rooted in Wesley's earlier demand that Williams stop printing Methodist books in America because such activities prevented the equitable distribution of profits. In the face of the Methodist Book Concern's mounting liabilities, Dickins seems to have realized that there was an important difference between directing profits back into the wider Methodist Episcopal Church and loudly proclaiming that one was doing so. In 1793, Dickins issued the Concern's first catalogue as an appendix to his edition of John Fletcher's *Posthumous Pieces*. It contained something far more important to the Concern's long-term survival than the twenty-three titles actually listed for sale. Almost half of the catalogue's allotted two-page space was occupied by a kind of advertisement in which Dickins attempted to explain why his books were more desirable than those of his competitors:

> The Following BOOKS are published by John Dickins, No. 118, North Fourth-Street, near Race-Street, Philadelphia; for the use of the Methodist Societies in the United States of America; and the profits thereof applied for the general benefit of the said Societies. Sold by the publishers, and the Ministers and Preachers in the several Circuits.
>
> [...]
>
> As the Profits of these Books are for the general Benefit of the Methodist Societies, it is humbly recommended to the Members of the said Societies,

that they will purchase no Books which we publish, of any other person than the aforesaid *John Dickins*, or the Methodist Ministers and Preachers in the several Circuits, or such Persons as sell them by their Consent.[30]

By connecting the sale of his books to the welfare of the Methodist Episcopal Church in a document read not only by preachers, but also by all his potential customers, John Dickins took a critically important step towards equating patronage of the denominational publisher with loyalty to the Church itself. No other publisher could make a similar claim. Every book the Concern published, whether authored by a Methodist or a non-Methodist, a living or a dead author, an American citizen or a British subject, conferred in equal measure the same denominational distinction on the purchaser. This set apart not only the Concern's Methodist hymnbook from the rival hymnbooks that were beginning to flood the market, but also from the spiritual classics popular among Methodist readers but over which they had no special claim of ownership, such as Richard Baxter's *Call to the Unconverted* – a book that the Roman Catholic publisher Matthew Carey would soon issue in Philadelphia in the hope of selling it across denominational lines. Tellingly, Dickins made no effort to describe his texts as more accurate, less expensive, or of a superior manufactured quality. The one and only reason Methodists ought to prefer his books over those published by others was that Dickins's books conferred financial benefit on the wider Methodist Episcopal Church. To open an edition of Baxter's *Call* and see the name John Dickins on the imprint conveyed to anyone who had read Dickins's catalogue a message about the denominational identity and loyalty of the owner of that book.[31]

For decades to come, Dickins's language, or language inspired by it, appeared at the head of all the catalogues and in many of the prefaces to the books published by the Methodist Book Concern. Meeting in Baltimore in 1800, the General Conference of the Methodist Episcopal Church took this principle about the proper use of profits derived from Wesley one step further by instituting a commission on the sale of all books to Methodist preachers who were also now required to sell the Concern's wares wherever they went. The amount of the payable commission varied but typically fell somewhere between 15 per cent and 25 per cent. A portion of this was also reserved for presiding elders – senior preachers who bore responsibility for overseeing a group of preaching circuits. The result was an unintended ironic twist on Dickins's rhetoric and Wesley's original language inasmuch as the wider Church now assumed responsibility for the Concern's debts, and preachers became commissioned salesmen rather than straightforward beneficiaries of the Concern's bounty.[32]

In the end, the arrangement was not much different from the one Robert Williams had pioneered decades earlier: the more books a preacher sold, the more money he could put in his pocket. While not without spiritual dangers, this was a recipe for placing books in the hands of readers and visibly strengthening the role that those books played in the Methodist economy as denominational status objects. The efficacy of that rhetoric, moreover, proved to be as powerful in Upper Canada's backwoods as along any preaching circuit in the new United States of America. The colonists may have identified as British subjects, but they also understood themselves to be loyal Methodists with a moral duty to support their own denominational publisher. As the number of Methodists in the colony grew, the demand for these books printed on American presses would expand rapidly. Not everyone, however, welcomed a growing Methodist influence in Upper Canada.

II

"With respect to Religious Instruction," Bishop Jacob Mountain fumed in a letter to the British Secretary of State for Home Affairs penned in 1794, "the state of these settlers is, for the most part, truly deplorable. From Montreal to Kingston, a distance of 200 miles, there is not one Clergyman of the Church of England, nor any houses of Religious Worship except one small Ch[urch] belonging to the Lutherans & one or perhaps two belonging to the Presbyterians." As if that were not bad enough, the Methodists were also making worrying and unwelcome inroads. "The greatest bulk of the people," Mountain continued, "have and can have no instruction but such as they receive occasionally from itinerant and mendicant Methodists, a set of ignorant enthusiasts whose preaching is calculated only to perplex the understanding, & corrupt the morals & relax the nerves of industry, & dissolve the bonds of society."[33]

Jacob Mountain had good reason for not liking the Methodists. Unlike them, as least as far as he was concerned, he had worked long and hard to get where he was. A graduate of Caius College in Cambridge, he had already put in many years patiently climbing the ecclesiastical ladder in England as deacon, curate, vicar, and chaplain before being appointed bishop of his new Upper and Lower Canadian diocese in 1793. As Mountain surveyed the tiny settlements scattered across the first of these, the essence of his mission seems to have struck home: first, place the Church of England on a surer footing here than ever it had been in the American colonies; and, second, beat back its denominational competitors at every opportunity. For Mountain, something more than just the welfare of the Church rested on the successful execution of this plan. The survival of the colonies themselves hung in the balance. In this conviction, Mountain was not alone.

Jacob Mountain owed his appointment in large part to a request made by the colony's first lieutenant governor, John Graves Simcoe, some years earlier when he petitioned for a Church of England bishopric in Upper Canada. Lord Dorchester, then in charge of the colonies, was only too happy to oblige. As astonishing as it may seem, throughout the entire period before the American Revolutionary War, such an office had never been established by the British authorities in a single North American colony – not even in colonies such as New York and Virginia where the Church of England held forth real pretentions to establishment. After the war, bureaucrats in England, under the belated influence of William Warburton's writings, determined that the presence of such an ecclesiastical figure would have done much to impede the cause of the rebels. Warburton, a man of considerable ecclesiastical and literary reputation in the eighteenth century, served in a variety of offices from chaplain to bishop while finding time to publish works against both deism and Methodism. By Jacob Mountain's time, he was best remembered for his 1739 treatise on religious establishments titled *Alliance between Church and State*. "When religion is in Alliance with the state," Warburton wrote, "as it then comes under the magistrate's direction, those holy leaders have neither credit nor power to do mischief, its purity must needs be reasonably well supported and preserved." In other words, church and state functioned best as mutually reinforcing institutions. In that spirit, the colonial authorities came to believe that when they gave the Church of England a boost in the Canadas, they were helping to eliminate subversive influences – including those emanating from religious quarters – that might encourage a second revolution.[34]

With that disagreeable thought in mind, the administration of British Prime Minister William Pitt the Younger charted a legislative course to advantage the Church of England by setting aside a seventh of all public lands "for the Support and Maintenance of a Protestant Clergy" in the Constitutional Act of 1791. That particular wording would eventually lead to endless wrangling on the part of denominational leaders and politicians – who exactly were the "Protestant Clergy" anyway? For the time being, however, it was generally understood that the Church of England was the sole intended beneficiary of the Act's largesse.

Lieutenant Governor Simcoe, a fervent Anglican who also happened to subscribe to Warburton's political ecclesiology, took his own steps to unbalance the playing field when the first session of the colony's tiny sixteen-member Legislative Assembly met in Newark in 1792. Simcoe not only granted the Church of England land and financial assistance to aid in the erection of churches and rectories, he also set about drafting a Marriage Act that restricted the solemnization of marriages to Church of England clergymen alone. Meanwhile, clergymen like Jacob Mountain kept their criticism of the Methodists and other "dissenters" largely to themselves and a small handful of government officials before the War of 1812. Why? They were confident that, once the dust settled and they finally secured the resources they needed from the British Parliament, the colony's settlers would inevitably flock to their banner. It would be another two decades before they finally admitted to themselves that these beliefs about the actual religious preferences of Upper Canadians were badly mistaken.

It really should have come as no surprise to anyone that Upper Canada was as religiously eclectic as any of the former North American colonies. After all, almost everyone who settled there after the Revolutionary War had come from those colonies. By the time Bishop Mountain began his episcopal oversight of the Canadas, the upper province was already home to Moravians from Ohio, Lutherans and Presbyterians from New York, Mennonites and Quakers from Pennsylvania, and Baptists from Vermont. While the colony's tiny handful of Church of England clergymen viewed this eclecticism with an equal measure of religious disdain and political dread, the Methodists saw in it nothing more than a routine field of religious competitors. The First Amendment to the Constitution of the United States of America – "Congress shall make no law respecting an establishment of religion, or prohibiting the free exercise thereof" – had no legal force north of the US border, of course, but preachers arriving from the United States behaved as though it did. For them, the whole of North America was a single and unfettered religious marketplace.[35]

Michael Smith, a Baptist preacher from Pennsylvania who temporarily settled in the colony before the War of 1812, put it most succinctly when he observed that Upper Canadians "enjoy full liberty of conscience to worship God as they please, and are protected by law from penalties, impositions, or burthens of any kind relative to religious concerns." Confronted by this reality on the ground, Methodists, like other religious leaders, paid little heed to Simcoe's legislation, less to Pitt's Constitutional Act, and none at all to the abstruse theories advanced by Warburton fifty years earlier. Instead, they directed the whole of their energies to blazing preaching circuits across Upper Canada's almost trackless stretches of wildness, drawing colonists together into denominational communities wherever they found them, recruiting promising candidates for local and itinerant preaching, and selling as many books as they could from the Methodist Book Concern's growing catalogue of titles.[36]

William Losee was the first Methodist preacher to cross the US border into Upper Canada. A tall man in his late twenties and hampered by a withered arm, Losee traversed the frozen St Lawrence on horseback near Matilda, present-day South Dundas, in the winter of 1790 to preach to family and friends. When he returned to the United States later that spring, he obtained permission from the New York Conference to establish a formal preaching circuit in the region. The following year, in 1791, he arrived back in Upper Canada and in no time had attracted more than 150 new members to the cause from as far away as the Bay of Quinte and even Niagara. Not incidentally, as least as far as Losee was concerned, he also managed to draw the eye of a pretty young woman along the way. Sadly, she transferred her affections to another Methodist preacher, Darius Dunham, who happened to have a particular flair for the dramatic – including the performance of public exorcisms. Although Losee abandoned the work with a broken heart, and despite a serious shortage of preachers in the United States, dozens followed Losee's example by accepting preaching circuits in British North America as Upper Canadian Methodism entered a period of unrivalled expansion.[37]

During the first decade of the nineteenth century, Upper Canada attracted tens of thousands of settlers from the New England and mid-Atlantic states who took up land grants chiefly in the western portions of the province. Michael Smith went so far as to conjecture that "if all the inhabitants of Upper Canada were divided into 10 parts, 6 parts would be natives of the United States." Those living in Upper Canada during these early years – especially those who chose to put down stakes outside the province's tiny urban settlements at Kingston, York, and Niagara – might have been forgiven for feeling as though they lived in a corner of British North America that had been effectively transformed into a demographic, if not a political, extension of the United States. The religious makeup of the province was also undergoing a major shift. By 1810, 3.7 per cent of the province's total population belonged to the Methodist Episcopal Church's formal membership – a remarkable figure when one considers that in the United States that statistic stood at only 2.5 per cent. Historians estimate, moreover, that for every formal member there were as many as eight additional adherents. Thus, the total proportion of Methodists and Methodist adherents in Upper Canada's population may well have been closer to 30 per cent before the War of 1812. No wonder Bishop Mountain and his fellow clergymen were looking over their shoulders.[38]

Needless to say, this shift in the colony's population also worried Upper Canada's governing class. Yet, in spite of the colony's increasingly complicated and precarious political footing, uncertainty about the loyalties of the majority of its inhabitants, and a steadily growing chorus of animadversions directed against at least some factions of the United States, Methodism continued to attract converts more quickly than any of its denominational rivals. Even Michael Smith admitted as much. "The Methodists," he wrote, "are the most numerous, and are scattered all over the province." The willingness of these "itinerant and mendicant Methodists" to pursue potential converts to the limits of white settlement was all but legendary. Indeed, they typically arrived in tiny new settlements years and even decades ahead of their religious competitors. But there was more to their success than simply a propensity to travel light. They were also willing to adopt almost any innovation that promised results.[39]

One of the most successful of these innovations was the American-style camp meeting. Planned months in advance, these events typically continued for days in remote locations where settlers pitched tents to listen to impassioned preachers extemporize from a make-shift platform while they sang rousing hymns, had their maladies miraculously cured, and even witnessed the occasional demonic exorcism. Dozens upon dozens of these raucous meetings were held across Upper Canada in the first decades of the nineteenth century. Something of their breathlessness and zealotry can be detected in a rare eyewitness account surviving from the first such event held in the colony over a period of nearly four days and three nights in the autumn of 1805. A stage was erected in a field, and tents were pitched around it to accommodate worshippers. The proceedings continued well into each night as "the power of God descended upon the Camp," while "songs of praises to God for Salvation found" rose into the starry sky.[40]

This event attracted thousands – believers and unbelievers alike. As the preachers in attendance no doubt hoped, conversions abounded. But so did conflict. "The people of God were chiefly in a bunch by themselves when the camp took fire and the wicked formed a circle round about where they stood with astonishment to see the exercise, whilst many of them were constrained to cry aloud for mercy." By the time the sun rose on the third day, the spiritual warfare was in full swing. One young woman "of a high rank" was suddenly and unexpectedly "struck by the power of God" and fell weeping to the ground. Her unrepentant sister, horrified by her sibling's improper behaviour, pulled her away from the stage. But the two were pursued by another group of women, "the daughters of Jerusalem," and forcibly returned to the camp. Meanwhile, the unrepentant sister, "the wolf who stole away the lamb," found herself "shot with an arrow from the Almighty" as "her ferocious nature" was miraculously changed "into the lamblike nature of Christ." Astonishingly, that was not the most dramatic event of the day. A few hours later, a young man could be seen being dragged to the meeting against his will by those who believed he was possessed by a demon. Darius Dunham, famous for his exorcisms in the Upper Canadian backwoods, went to work as the other preachers held the young man down. Unrepentant onlookers were aghast. "The wicked Children of the Devil were so enraged because he was brought there that they came upon us, and would have taken him away with violence, had we not formed a ring around him of 5 or 6 deep in order to keep them off." Amazingly, once the exorcism was complete, the young man appeared to be fully restored to his senses and joined the other believers in prayer and worship.[41]

Those belonging to Upper Canada's more staid denominations would have none of it. "You can have almost no conception of their excesses," lamented one disgusted Church of England clergyman, "They will bawl twenty of them at once, tumble on the ground, laugh, sing, jump, and stamp, and this they call the working of the spirit." Years later, the same clergyman went further, describing these spectacles as little more than "animal fervour." British Wesleyans were equally appalled. In 1807, they banned such meetings outright, condemning them as "highly improper ... and likely to be productive of considerable mischief." Respectable members of the laity agreed. "Nothing, believe me," railed one women in a letter sent from Upper Canada to an overseas correspondent, "that you may have heard or read of the frantic disorders of these Methodist love-feasts and camp-meetings in Upper Canada can exceed the truth!" Interestingly, these accusations were remarkably similar to those levelled against Wesley himself by the Bishop of London, who chastised Methodists for their "Cryings out, Screamings, Shriekings, Roarings, Groanings, Tremblings, Gnashings, Yellings, Foamings, Convulsions, Swoonings, Droppings, Blasphemies, Curses, dying and despairing Agonies, Variety of Tortures in Body and Mind."[42]

However dismissive the more respectable members of society might have been about this kind of unhinged religious revelry, camp meetings worked. Gains in Methodist membership became so pronounced over the following years that the entire period before the War of 1812 came to be known simply as the "Canada Fire" among North American Methodists – a phenomenon that spread "like a conflagration over the Canada circuits." Recognizing that it would have been easy for these new converts to slip through their fingers once all the excitement subsided, the Methodists were careful to take steps to cement their gains by organizing all new members into weekly classes under the direction of local preachers to oversee the growing Methodist congregations while the itinerant preachers were absent.[43]

With so many flocking to their banner, Methodist preachers soon began to see evidence that their activities had attracted not only the notice of their religious competitors, but of their infernal Adversary as well. "Drive the devil out of the country!" roared Henry Ryan, a hulking preacher who had exchanged his boxing gloves for a Bible years earlier, "Drive him into the lake and drown him!" And drive out the Devil they did. One young preacher, hindered by an impish fiddler whose rousing tunes drew hearers away from religious services, castigated the player as "the devil's musician" and threatened darkly that God would either "convert him or take him out of the way." Thus chastened, the man fled the scene, burned his fiddle, and never interfered with the Methodists again. Another itinerant, frustrated by the repeated interruptions to his sermon occasioned by a howling baby, advanced on the disruptive child, *"and rebuked the Devil in it, and commanded him to come out."* Needless to say, "the child ceased to cry, and never disturbed the congregation more." Yet another preacher, heckled by the profane jeers of a young sinner, pointed an accusing finger at the miscreant while thundering, *"My God! smite him!"* When that young man dropped dead on the instant, "as if shot through the heart with a bullet," it became the stuff of Methodist legend. But these preachers had more than just their own loud voices, extemporaneous preaching, and an occasional supernatural intervention to counter both the interruptions of the Devil and the calumnies of conservatives like Bishop Jacob Mountain. They also had books.[44]

III

The families of Barbara Heck and Philip Embury, settling north of the St Lawrence River in the summer of 1785, were probably among the first Methodists to bring religious books printed on American presses into post-Revolutionary British North America. Among the small library of books they carried with them were almost certainly the American editions of Wesley's works that Robert Williams had published some sixteen years earlier in New York, with Embury's help. At this early date, the association of these editions with Williams would probably have meant more to the Hecks and Emburys than that they were published in territory belonging to the new United States. After all, George Washington's inauguration was still four years away, the Methodist Book Concern did not yet exist, and Loyalist refugees streaming north would have found books among the easiest of their movable possessions to transport.

What remained to the British in North America after the Revolutionary War could hardly be described as a vibrant intellectual culture. Literacy rates among French Canadians, in particular, were notoriously low. Although Champlain had founded Quebec in 1608, just a year after the English established a colony at Jamestown, there never was a French Canadian equivalent of *The Bay Psalm Book*. As remarkable as it may seem, not a single printing press was set up in the whole of New France before General Wolfe captured Quebec for the English at the Battle of the Plains of Abraham in 1759. That was in sharp contrast to those parts of the continent controlled by the English. Halifax was the first northern colony to have its own newspaper, the *Halifax Gazette*, established by former Bostonian John Bushnell in 1763. Shortly after that, migrants from Philadelphia established English newspapers in both Quebec City and Montreal. By January 1793, Upper Canada's first printer, Quebec-born Louis Roy, had set up a press in the colony's tiny capital in Niagara to print the government's weekly *Upper Canada Gazette*.[45]

Upper Canada certainly had its detractors – among them Anna Jameson who, regarding herself as a kind of cultural exile from the British metropole in the 1830s, repeated reports that not one in twenty or thirty, indeed, not even one in seventy, could read or write. Demographic evidence, however, suggests that literacy rates in the colony were, in fact, quite high. Unlike Lower Canada, where the Catholic Church did little to encourage reading among parishioners, most of the Loyalists and so-called late Loyalists were refugees or migrants from American colonies that had established strong traditions around the importance of common (public) schools far back into the eighteenth century. Those traditions meant that wherever these colonists arrived, printing presses were soon to follow.[46]

Yet, unlike those who plied their trade in the new United States, printers across British North America continued to be bound by those laws that privileged the London Stationers' Company in the transatlantic book trade. Thus, like American printers before the 1760s, printers who set up shop in Upper Canada were largely confined to producing local newspapers, broadsides, and documents requested by the colonial administration. The vast majority of settlers, like the Hecks and Emburys, relied for their reading material on the small libraries they brought with them from the United States to their new homes in British North America. With only a tiny commercial infrastructure and just three small towns at Kingston, York, and Newark, opportunities to purchase books in these early years were few and far between. The book trade in British North America was, as one scholar notes, "severely constrained, prior to the burgeoning immigration of the 1820s and the beginnings of railway building in the 1830s, by a relatively low and widely scattered population coupled with limited and slow transportation."[47]

Books and other manufactured commodities remained scarce for decades, and were valued in ways incommensurate with their actual commercial worth. Amelia Harris, daughter of Samuel Ryerse, underlined the value her family had come to place on all material commodities – but especially on books – in her description of the destruction of her family's house by fire in 1804. In addition to the loss of precious linens, bedding, and articles of furniture, she noted, "The greatest loss was a box or two of books. These were not to be replaced this side of New York, and to a young family the loss was irreparable." Shortly after settling in Upper Canada in 1799, Nathan Bangs was unable to obtain any books at all except by borrowing reading material from a local family, who he was delighted to find, possessed a "small library" that included works by Milton, Bunyan, and James Hervey. Andrew Prindle, born in Prince Edward District in 1780, and one of the first Canadians to serve as a Methodist preacher, put it even more bluntly when he complained that he had "received his education in Canada, when there were no schools and no books."[48]

Religious organizations were typically at the forefront of efforts to supply colonists with those books, tracts, and periodicals that they believed would furnish readers with the greatest spiritual benefit. But even these organizations were relatively slow off the mark in Upper Canada. The Society for Promoting Christian Knowledge, the Society for the Propagation of the Gospel, the Religious Tract Society, and the British and Foreign Bible Society were all severely constrained in their work while the colony lacked an efficient infrastructure of volunteers to assist them in distribution – an infrastructure that did not begin to emerge, even in a primitive form, until the 1820s. Indeed, it was not until the 1840s that even the boldest of these organizations were able to reach the more remote corners of the province through the use of travelling agents and paid colporteurs.[49]

Thus, the market for books in Upper Canada remained all but devoid of serious competitors when the General Conference of the Methodist Episcopal Church passed a resolution in 1800 intended to transform its growing corps of itinerant preachers into a travelling sales force on behalf of the Methodist Book Concern. "It shall be the duty of every preacher," ran the declaration, "who has the charge of a circuit, to see that his circuit be duly supplied with books, and to take charge of all the books sent to, or that may be in his circuit, and account with the presiding elder for the same." When a preacher left a circuit, all the books in his charge would be inventoried and warehoused somewhere along that circuit until a new preacher assumed responsibilities. Those who were derelict in their bookselling duties could be removed at the discretion of the presiding elder. The wording of this resolution leaves little doubt that the General Conference hoped to make presiding elders and preachers personally responsible for the sale as well as the stewardship of the Methodist Book Concern's books. Selling books now became as integral a part of an itinerant's duty as preaching itself. In Upper Canada, where books were particularly scarce, this was a very welcome change in policy. But Methodists books were not the only books in circulation. Their detractors also used print to counter the advances these itinerants were making across the colony.[50]

IV

When Nathan Bangs was licensed to preach, in August 1801, he sold all he owned and used the money to purchase a horse, a preacher's outfit, and the "indispensable saddle-bags" in which to carry the Methodist Book Concern's wares along his rounds. Bangs's first circuit was along the Niagara River, where he laboured under the supervision of his beloved mentor Joseph Sawyer. And as long as Bangs remained close to his brethren everything seemed to go well. "The settlements in this country were new, the roads bad, and the fare very hard," he later recalled, "but God was with us in much mercy, awakening and converting sinners, and this was abundant compensation for all our toils." Unfortunately, things took a turn for the worse shortly after Sawyer appointed the young preacher to set out on his own and break new ground north of Lake Erie. Bangs fretted over the slowness of his progress in the new region and attempted to assuage his loneliness by daydreaming about Niagara as he traversed the extensive tracts of unbroken wilderness between settlements. Soon, however, the young preacher had a much more serious challenge with which to contend. "An enemy," he wrote, "introduced Lackington's Memoirs among us, and it passed from house to house, from hand to hand, counteracting our labors." Lackington's *Memoirs* turned out to be a very dangerous book – so dangerous that it almost destroyed the young preacher's faith.[51]

James Lackington was best known as a successful bookseller in London who had converted to Methodism decades earlier while apprenticing as a cobbler. His *Memoirs*, published the year John Wesley died, in 1791, went through several editions on both sides of the Atlantic. Lackington used his *Memoirs* to recount in the most cynical terms how Wesley's preaching transformed him from "a gay, volatile, dissipated young fellow" into "a dull, moping, praying, psalm-singing, fanatic, continually reprehending all about me for their harmless mirth and gaiety." He described in detail the moment of his own spiritual crisis, his awakening to his sinful nature, and how he managed to work his imagination up to "the proper pitch" before persuading himself that he had become "a very great favourite of heaven." The narrative trajectory, minus the sarcasm, was identical to those found in countless Methodist tracts. It also captured the essence of Bangs's own spiritual experiences.[52]

Alas, Lackington's conversion did not last. When he later began to question Methodist beliefs and practices, he found himself shunned by his former coreligionists. Away from their regular company, his "mind began to expand, intellectual light and pleasure broke in and dispelled the gloom and fanatical melancholy; and the sourness of [his] natural temper (which had been much increased by superstition, which Swift calls, 'the spleen of the soul') in part gave way, and was succeeded by cheerfulness, and some degree of good-nature." The final result? Lackington threw off the Methodists completely, "determined to laugh at all their ridiculous perversions of the scripture, and their spiritual cant."[53]

Nathan Bangs, of course, was well acquainted with the fact that the world contained no shortage of books that took a dim view of his faith. But unlike those authored by the more famous Enlightenment critics such as Voltaire, Thomas Paine, and David Hume, James Lackington was a genuine insider. As a result, the criticisms contained in his little volume were as informed as they were devastating. Inevitably, Bangs began to question whether he might not be on the same path – just not quite as far along – as Lackington himself. "Which way to look for relief I knew not," Bangs reflected after poring over every page of the little book, "for I thought God had deserted me." And even if God had not, his fellow preachers certainly had. Bangs's tiny isolated flock turned to him to refute what they claimed were Lackington's "plausible impeachments." He could not. Instead, he hung his head, left for a neighbouring settlement, and sank into a protracted lethargy. His prayers went unanswered, and soon Nathan Bangs began to despair of his very salvation. "Such torment I am sure I could not have endured for many days," he wrote, "I thought that the lost could experience no greater misery. Frequently I was tempted to open my mouth in blasphemy against God, and to curse the Saviour of men."

As it turned out, however, the help Bangs so desperately needed to overcome his doubts was closer than he could have imagined. Although he found some consolation in the company of others, the disaster threatened by Lackington's book was not fully averted until he finally reached down into his saddlebags and withdrew the Methodist Book Concern's hymnbook. Together with the Bible, the hymnbook was the one book sure to be found among the small library of offerings that every Methodist preacher carried wherever he went. "As I read," Bangs recalled, "such a sudden glow of joy filled and overflowed my soul that I praised God aloud, and I rode on triumphing in his goodness to me and to all men."[54]

Bangs learned from his painful experience that books could be potent tools for both good and ill. Just as surely as one book could tear down, another could build up. Importantly, the hymnbook that Bangs pulled from his saddlebags did more than help him recover his faith. It also reminded him of his membership and role in the Methodist Episcopal Church. Almost certainly, the edition Bangs carried along with him was Ezekiel Cooper's 1802 *Pocket Hymn-Book, Designed as A Constant Companion for the Pious*. Based on a pirated edition of Wesley's hymnbook first published by Robert Spence in London in the early 1780s, the *Pocket Hymn-Book* was accompanied by a special preface signed by bishops Thomas Coke and Francis Asbury that urged the singer, the reader, and most importantly the purchaser, of his or her role in Methodism's wider economy. "For after the necessary expenses of printing and binding are discharged," the text ran, "we shall make it a noble charity by applying the profits arising therefrom, to religious and charitable purposes ...

We must therefore earnestly entreat you, if you have any respect for the authority of the Conferences, or of us, or any regard for the prosperity of the Connection, to purchase no Hymn-Books, but what are signed with the names of your two Bishops." Thus, on both sides of the border, the circulation of books such as these, books that provided not only nourishing spiritual fare, but that also reinforced the denominational identities of readers, played a vitally important role in not only attracting, but also holding Methodist converts – and in this particular case one very promising Methodist preacher.[55]

Methodist itinerants criss-crossing the colony in those early days were, in the words of one Canadian preacher, "indefatigable sales-men of good books, which they carried about with them in their saddle-bags." In this, the same preacher elaborates, they had little choice: "To this they were impelled, partly by a sense of duty and respect to the rule of Conference on the subject, and partly by necessity; for the little profits they made on books sold, went to supplement their very small allowances." Driven on by duty and need in equal measure, the result was that "the principal Methodist family in the early days was better supplied with standard books in theology and religion than similar families are now – not only relatively, but often really. What a boon were these publications in the then tardy state of communication with the outside world."[56]

Not incidentally, as these preachers travelled their extensive circuits, crossing wide tracts of tedious wilderness between settlements, they also "had the use of the books themselves" to improve the hours and pass the time. These circumstances not only helped them fulfil the *Discipline*'s requirement that they spend a portion of each day in study, they also afforded an essential opportunity for Methodist preachers to become intimately familiar with the products they were offering for sale. It is hard to imagine that references to the contents of these books did not routinely leaven their sermons and inform their conversations as they led local Methodist societies in worship, in classes, and at quarterly meetings along their isolated circuits. This, in turn, would have helped to shape and homogenize the market demand for books by encouraging readers to develop a particular taste for the Methodist Book Concern's steadily growing list of titles.

As Methodists itinerants lingered on horseback, poring over the *Discipline*, the hymnbook, and the catalogues of offerings printed at the rear of these and other texts, they no doubt would have come to think of their auditors as potential customers as well as spiritual charges. The dual role filled by the preachers meant that spreading the Methodist gospel both increased the denomination's membership rolls and expanded the Concern's market. The two could no longer be separated. Thus, it is not surprising to discover that those who converted to Methodism typically remarked a significant change in their reading habits and tastes. There is little evidence, however, to suggest that these books were much circulated outside Methodism's denominational boundaries. On the contrary, there were compelling reasons for preachers not to attempt to sell the contents of their saddlebags to all and sundry.

Already objects of political suspicion on the part of the governing authorities and the few Church of England clergymen assigned to the colony's small settlements, Methodist preachers knew well that they were not always welcome figures. The intense form of "experimental religion" they peddled was particularly unpalatable to those who were, at least as far as these preachers were concerned, little more than hardened sinners. "When you consider that I came alone into this almost savage land," wrote William Case, an early American preacher who took up a preaching circuit in Upper Canada shortly after 1800, "two hundred miles from my brethren, and among a people, not one of whom I had ever seen before, and had not a friend, save one, with whom I could converse freely on the subject of experimental religion, you may guess what were my feelings. It was soon told me that there were some who would not hesitate in taking my life if they could do it without being detected."[57]

This was more than idle fear on Case's part. On one occasion, a man carrying a noose threatened to hang the young preacher if he didn't like the sermon. On another, a small crowd that gathered to hear Case in Kingston suddenly turned ugly and tried to topple him from a makeshift pulpit and set his hair on fire. George Neil, another of the province's earliest preachers, reported being pelted "with stones till the blood flowed down his face" after "preaching against the prevailing vices of the country." Nathan Bangs also described unwelcome physical opposition to his efforts, among them a narrow escape from some "ruffians"' who disliked his preaching and set an ambush to "wreak their vengeance" with an eye to stealing his horse as well as the contents of his saddlebags. In an environment this isolating and this fraught with danger, the imprudence of openly displaying fragile printed wares for which individual preachers had been made financially responsible by the American General Conference, and that they would have found impossible to replace if stolen or destroyed, would have been only too obvious to these young men. It comes as no surprise, then, that Nathan Bangs and his fellow preachers suggested in their journals and reports that bookselling activities took place in denominationally sequestered settings such as Methodist class meetings and at other gatherings characterized by a high degree of religious homogeneity. The end result was that the Methodist Book Concern's market in Upper Canada, although largely coextensive with white settlement, remained culturally isolated and denominationally insular for decades to come. As long as that market remained hidden from public view, moreover, Methodism's conservative and Anglican detractors would be unable to condemn Methodists for scattering these purportedly seditious and reputedly fanatical books of republican manufacture across the land.[58]

Thus, undisturbed by their critics, Methodist readers across Upper Canada found that their piety and their reading practices soon became mutually reinforcing. The more they read, the more entrenched their Methodist faith became, and the more ardently they coveted the books that Methodist preachers offered for sale to members of the local societies. At the same time, Methodist readers were continually reminded by the texts found in the Methodist Book Concern's catalogues, by the prefaces to its hymnals and other books, by printed polity documents, and even by the imprints on title pages, that the purchase of these books conferred a financial benefit on the work of the wider Methodist Episcopal Church in North America. Participation in this market was, in other words, a powerful act of denominational solidarity. The Concern's books were to be purchased chiefly for this reason and not simply because those books were useful, handsome, or inexpensive. At the same time, the preachers who functioned as the Concern's travelling points of contact had their own reasons for underscoring this relationship between patronage and denominational identity: although it certainly assured the Methodist Episcopal Church of a steady stream of revenue for its charitable work, this relationship also served as the only way to supplement incomes so meagre that without them these preachers could hardly have kept body and soul together.

As Methodism continued to expand across the colony, it would have become increasingly difficult for anyone brought into the Methodist fold to remain unconscious of the denominational rhetoric the Methodist Book Concern used at every opportunity to set its books and later periodicals apart from the products of rival printers in places like New York, Boston, Philadelphia, and Baltimore. Although the Concern had almost no competition to speak of in Upper Canada's backwoods, the denominational implications of that rhetoric would have remained undiminished: by continuing to purchase books bearing the Concern's imprint, Upper Canadian Methodists knowingly shored up the interests of an American religious institution by confirming, through these transactions, membership in the Methodist Episcopal Church. In a province as religiously eclectic and demographically diverse as any American state, the transnational nature of this insular market continued to be largely unproblematic – at least before the War of 1812. The outbreak of hostilities would do much to change that.[59]

Chapter Two

"Rekindling the Canada Fire": Books, Periodicals, and the Revival of Methodism after the War of 1812

In January 1819, the United States stood on the precipice of its first major peacetime financial crisis. Methodist preachers across North America hardly noticed. They were too busy fanning the flames of revival and stuffing their saddlebags with copies of the first anniversary issue of the *Methodist Magazine* for eager subscribers along the denomination's expanding network of preaching circuits. A modest octavo of about forty pages, the issue featured an engraved frontispiece of William McKendree, the first American-born bishop of the Methodist Episcopal Church, together with the usual miscellany of articles, sermons, extracts, and missionary correspondence. Yet, towards the end of the issue, readers would have encountered a series of narratives so improbable that their contents must have struck many as nothing short of miraculous. Written from Augusta, a town on the St Lawrence River, by Upper Canada's presiding elder, William Case, these accounts described a series of mighty Methodist revivals then sweeping across the whole of the province that had already more than made up for all the enormous losses suffered as a result of the War of 1812.

With American preachers absent during that entire conflict, Upper Canadian Methodists found few opportunities to gather for religious services. For the first time since William Losee began preaching near Matilda in the winter of 1790, church membership plummeted. For a religious denomination that had spread from the United States and that had relied on foreign preachers to sustain its momentum, even more worrying was an emergent but unmistakable shift in Upper Canada's political complexion that divided a period of relative ideological diversity from one increasingly dominated by the views of an influential conservative leadership that shared the anti-American prejudices of the colonial administration. As if this were not enough, British Wesleyans – to whom American preachers had already ceded control over the Maritime colonies in 1800 – took the opportunity of Methodism's wartime decline to establish rival preaching outposts in both Upper and Lower Canada, with an eye to displacing American Methodism from British North America altogether.

Yet, here in this last problem lay a solution to all the others. After all, a growing British Wesleyan presence promised Upper Canadian Methodists a relatively easy and straightforward path to postwar recovery. The Wesleyans would furnish the colony with a ready supply of paid missionaries while at the same time providing Canadian Methodists with the bona fide conservative and Loyalist credentials they so desperately needed to counter mounting political suspicions about individual believers who would otherwise be obliged to continue taking their marching orders from American bishops. But, in a move that can only be described as dumbfounding, Canadian Methodists turned their backs on British Wesleyan missionaries, and in the years following the War of 1812, insisted on maintaining their membership in the American Methodist Episcopal Church. How can this be accounted for? Either Canadian Methodists were stunningly ignorant of the political realities they faced, or there was a strong counterweight to these conservative forces that was responsible for shaping their religious and denominational identities in a decidedly transnational way.

As this chapter will show, the *Methodist Magazine* did more than announce the remarkable revival of Episcopal Methodism in Upper Canada: it helped to bring it about. The *Magazine*, together with the Methodist Book Concern's other offerings, although produced in New York and distributed mostly by American preachers assigned to Upper Canada during the immediate postwar years, consistently presented Methodism as a movement that transcended political boundaries, identities, and allegiances. The *Magazine*'s editors also encouraged preachers to promote the periodical by framing the act of subscription as a potent sign of denominational solidarity. This mirrored and reinforced ongoing reminders to readers in prefaces, editorials, and other documents that all profits derived from the purchase of the Concern's books and periodicals furthered Methodist efforts across the whole of North America. In this way, the Concern's transnational market came to function as a powerful centripetal force uniting the Methodist Episcopal Church's extensive North American congregations. As these rhetorical linkages between religious identity and the consumption of printed matter were strengthened on an iterative basis, they played a central role in reducing what would otherwise have seemed an ever-widening ideological gap separating the inhabitants of British North America from citizens of the United States of America.

I

The United States declared war on Britain in June 1812, and Methodist expansion in Upper Canada came to a sudden and abrupt halt. At the same time, the Methodist Book Concern's access to its Canadian readers was unexpectedly severed. The causes of the war – British naval blockades of continental Europe, the impressment of British-born sailors serving on American ships, President Jefferson's Embargo Act – must have seemed unutterably remote to many settlers toiling in the Upper Canadian wilderness. The war's effects, however, were immediately felt when the province's farmers, merchants, labourers, and artisans were organized into militias while the vast majority of Britain's professional military force was busy contending with Napoleon in Europe.[1]

After the outbreak of hostilities, most of the colony's preaching circuits were abandoned as American Methodist itinerants fled for the safety of the United States. One of the few who remained behind was Upper Canada's presiding elder, Henry Ryan – that former stage boxer turned evangelist – who insisted that his birth in Massachusetts before the Revolutionary War was over rendered him as much a British subject as any Loyalist. Ryan's extraordinary tenacity and decisiveness was fuelled by a fierce sense of mission. It also helped that he was not afraid to get his own hands dirty when it came to enforcing discipline. "He was known in his prime to throw ordinary sized men over the enclosure of the Campground, who were found disturbing the order and solemnity of the services within," one contemporary noted with equal parts astonishment and admiration. Francis Asbury rewarded Ryan for his dedication by promoting him from his preaching circuit in Niagara to serve as presiding elder when Upper Canada became a separate district in the new Genesee Conference, in 1810. In that role, Ryan became responsible for overseeing the ministry and bookselling activities of about a dozen or so travelling preachers working from Augusta to the province's furthest western settlements.[2]

On the eve of the War of 1812, Methodists counted almost three thousand members across Upper Canada as well as about three hundred more in Lower Canada. When hostilities commenced that June, Henry Ryan suddenly found himself almost alone and with far more on his plate than any one man could be expected to handle. Nor were all his troubles on the supply side of the equation alone: Ryan also had to contend with a political landscape that was increasingly hostile to his mission and its roots in the United States. In addition to the well-known antipathies harboured by the province's slowly growing number of

Church of England clergymen and British Wesleyan missionaries – who in their more candid moments characterized Methodism as little more than "deplorable fanaticism" – the colony's senior administrators began to nurture a sturdy distrust of Methodism on the grounds that it had spread to British North America from the United States. Even Isaac Brock, Upper Canada's ranking military officer at the outbreak of war, remarked in official correspondence to the secretary of state of the Colonial Office that these American-based preachers espoused political views that were "highly prejudicial to the peace of Society."[3]

Fortunately, Ryan had more than just his remarkably forceful personality to sustain Methodism. He also had a surprisingly large inventory of the Methodist Book Concern's books on hand to fortify the hearts of readers while underwriting costs associated with carrying on his ministry. That was fortunate because there were few, if any, opportunities while the conflict lasted to replenish his stock. Isaac Brock, in his first public proclamation after the US Congress's declaration of war, ordered those in the province to "forbear all Communication with the Enemy or Persons residing within the Territory of the United States and to manifest their Loyalty by a zealous Cooperation with His Majesty's Armed Forces in Defence of the Province, and Repulse of the Enemy." In probable deference to Brock's edict, not a single preacher from Upper Canada attended the second annual Genesee Conference that took place later that summer, even though it was held just across the Niagara River. Indeed, Ryan and his preachers would make no effort to cross the border or to attend any of the annual Genesee conferences until hostilities finally and officially ceased, in March 1815.[4]

These wartime years have sometimes been referred to as the "*non-historic period*" of Canadian Methodism because during this time Henry Ryan kept no membership statistics and recorded no minutes of the three annual conferences he claimed to have held with his own preachers each July. By the time the War of 1812 ended, it was clear that Methodists – together with the province's Baptists and Presbyterians – had suffered major reversals across the colony. "The sudden and repeated calls of the militia in cases of alarm," explained William Case, Ryan's successor as Upper Canada's presiding elder after the war, "rendered it extremely difficult, at times, and especially in some circuits, to get many together for the purpose of religious instruction. Frequently none but women and children could attend preaching." Regular membership in Upper and Lower Canada declined from a high of 3,293 before the war to only 1,785 by the time the Genesee Conference met in June 1815.[5]

Money was almost as scarce as converts in wartime Upper Canada. Even the formidable Henry Ryan had a hard time making ends meet under these conditions. In the winter, when the difficulties attendant on itinerant preaching were at their worst, he turned to hauling goods across both Upper and Lower Canada in order to support his family. Ryan also supplemented his income by continuing to sell a surprisingly large quantity of the Concern's books and tracts to the colony's declining number of Methodists. By the time Ryan turned up at the General Conference of the Methodist Episcopal Church in Baltimore in May 1816, he owed a considerable debt to the Concern for the bookselling proceeds that he and his preachers had pocketed to sustain themselves.[6]

A committee appointed to examine the affairs of the Methodist Book Concern reported, "While [Ryan] and the preachers on his district were traveling in Upper Canada, they were, in consequence of the prevailing distress and scarcity, reduced to the unavoidable necessity of supporting themselves, in part, by means of book-money, or of leaving the work." The committee went on to note that Ryan and his preachers had appropriated no less than $700 during the conflict and that, since the cessation of hostilities, Ryan, who as presiding elder was responsible for the entire outstanding sum, had paid back all but $227. To set that overall figure in context, at the General Conference of 1816 the salary of travelling preachers was raised from $64 to $100 per annum. Out of this modest sum each preacher had to "furnish himself with clothes, horse, and traveling apparatus, his board being included among his travelling or extra expenses." For the time the conflict lasted, then, the amount of money appropriated from the sale of the Concern's books in Upper Canada was the equivalent of more than ten years' worth of salary for a typical travelling preacher. Fortunately for Ryan, the committee recommended that his debt be forgiven in view of his service to Methodism during these difficult years.[7]

How many books and tracts did Henry Ryan and his small handful of preachers actually sell during the War of 1812? By extension, how large were the inventories that were being maintained in British North America as a matter of routine before the war broke out? Wartime catalogues published by the Methodist Book Concern between 1810 and 1816 are suggestive. James Lackington's *Confessions* – a dramatic retraction of that earlier title that had almost destroyed Nathan Bangs's faith while he was in the Upper Canadian wilderness a decade earlier – could be had for anywhere between 25¢ and 37½¢. William Law's *Serious Call to a Devout and Holy Life* was offered for between 50¢ and 75¢. And Elizabeth Rowe's *Devout Exercises of the Heart*, another popular title among Methodists throughout the early nineteenth century, was priced at 25¢. Assuming that Ryan and his preachers sold books without any wartime discount and at an average price of 40¢ each, and taking into account the 18 per cent bookseller commission the committee would have excluded from the total figure owed, Ryan and his preachers probably sold about two thousand books between the summers of 1812 and 1815.[8]

All of this strongly suggests that some kind of provincial depot or depots must have been in operation during, and probably well before, June 1812. It also indicates that a relatively robust denominational market for the Methodist Book Concern's books had been successfully established in Upper Canada during the first decade of the nineteenth century. By 1815, however, profound changes were in the offing. Not only was the political mood of the colony becoming markedly more conservative, but the Methodist Book Concern was about to enter a new period of unprecedented growth – and at the heart of that growth was a new periodical that would unite Methodists across North America as never before.[9]

II

Church of England clergyman John Strachan was accused of many things throughout the course of his long lifetime, including greed, arrogance, hypocrisy, intolerance, corruption, tyranny, and bigotry. But, no one ever accused Strachan of cowardice. In April 1813, Upper Canada's capital was in flames. Major General Isaac Brock had been killed at the Battle of Queenston Heights the previous autumn, and his replacement, Loyalist Major General Roger Hale Sheaffe, was unlucky enough to find himself in Little York on that fateful spring day when an American flotilla of fourteen ships carrying almost two thousand troops came looming over the horizon. Outnumbered by more than two to one, it did not take long for things to go sideways for the British. After a series of reversals, Sheaffe beat a retreat to Kingston, burned the wooden bridge over the Don River to frustrate his pursuers, and issued an order for Fort York's magazine to be fired.

With no one but members of the militia left to negotiate terms of surrender, much less protect the lives of the inhabitants, John Strachan marched out to confront the enemy and demanded to be taken aboard the principal American ship commanded by General Henry Dearborn. Once there, he insisted on immediate terms in order to prevent American troops from looting the town. So taken aback was Dearborn by the audacity and vehemence of this seemingly inconsequential clergyman that he capitulated. When the Americans returned again later that summer, Strachan played a similarly heroic role when he managed to extract a promise that the volumes purloined from colonial libraries the previous spring by mischievous – if wholesomely bookish – American soldiers would be returned. Why did Strachan risk his own life not once but twice to protect the interests of the colonists? In the end it didn't matter. He was a hero. And the events playing out all across the colony proved that Strachan and his fellow clergymen had been right all along: the Americans really were a treacherous lot.[10]

The nature of the immediate impact of the War of 1812 on Upper Canada's political temper and the way in which it provoked a rise in anti-Americanism across the colony are subjects of disagreement among recent scholars. In the main, however, religious historians generally concur that there was a causal relationship between the two. "The War of 1812 displayed citizens of the United States in a new role as invaders from without," observes one scholar emblematically, "and the result was to make possible a sentiment that was not merely anti-republican, or anti-democratic but specifically anti-American." Whether the change was immediate or protracted, the War of 1812 undoubtedly opened a new phase of development in Upper Canada's political character that led to the eventual hegemony of a conservative ideology at odds with the steady decline of Federalism in the United States.[11]

These opposing trends helped to foreground political antipathies in the postwar period at a time when distinctions between American Republicans and American Federalists were invoked less and less frequently in the newspapers published in Kingston, Niagara, and York. Indeed, the artillery was hardly cool before the *Kingston Gazette*, the only Upper Canadian newspaper to be published continuously throughout the conflict, reprinted a letter from the *Montreal Herald* complaining about the poisonous influence of Americans and American books. "They teach us to hate the government that we ought, and are bound, to support," complained the writer, "to revile the country that we are bound to love and respect; and to think that there is nothing great or good, generous or brave, anywhere to be found but in the United States."[12]

Just as participation in the War of 1812 eventually became a symbol of one's colonial loyalty to the British Crown and constitution, those individuals remembered for playing a standout role in the defence of Upper Canada found their own status enhanced considerably. John Strachan, that Church of England clergyman who had had the temerity to face down American General Henry Dearborn on his own vessel, was by far the most prominent and influential of these figures. Indeed, Strachan made sure to take great credit for the part he played and his bravery was soon rewarded with appointments to the Executive Council in 1817 and the Legislative Council in 1820. The first of these functioned as a kind of cabinet for the colony's lieutenant governor and the second as an upper house relative to the province's elected Legislative Assembly.

Strachan's influence in the councils of church and state continued to grow in the following years when he was appointed archdeacon in 1827 and secured prominent posts for many of the former students he had once taught while a schoolmaster in Cornwall. These men included Sir John Beverley Robinson, who served as the colony's attorney general between 1818 and 1829, as well as Christopher Hagerman, Charles Jones, and George Markland, all of whom went on to secure seats in either the Legislative Assembly or on the Executive Council. Strachan also won the unswerving confidence of Sir Peregrine Maitland, the lieutenant governor of Upper Canada between 1818 and 1828. Indeed, so pervasive did Strachan's influence become in these postwar years that subsequent historians have sometimes referred to him as the province's first unofficial premier. As the acknowledged leader of this powerful oligarchy – referred to by its detractors in the press as the "Family Compact" – Strachan was able to shore up the interests of the Church of England while beating down the Methodists, his chief religious rivals, for their disloyal connections to an American church.[13]

John Strachan's dislike for the inhabitants of the United States was both long-standing and visceral. "They have frequently got no education at all," he blustered in a letter written just a few years after President Thomas Jefferson took office in 1800, "or so little, that it cannot be known in conversation. And yet like all the ignorant, they know everything." As the years passed, Strachan seems to have concluded that the only thing worse than an American citizen was an American preacher – especially if he happened to be a Methodist. "The Methodists are making great progress among us and filling the country with the most deplorable fanaticism," he seethed. Even worse than their unseemly and unbridled religious enthusiasm, however, was that their American roots caused them to be "tainted by religious dissent and republicanism." The ultimate purpose of these preachers, as far as this rising clergyman was concerned, was to "pull down all establishments, undermine the loyalty of the people and constitute us a province of the United States." Strachan was vehement, persistent, and persuasive on these points. As his influence in government grew, he took steps whenever possible not only to frustrate the Methodists, but also to staunch the flow of American immigrants to the colony. How else, Strachan reasoned, could loyal subjects put a stop to these republicans' becoming involved in politics themselves and ultimately turning over the whole colony to Washington?[14]

Strachan and his allies received another boost when the Society for the Propagation of the Gospel in Foreign Parts began in 1813 to receive annual grants from the British Parliament – money that was used, in part, to support Anglican missions in Upper Canada. This increase in funding, together with Britain's protracted postwar economic depression after the defeat of Napoleon, resulted in five additional clergymen being appointed to Upper Canada between 1818 and 1819 – bringing the provincial total to thirteen. This period also marked a shift in the Church of England's strategy for dealing with the Methodists as Jacob Mountain, John Strachan, and others began to face the fact that Anglicanism, even with a supply of priests sufficient to match Methodist preachers man for man, would be hard-pressed to stamp out their competitors. Up until this time, these clergymen had decorously confined their growing disquiet to the letters they had written to one another and, on occasion, to distant government officials in the British metropole. No more. With the Methodists once again expanding their numbers and their influence, Strachan and his supporters began denouncing this resurgent religious rabble from the pulpit and in the press.[15]

Pressures of this kind fostered a growing awareness among Upper Canadian Methodists of the liability their ongoing connection to the American Methodist Episcopal Church – and the Methodist Book Concern – posed to their postwar recovery and expansion. These changing circumstances formed a subject of serious discussion when the preachers who together made up the Genesee Conference – embracing parts of both the State of New York and the province of Upper Canada – convened together in Lyons, New York, in June 1815. Delegates at that meeting of the Genesee Conference remained as committed as ever to winning souls north of the border, while at the same time acknowledging that the conditions on the ground called for circumspection and delicacy. Thus, they resolved together "to go on with the work in Canada; but to be careful in the choice of preachers, that offence, as far as possible, might be prevented."[16]

Alas, offence was not prevented. Episcopal Methodists attempting to revive religion along their preaching circuits encountered surprisingly stiff opposition – especially from their British Wesleyan counterparts in the metropole who had dispatched several of their own missionaries to the Canadas after most of the American preachers had fled. When Henry Ryan arrived in Montreal in September 1815 to begin his term as Lower Canada's new presiding elder, he was stunned to discover that the Wesleyans had locked him out of the Methodist chapel. Montreal Methodists, who had welcomed the Wesleyans with open arms during the War of 1812, protested Ryan's presence by chanting "I am a true Britton." Faced with a problem that could not be solved either by a rousing sermon or by the application of brute strength, Ryan was reduced to protesting meekly that the Wesleyans and their ilk had no proof that he and his fellow preachers had "not been conscientious in praying for Kings and all that are in authority."[17]

As both parties dug in their heels, it became clear that this dispute would not be easily remedied. The Wesleyans refused to retreat and the Episcopal Methodists, meeting for their General Conference in Baltimore the following May, resolved, in the presence of two delegates from the Wesleyan Methodist Missionary Society no less, to continue their work in the Canadas on the grounds that "it is the desire of the great majority of the people in Upper and Lower Canada to be supplied, as heretofore, with preachers from the United States." Nathan Bangs, together with two other preachers, drafted a letter to the Wesleyan Methodist Missionary Society in London declaring their resolve. Undeterred, the Wesleyans increased their postwar efforts to displace their American competitors, and by 1817 had ten missionaries stationed in the Canadas – including at Kingston and Cornwall. The following year, they spread further west to the Bay of Quinte and the Town of York, and by 1818 had come as far as Niagara. Henry Pope, who spearheaded Wesleyan advances at Cornwall, York, and Niagara, did so in the firm conviction that the Americans were, in words that might have been borrowed from John Strachan himself, "by no means acceptable, partly owing the late war [...] and partly owing to their extensive ignorance and uncouth conduct."[18]

In May 1820, delegates attending the General Conference in Baltimore approved new language for the *Doctrine and Discipline of the Methodist Episcopal Church*: "As far as it respects civil affairs," the revised text read, "we believe it the duty of Christians, and especially all Christian ministers, to be subject to the supreme authority of the country where they may reside ... and therefore it is expected that all our preachers and people who may be under the British or any other government, will behave themselves as peaceable and orderly subjects." This new clause meant more than that the bishops expected preachers in the Canadas to mind their manners and refrain from antagonizing local authorities. It also signalled that the Americans were as determined as ever to regain control of their preaching circuits north of the border.[19]

Later that year, a young preacher named John Emory – one of American Methodism's brightest lights, who would later serve a term at the head of the Methodist Book Concern before being ordained a bishop – travelled to London to meet with members of the Wesleyan Methodist

Missionary Society. Placing his finger on this new passage in the *Discipline*, Emory "asserted that his brethren were grievously wronged by the insinuation that they had acted in a manner inimical to the established Government of Canada," and he somehow managed to persuade his Wesleyan listeners that "in Upper Canada at least, his Church was competent for the work it had undertaken." In the spring of the following year, Bishop Enoch George wrote to the Missionary Society confirming the agreement between the British missionaries and "the preachers of the American connexion" to divide the Canadas between them – the former occupying Lower Canada and the latter Upper Canada. "The prejudices which may exist in the minds of some of the members, on both sides," the bishop wrote, "and which may have originated in the unpleasant state of things in the Canadas, will require time to remove them [*sic*]: but with a prudent administration, it is believed they will subside."[20]

In the following years, despite increased rancour directed against them by Church of England clergymen, together with a rising tide of anti-Americanism across the British colony more generally, the Methodist Episcopal Church reported impressive gains at the annual meetings of the Genesee Conference. Charles Stuart, a young man who immigrated to Upper Canada after the War of 1812 and who held out hope for eventual ordination in the Church of England, was clearly more than a little surprised at this. "The American Methodist church of the United States," he remarked, "a society without public funds; without any public constituted authorities; the members of a state severed from us by the reminders of civil wraths, and by mutual intolerance, and emulation, and pride, hath been the chief (by no means the only) medium, under God (particularly to the westward) of fostering in our districts the spirit of the Gospel." Needless to say, William Case was in complete agreement – at least with Stuart's conclusion. "The last four years have been a season of harvest indeed," enthused Case, "and revivals are still going on." With more than five thousand formal members now living west of the Ottawa River, Methodism's resurgence had once again made it the British colony's most vigorous denomination.[21]

These impressive gains amid so many headwinds were not realized by preaching alone. The Methodist Book Concern's infrastructure for book distribution had also been rebuilt, and now, for the first time, Methodists could boast of a successful denominational periodical in which to tell tales of religious revival. The colony's growing corps of travelling preachers, men who were already practised booksellers, became the *Methodist Magazine*'s sole subscription agents and took copies with them wherever they went. Back in New York, the editors of the *Methodist Magazine* used the new periodical to promote nascent missionary work among Native groups, to encourage the adoption of courses of study for preachers and ministerial candidates, and to stimulate the spread of Sunday schools and Sunday school libraries. In all this, the editors took advantage of the *Magazine*'s rising popularity to shore up the denominational loyalties of readers on both sides of the border by continually emphasizing the relationship between patronage of the denominational publisher and the religious identities of its customers.[22]

By the end of 1824, William Case was able to report that even around Kingston, an area typically more resistant to Methodism than other parts of Upper Canada, the *Magazine* had found a significant number of subscribers. "Sixty-four subscribers," he wrote, had "given in their names for the Magazine" in that region, together with seventy in "Bay of Quinty [*sic*] circuit alone." "The list of subscribers," he went on to add, "might be easily increased, greatly to the advantage of the cause of religion, as well as the interests of the concern, if an active part were taken by the preachers in the circulation of this valuable work." At the time of Case's letter, Kingston and the Bay of Quinte had a combined Methodist membership of 652. A conservative extrapolation of these subscription figures across the rest of the colony's preaching circuits embracing 6,357 formal members of the Methodist Episcopal Church suggests that the total number of active Canadian subscriptions to the *Magazine* was upwards of 1,500. By comparison, the *Upper Canada Gazette*, the province's official weekly newspaper, was printed in runs of only 300 copies. Around the same time, William Lyon Mackenzie's more popular *Colonial Advocate* counted not more than about 400 subscribers. Through its denominational network of preachers functioning as subscription agents and colporteurs, then, it appears that by 1825 the *Methodist Magazine* was reaching a significantly larger number of paying subscribers in Upper Canada than any periodical produced by Canadian printers.[23]

The *Magazine*'s remarkable popularity among the colony's Methodists can be accounted for in several ways. For one thing, Methodist preachers were notoriously underpaid for their efforts and found themselves regularly obliged to make up shortfalls in their salaries by selling the Methodist Book Concern's books and periodicals along their circuits. Since the General Conference of 1800, preachers had been paid commissions of between 15 per cent and 25 per cent on whatever they sold. With not only the welfare of the denomination, but also their own personal financial interests to consider, it seems probable that Methodist preachers would have promoted subscriptions to a regular periodical, and therefore a regular revenue stream, with some energy "to supplement their very small allowances."[24]

Motivated subscription agents alone would not have been enough, however, to account for this degree of success. It is highly probable that Canadian Methodists also took such an active interest in reading the *Methodist Magazine* because they saw for the first time their own stories reflected in its pages. The way for this was opened when the Book Committee, reporting at the General Conference of 1816, determined that "it shall be the duty of each annual conference to appoint a committee of three, who shall receive communications from their brethren, and correspond with the editor in order to furnish him with materials proper for publication."[25] As one of three preachers assigned by the Genesee Conference to supply the new periodical with content, William Case authored many pieces about Canadian Methodists that appeared alongside American narratives.[26]

Case's enthusiastic report on the postwar Canadian revivals in January 1819 was only the beginning. In subsequent years, minutes of meetings, missionary reports, revival narratives, and other stories written by and about the affairs of Upper Canadian Methodists appeared regularly in the *Methodist Magazine*. In the summer of 1820, for example, William Case and Henry Ryan submitted a report to the *Magazine* describing the success of the proceedings of the annual meeting of the Genesee Conference while noting that, despite its American majority, delegates met on the Canadian side of the border, in Niagara. "Religion in this province we think to be on the rise." The authors went on to note proudly, "The last four years have been a season of harvest indeed, and revivals are still going on." The lesson that these preachers wanted their Canadian and American readers to draw from this was clear: Methodist interests were being advanced with as much energy, enthusiasm, and effectiveness north of the border as they were south of it.[27]

III

In the same year that John Emory crossed the Atlantic to negotiate Wesleyan withdrawal from Upper Canada, Nathan Bangs was elected senior book agent of the Methodist Book Concern. He also assumed the editorial reins of the *Methodist Magazine*. After his conversion in Niagara, Bangs had proven himself to be an itinerant without peer during those early years of the nineteenth century as he blazed new preaching circuits in the province's furthest western reaches and played a starring role in Upper Canada's earliest revival camp meetings. Bangs's election thus signalled an important development in the North American market for Methodist books inasmuch as his formative spiritual experiences had taught him to recognize Methodism as a denomination without borders. Indeed, he never ceased to regard the British colony as his spiritual birthplace and even married a Canadian woman before returning to the United States a few years before the War of 1812. There can be little doubt, then, that Bangs was just as committed to forwarding the Concern's interests in Upper Canada as he was in the United States.

When Upper Canada was finally set apart as an independent annual conference of the Methodist Episcopal Church, in May 1824, support for the *Methodist Magazine* remained undiminished. As a growing number of preachers, following the example first set by William Case, began to submit copy to New York for publication in the periodical, so too did delegates attending the inaugural Canada Conference. Indeed, the ink recording its official minutes had hardly been allowed to dry before delegates whisked a copy off to New York for publication in the *Magazine.* As readers in the thousands on both sides of the border read with increasing frequency articles recounting Canadian Methodist exploits, the *Methodist Magazine* might be said to have functioned not only as a venue, but as a symbol in its own right, for demonstrating the degree to which North American Methodism annulled and surmounted mere political differences.[28]

The *Methodist Magazine* was especially important for preachers and laypersons in Upper Canada wishing to stay apprised of Methodist missionary activities among the colony's Natives along the Grand River, the Thames, and the Credit. Before the early 1820s, Methodists had shown only sporadic interest in evangelization outside the boundaries of white settlement. Nathan Bangs and David Sawyer were the first to preach to some isolated Native communities as early as 1800. William Case was known to do the same when circumstances allowed. Anything like a more systematic approach, however, did not finally begin to take shape in Upper Canada until midsummer 1823, when Alvin Torry began to preach more consistently among the Mohawks living along the banks of the Grand River in the western portion of his Lyon's Creek circuit. Still only in his mid-twenties, Torry was already a relatively experienced itinerant who by that time had ministered along circuits in both the United States and Upper Canada. Mohawks in this region of the colony had long been identified with the Anglicanism of Joseph Brant, but Torry concluded on his own evidence that their Christian convictions were largely perfunctory. And he was determined to change that.[29]

Sometime later, Nathan Bangs appears to have solicited from Torry an account of his work for the *Methodist Magazine*. Torry's response, which became the first printed record of Methodist missionary activities among Natives in Upper Canada, appeared in the *Magazine*'s January issue of 1824. Torry described at length "a powerful awakening" sweeping over the mission. He also included a long letter written by Seth Crawford describing a camp meeting revival that had taken place at the Mission the previous summer. Torry mentioned nothing about the government in his first report. The following year, however, in December 1825, he noted that Upper Canada's government was showing "good will" towards Native converts "on account of their reformation and disposition for civilization," and he described a visit paid to the Mission in June 1825 by "several gentlemen from York, of high respectability" to distribute "presents."[30]

Within a few short years, Torry's optimistic assessment of the government's intentions proved to be embarrassingly naive. Yet, his rhetorical approach in these articles is telling. In the first report, he drew no attention to the fact that his Mission was situated in a geopolitical context quite different from that informing the lives of most of his readers. In the second, while commenting on the apparently smiling presence of several government officials, Torry omitted anything to demarcate for his readers how these officials might differ from Americans on their views about the relationship between church and state. Instead, brushing all that complexity to one side, both Torry and Bangs left their readers to infer simply that a favourable disposition on the part of the government was something to be valued. The actual contribution of these officials to the real work of conversion – notwithstanding their distribution of "presents" – was left unaddressed.[31]

In the end, the reports that Torry authored for Bangs seem to have been written – consciously or unconsciously – with an eye to leaving readers with the impression that, to whatever extent any ongoing relationship between church and state in Upper Canada may have interfered with Methodist ambitions, it had little real impact on what in actual practice was a functioning religious free market indistinguishable from that in the United States. In this way, the *Methodist Magazine* once again became a locus for softening political differences in the minds of readers while foregrounding precisely those things that Methodist subscribers across North America held in common: an equally vigorous dedication to Native missions that simultaneously reinforced their own sense of participation in a transnational community of common spiritual purpose and shared denominational identity.

IV

Under Nathan Bangs's editorial direction, the *Methodist Magazine* also began to function as a public forum in which preachers assigned to Upper Canada's expanding network of preaching circuits could appeal to the Methodist Book Concern, the Methodist Missionary Society, and other denominational organizations located in the United States for help. Bangs knew Upper Canadians were particularly desperate for books. His own experience in the colony almost two decades earlier had taught him how miserable life could be without access to edifying reading material. Thus, when Fitch Reed, who travelled to Upper Canada from New York as a missionary in July 1820, wrote an impassioned letter describing his struggles on behalf of the Missionary Society in the province's backwoods, Bangs wasted no time publishing it in the *Methodist Magazine.* The problem as Reed saw it was a truly distressing lack of books: "We have none to read in our families" was the cry all along his circuit.[32]

Bangs answered Reed's plea by sending bibles and continuing to keep a close eye on developments in Upper Canada. About a year later, another letter appeared in the *Methodist Magazine,* this one written by William Case, acknowledging the receipt of another shipment of bibles and New Testaments, adding that they "will be joyfully and thankfully received." In that same issue, Bangs published a second letter written by Reed, describing the establishment of six new societies in Upper Canada, the addition of seventy new members, and the formation of two new Sunday schools. "Surely the Lord is at work among the people," Reed summarized, "and I believe he will perform gloriously in this country."[33]

Bangs knew, however, that merely responding to requests for books he received from preachers, whether in Upper Canada or the United States, would never be enough to achieve the kind of commitment to reading and study that would ultimately be required to once and for all silence critics like John Strachan who continued to denounce the Methodists as "ignorant enthusiasts." In the continued absence of a prescribed reading list for aspiring preachers with the force of polity behind it, Bangs used his complementary roles as both editor of the *Methodist Magazine* and senior book agent of the Methodist Book Concern to stimulate and to satisfy a demand for specific books within the denomination. The first in a series of a dozen articles Bangs wrote with that agenda in mind appeared in the September 1822 issue of the *Magazine* under the title "The Importance of Study to a Minister of the Gospel." In this and each subsequent article in the series, Bangs presented his readers with a narrative bibliography organized around a variety of subjects intended to help them "explain," "defend," and "enforce" the Holy Scriptures.[34]

By the time the final article appeared, almost a year later, Bangs had enumerated and described a total of some two hundred titles ranging from Wesley's *Notes on the New Testament* to Webster's *Dictionary*. Most were drawn from the Concern's existing catalogue. The rest Bangs offered to obtain on behalf of Methodist preachers in his role as senior book agent. Clearly, Methodist preachers were intended to be his primary audience, but Bangs knew that others in the Concern's denominational market – local preachers, class leaders, exhorters, members, and even adherents – would inevitably follow his advice as well. In this way, the market for Methodist books was made to conform not to the untutored demands of consumers, but to the catalogue of titles that Nathan Bangs chose to publish and promote. This effect was further amplified when annual conferences across both the United States and Upper Canada began using Bangs's *Methodist Magazine* articles as a basis for constructing their own formal courses of study for ministerial candidates.[35]

When the preachers of the newly formed Canada Conference convened for their second annual conference, in September 1825, it was resolved, in view of an improvement in "literary acquirements" among Upper Canadians more generally, that "our young men should have more advantages for the improvement of their minds." To that end, presiding elders and other "senior brethren" were instructed "to pay special attention to this matter; taking the oversight of, and affording to, our young men all the aid in their power for the attainment of this object." These resolutions were not much different from those adopted by the General Conference in 1816 except in one important point. The manuscript minutes for 1825 indicate that a "Committee on a Course of Study" was struck to provide an actual list of texts on which ministerial candidates would be examined.[36]

The Committee on a Course of Study relied heavily on Bangs's articles. Indeed, Canadian delegates attending the Conference that year specifically requested that the New York Book Concern "republish in a convenient volume, the course of study published in the late Vol. of Methodist Magazine." The following year, and partially in response to this request, the Methodist Book Concern did indeed publish a small book under the title *Letters to Young Minister of the Gospel on the Importance and Method of Study*. This book included Bangs's twelve original articles as well as three additional chapters and an injunction to a "junior preacher" to "Circulate good books" while letting it be known that "you do not do this on account of the profits of sale." In the preface, Bangs publicly acknowledged the encouragement he received from the New York and Canada conferences. More than that, he even reproduced in full the Canada Conference's resolution that had been forwarded to him in a letter by the Conference secretary, William Case.[37]

Nathan Bangs's new book was not among those included on the course of study list. Yet, many preachers received on trial in Upper Canada from that time onward seemed to have been remarkably familiar with it. Indeed, the Canada Conference's very resolutions, and Bangs's public acknowledgment of the role that Canadian Methodists played in bringing the book to market, amounted to its unofficial endorsement as a textbook for aspiring ministerial candidates in Upper Canada. In a letter written in April 1826, William Case made reference to having several copies of "Bangs's Course of Study" on hand for distribution among Canadian preachers. Egerton Ryerson, who came to occupy a position of singular importance in Canadian Methodism, seems to have been among the newly inducted preachers provided with a copy. Years later, in 1841, Ryerson wrote to Nathan Bangs to thank him for his efforts on behalf of Upper Canadian Methodism and "for your '*Letters to Young Ministers of the Gospel*,' which were the first I recollect of reading on the subjects of which they treat. Many of your remarks & suggestions have been of great service to me." No doubt the book was of even greater service to Bangs and his successors. As the attentiveness of young preachers like Ryerson to his "suggestions" grew, and as the market in Upper Canada correspondingly evolved to conform ever more closely to the Concern's catalogue of offerings, it became progressively less difficult for Bangs to meet, and to continue to shape, its demands.[38]

V

In 1826, Nathan Bangs set about publishing the Methodist Book Concern's first weekly newspaper, the *Christian Advocate*. He took far more trouble to cultivate the new periodical's market in Upper Canada than had his predecessor Joshua Soule with the debut of the *Methodist Magazine* in 1818. Certainly, Bangs's emotional attachment to Upper Canada might have encouraged this kind of attentiveness, but he also had compelling business reasons for directing serious attention to his market in British North America. After all, the *Methodist Magazine* was already a great success in Upper Canada. Methodist appetite for the Concern's books was also growing steadily. Methodists in Canada, however, were undoubtedly becoming increasingly convinced that ongoing membership in the Methodist Episcopal Church, even as an independent annual conference, continued to impede their political prospects. Indeed, Henry Ryan and others were beginning to make some very loud noises about that very thing as they mounted an increasingly strident campaign to agitate for complete separation from American Methodists.[39]

Attentive to both the opportunities and the challenges in Upper Canada, and a steadfast opponent of ecclesiastical separation along the border, Nathan Bangs probably hoped that the widest possible circulation of the *Christian Advocate* north of the border might help to strengthen the Church's transnational bonds in much the same way that the *Methodist Magazine* had tempered political differences throughout the previous eight years. It is probable that Bangs was also coming to realize that Upper Canadian Methodists, hindered as they were by increasingly outspoken political opponents and beleaguered by growing internal dissent, formed a market that the Concern could no longer take for granted. All these reasons invited a greater effort on his part to gain the cooperation of the Canada Conference and its preachers in this new endeavour. When the Canadian preachers met for their annual conference in Hamilton in August 1826, Bangs took the trouble to make a personal appearance. Standing on British North American soil for the first time in many years, Bangs told the gathered delegates that the Methodist Book Concern had "resolved on publishing a weekly religious newspaper in New York, for the benefit of the general work in the United States and Canada, and hoped for the approval and aid of the Provincial Conference in the undertaking." No doubt Bangs breathed a sigh of relief when the Canadian delegates, in spite of growing pressures from within and without to sever ties with their American brethren, finally resolved, "That we highly approve of the publication of said paper; and we pledge ourselves to encourage its circulation." Subscriptions in large numbers soon followed and, as Thomas Webster noted, "The paper was well received throughout the province."[40]

The *Christian Advocate,* like the *Methodist Magazine,* was distributed exclusively through Methodist preachers who served as subscriptions agents. In this way, like the Methodist Book Concern's other publications, the newspaper was shielded from much of the criticism it might otherwise have attracted from the province's conservative elite. Anson Green, an American-born preacher received on trial by the Canada Conference in 1825, described his own efforts to promote it along his first preaching circuit in Ancaster (near Hamilton) at a price of $2.50 per year or $2.00, if paid in advance. "I read portions of it in my congregations," wrote Green, "and obtained quite a number of subscribers, advancing the pay for those who were not prepared to do it themselves – most of whom paid me during the year. It is an excellent paper and much needed." No doubt Green also gave away the many free copies he would have received for every six subscriptions he obtained.[41]

Methodists in Upper Canada quickly fell into the habit of submitting copy to New York for publication in the *Christian Advocate*. In less than a month, the first article concerned exclusively with Methodism in Upper Canada appeared, describing the annual meeting of the Canada Conference Bangs had attended in Hamilton the previous August to encourage preachers to circulate the *Christian Advocate*. Dozens of additional articles appeared in the paper's first year. Some of them were concerned exclusively with Upper Canada, while others combined events north and south of the border into a single narrative. These articles described the lives of individual preachers, religious revivals, and missionary work. In one typical example, descriptions of revivals in Virginia, New York, and Mississippi were bracketed with accounts of revivals in Ancaster and Hallowell (present-day Picton). Such juxtapositions conveyed the tacit but clear message that Methodism's advance in both the United States and Upper Canada evidenced a single outpouring of divine grace on the Methodist Episcopal Church across North America.[42]

Nowhere was the shared struggle of American and Canadian preachers more evident than in the narratives that Nathan Bangs published describing the emergence of a strong denominational Sunday school movement and the establishment of thriving Sunday school libraries on both sides of the border. The new *Christian Advocate* played no small role in promoting those interests and fostering a shared sense of ownership over the movement as a whole. Writing from Upper Canada in the spring of 1827, for example, Anson Green noted that the progress Sunday schools had made along his Ancaster circuit had much to do with American examples. Without the *Christian Advocate* – and Green's enthusiastic pursuit of a large audience for it along his circuit – that example would have been less well known and the Methodist Book Concern's market for Sunday school books perhaps less well developed. "Such a Sunday School Union as you have now formed in New-York has, for some time, been a desideratum in the economy of our Zion. It has already given a zest to the cause of Sabbath Schools on this circuit, which it never possessed before; and, I trust, it will give an importance to the institution which will not soon be forgotten." Green also stressed for his readers the central role that books played in stirring up this enthusiasm: "Many are hastening to form auxiliaries, and avail themselves of the books which you offer them," he continued, "Our Sabbath schools on this circuit have increased, the present year, from two to ten, and all are earnestly wishing to have a box of books deposited in this district, as considerable money is collected for the purpose of establishing Sabbath School libraries."[43]

Green concluded his letter by noting that he had enclosed ten dollars collected from three new auxiliaries and asked Bangs to send that amount to him "back in books." Anson Green's trust in the Methodist Book Concern's agents to provide for the needs of Sunday school readers along his circuit in this brief passage is total and exemplary: total because he leaves the choice of what individual titles would fill the "box of books" entirely up to the Concern's agents in New York; and exemplary because, as its appearance in the *Christian Advocate* shows, Bangs was anxious to showcase his work as a salesman of the Concern's wares to subscribers everywhere. By the time Green's letter appeared in print, the Sunday school movement and the Methodist Book Concern's support for it was already building on past successes. Sunday schools – and the new market for books that accompanied their growth – existed along most preaching circuits in the United States already. Indeed, even in Upper Canada, Sunday schools had been in operation in some places for more than a decade.

VI

Partly in response to a call from the ecumenical itinerant Thaddeus Osgood, one of Upper Canada's first Sunday schools was established in York in 1818 – the same year Joshua Soule began publishing the *Methodist Magazine* in New York. John Carroll, who had until that time lurked along Methodism's periphery under his mother's pious influence, was among its initial students. Held "every Sunday afternoon in the new Methodist meeting-house on King Street," its teachers – including prominent York businessman, political reformer, and committed Anglican Jesse Ketchum – were drawn from a variety of denominations. In a few short years, Fitch Reed, assigned to the York circuit in 1820 and 1821, reported in the *Methodist Magazine*, "Sunday schools were fast rising in the estimation of the people, and increasing throughout the country."[44]

Upper Canadian Methodists did what they could to support the province's earliest nonsectarian Sunday schools. Yet, like their British Wesleyan counterparts in Lower Canada, they preferred to exercise full denominational control in order to promote Methodist expansion and, in Upper Canada, open new markets for the Methodist Book Concern's offerings. "Union" or nonsectarian Sunday schools were more common in rural areas of the province initially, while schools at York and Kingston bore a denominational character almost from the outset. But the province's Methodist preachers soon discovered that they had at their disposal a ready means for exerting a decidedly sectarian influence without provoking the ire of other denominational leaders. The establishment of libraries in small communities, like the ones Anson Green hoped to open with the help of the Concern, became unequalled in the province as inexpensive sources of reading material – often the only such sources available in some of the more far-flung parts of the province until as late at the middle of the nineteenth century. In a word, these libraries had the power to attract students. Methodists, who were more evenly spread across Upper Canada than any other denomination, who possessed the largest number of preachers, who boasted a practised sales force for the distribution of print, and who found in the Concern's periodicals a perennial source of encouragement and new ideas for stimulating the establishment of Sunday schools, were far better positioned to fill the empty shelves of these libraries than any other group.[45]

Despite these advantages, the capacity of the Methodist Book Concern to meet the demands of this new market did not evolve overnight. Initially, even Sunday schools operating under the direct supervision of Methodist preachers were obliged to rely on non-denominational societies to supply many of their texts. John Carroll notes that in the York Sunday school, for example, "There were few books of any kind in that early day, and not enough Bibles and Testaments. My first lesson was a fragment of a Bible, a psalm, pasted on a single sheet, which I read and committed to memory." Outside the province's principal towns the situation was even worse. Thomas Webster painted a gloomy picture of the way students growing up in the western regions of Upper Canada were obliged to work with an eclectic mix of texts that were always in short supply. "A few of the pupils," he recalled, "had Maver's Spelling book, others had Webster's Spelling book, and others had the English Reader, and most of those that could read had a copy, in whole or in part, of the New Testament, while several of the smaller children had to wait for a chance to borrow a book out of which they were to say their lessons. And in many cases two and sometimes three of the larger scholars had to use the same book." Even these few titles, he added, were available only by sending "to Niagara or Queenstown."[46]

Methodist preachers also believed that their Sunday schools were inadequately supplied with books, and they weren't shy about letting the book agents in New York know it. "If we listen again to the cry of the people," noted one Canadian itinerant in a letter to the editor of the *Methodist Magazine*, "we hear them inquiring for Bibles and Testaments. 'Have you none to give us, or sell to us at a small price? We have none to read in our families, or give to our children in the Sunday Schools.'" The preacher went on to appeal to the book agents to lay his case before the American Bible Society. A year later, another preacher wrote to the *Methodist Magazine* to relate, "The donation of the Bibles and Testaments from the American Bible Society has arrived." Yet, however joyful these students ought to have been, even in the colony's tiny urban centres they had little beyond these bibles to occupy their studies. Indeed, according to at least one former student at York in the early 1820s, the Sunday schools there remained, "entirely without hymnals, library books, and reward books."[47]

Despite what was clearly a significant problem in many Sunday schools, the Methodist Book Concern had taken the initiative to begin publishing a small trickle of books intended for younger readers after the establishment of the first Methodist Sunday school in New York in 1812. It was not, however, until the middle of the 1820s that Methodist preachers and the Concern's book agents decided that a far greater effort on their part was called for, if only to counter what was perceived by many Methodists as an unwelcome and growing Calvinist influence pervading the American Sunday School Union and the American Tract Society – ostensibly non-denominational publishers that both "specialized in providing cheap literature for Sunday school libraries, families, and communities."[48]

In 1824, the General Conference of the Methodist Episcopal Church passed a formal resolution requiring all Methodist preachers to "encourage the establishment and progress of Sunday schools" along their circuits. The Book Concern meanwhile was charged with responsibility to "provide and keep on hand a good assortment of books suitable for the use of Sunday schools" – not for free, but at "as low as they can possibly be afforded." Then, in April 1827, Methodists established their own Sunday School Union in order to throw off the American Sunday School Union completely. None of these actions was undertaken with a particular eye to Methodist interests in Upper Canada. Nevertheless, they combined to help foster the growth of a market for Sunday school books that was increasingly denominational in character and therefore largely protected by sectarian insularity from the censure of the colony's conservative elite. The Concern's willingness to provide Sunday school books as cheaply as possible also helped Upper Canadian Methodists to counter John Strachan's own state-sponsored efforts – in this instance a grant of £150 from Upper Canada's Legislative Assembly – to exert a distinctly Anglican influence over the province's Sunday schools beginning in the same year.[49]

As the Methodist Book Concern's Sunday school books became more readily available to Methodists in Canada, they seem to have had a remarkable impact on the reading tastes of at least some young converts – even in the province's few towns where readers had access to a somewhat larger variety of books than elsewhere. John Carroll, for example, after being converted by reading two Sunday school tracts distributed at the local Methodist Sunday school, set aside Richardson's *Pamela* and *Clarissa* as well as *Robinson Crusoe, Don Quixote,* and the *Buccaneers of America* – books he probably obtained from commercial sources such as the new circulating library established by York bookbinder George Dawson in 1818 – to take up "the precious Bible, the Methodist Hymnbook, Bunyan's *Pilgrim's Progress,* Doddridge's *Rise and Progress of Religion in the Soul,* the Lives of the Early Methodist Preachers, with many, many, other good books." Indeed, so dramatic was the change in Carroll's reading habits that his friends surmised he must have been dying. Otherwise, they reasoned, he "would not be so serious, and be reading the Bible so much."[50]

By the late 1820s, denominational Sunday schools were beginning to supplant "Union" or nonsectarian schools at a time when Methodists were becoming steadily more convinced of their utility to serve not only as nurseries of piety but, in the words of one historian, "nurseries of the church." They were also, as Carroll's experience demonstrates, potential nurseries of the Methodist Book Concern's denominational market in Upper Canada. By the time Anson Green had written to New York to order books in July 1827, Nathan Bangs had begun the practice of regularly publishing catalogues of Sunday school books in the *Christian Advocate.* The catalogue Green probably had in hand when he wrote to the Methodist Book Concern instructed purchasers to send cash with their orders for quantities of twelve to a hundred copies of any of its twenty-eight items. These ranged in price from 25¢ for a dozen copies of *Watt's Hymns for Children,* to $3.00 for the same quantity of *Youth's Instructor and Guardian.* Green's letter was soon followed by another from Upper Canada written by Thomas Demorest, a former Methodist preacher who had retired from the itinerancy in 1827, informing the Concern that "the schools here are well attended […] Measures have been adopted to furnish those infant nurseries with the advantages of a small library."[51]

The demand for these books in Upper Canada must have been considerable since, by August 1827, the Sunday School Union of the Methodist Episcopal Church had opened its own Sunday school book depository in Stoney Creek (near Hamilton) under the supervision of Anson

Green. But because all these efforts to establish schools and construct libraries took place in settings that were increasingly denominational in character, their growth went largely unnoticed and unremarked by the province's elite. It is almost certainly for this reason that the thunderous public backlash that erupted in the 1840s against the widespread use of American textbooks in Upper Canada's common schools seems not to have been anticipated by any similar reaction against what must have been at least as widespread a use of American Methodist Sunday school books a generation earlier – particularly at a time when Nathan Bangs, in the tradition of his predecessors, began using the *Methodist Magazine* and the *Christian Advocate* not only to disseminate information about the Methodist Sunday school movement, but also to reinforce that link between patronage of the Methodist Book Concern's Sunday school offerings and membership in America's Methodist Episcopal Church.[52]

VII

The successful introduction of two new periodicals, the adoption of a formal course of study for ministerial candidates, and an increasingly denominational Sunday school movement committed to the establishment of libraries all stimulated demand for Methodist books in Upper Canada. Nevertheless, the Methodist Book Concern's access to its Canadian market become steadily more fraught as pressures to sever ties with the American Methodist Episcopal Church mounted from both within and without. John Strachan continued to press his own arguments to a wider and wider audience by publishing belligerent sermons that accused Upper Canada's Methodists of political disloyalty for "gather[ing] their knowledge and form[ing] their sentiments" from the "republican states of America." Perhaps even more concerning, however, was that when the Genesee Conference failed to elect Henry Ryan as one of its delegates to the upcoming General Conference in 1823, that disgruntled preacher took it upon himself to publish a series of fiery pamphlets arguing strenuously for unilateral separation from the Americans – all in the hope that he might be appointed leader of an independent connection in Upper Canada.[53]

In this way, Henry Ryan and John Strachan found themselves in an accidental and strikingly awkward alliance as they both argued, for vastly different reasons, that the influence Americans continued to wield over the province's Methodists was a serious threat to peace, order, and good government. At the same time, a rising tide of anti-Americanism across the colony as a whole was making things even more difficult. In an account published in 1821, John Howison noted that "although the

Americans and Canadians upon the Niagara frontier, are not a quarter of a mile distant from each other, the difference that exists between them, in point of character and ideas, is as perceptible as the lines of demarcation which divides the two countries." In Upper Canada, he continued, "the people of the United States [are] mentioned with dislike and reprobation." That trend was not soon to abate. Writing in the late 1830s, Anna Jameson went even further, noting that the "very elements" out of which the Upper Canadian "social system was framed, were repugnance and contempt for the new institutions of the United States, and a dislike to the people of that country."[54]

Yet, in the face of such pressures, all evidence suggests that in the final months before the Canada Conference achieved ecclesiastical independence in the spring of 1828, the Methodist Book Concern's provincial market continued to expand largely unhindered. The most systematic proof of this trend can be found in the pages of the *Christian Advocate* itself, where Nathan Bangs and his successors published a regular column in tiny print listing the names of all those from whom the Methodist Book Concern had received letters as well as those to whom it had shipped books in the previous week. A selected review of these columns from the five-month period between 24 August 1827 to 18 January 1828 shows that approximately 20 per cent of Upper Canada's Methodist preachers were in direct correspondence with the Concern during that time and that a smaller, but still significant number were ordering books to stock provincial depositories in Upper Canada's two, and later three, districts.[55]

Not surprisingly, William Case, who was by then the most senior preacher in Upper Canada and presiding elder of the Bay of Quinte District between 1824 and 1828, was the most regular correspondent. He and two of his fellow presiding elders, John Ryerson and Thomas Madden, all received shipments of books during this period. Separate orders of books were sent to Case on 5 October, as well as on 2, 16, and 23 November in 1827. John Ryerson and Anson Green were each sent separate shipments of books by the Methodist Book Concern on 2 November that year "care of S. McAfee, Canada, opposite Black Rock." Ryerson was sent a second shipment of books two weeks later, on 16 November, this time care of S. McAfee "by tow boat." In addition to these, there are also two recorded shipments that year to David Wright of Kingston, on 7 September and 12 October. Finally, a single shipment of books was made to an unidentifiable person by the name of J. Rowell "by tow boat, Canada" on 14 December.

Such a steady flow of texts across the border, even as the province's political mood became steadily marked by growing levels of hostility towards the cultural and political influence of the United States, can only be explained by the fact that Upper Canada's conservative forces, reaching the pinnacle of their influence around this very time, were entirely unaware of what was going on. Although pioneered for purely practical reasons in the United States, the Methodist Book Concern's denominationally insular method for distribution proved itself to be an extraordinarily effective means for shielding Canadian Methodists from the criticisms they would otherwise have received for participating in a market characterized by rhetorical strategies that were stunningly ill-suited to Upper Canadian political realities.

Had John Strachan and other conservatives known the extent of the Methodist Book Concern's market in Canada, there can be no doubt that they would have been quick to point to it as yet another example of the way Americans continued to exert a dangerous influence over the province's largest "dissenting" religious denomination. However, because only those already committed to the cause of Methodism, either as members or adherents, were able to participate in the Concern's market, Strachan and other outsiders would have found themselves excluded even from knowing the full extent of its reach. Thus, the Concern's products – although they undeniably found a large audience in Canada – were, in practice, not a part of Upper Canada's public market for books and periodicals. Only in such a denominationally sequestered space could the Concern's market have continued to expand as Methodist societies and Sunday schools proliferated while the reading tastes of individual Methodists conformed ever more closely to the Concern's catalogue of offerings.

A situation like this one could not last forever. As Methodists in Upper Canada became steadily more aware of the extent to which their interests were hindered by their relationship to their American brethren, a small but influential coterie of new preachers began to take steps to reinterpret Methodism as a loyal segment of the province's religious mainstream. This, in turn, threatened to diminish the insularity of the Methodist Book Concern's market and increase the difficulties associated with its rhetorical strategies connecting patronage with denominational identity. The Concern's agents could only do so much to offset these problems. Nathan Bangs, for example, did far more to court Upper Canadian patronage of the *Christian Advocate* in 1826 than had Joshua Soule in introducing the *Methodist Magazine* in 1818. Yet, such direct appeals, however sincere, could not diminish the damaging effects that the Concern's rhetorical strategies were having on the viability of the Concern's market in Upper Canada. Travelling to Upper Canada to solicit support for a new publication was one thing. Altering the strategies by which that publication was promoted in the wider and far larger American market to accommodate a minority of preachers and readers in Upper Canada was quite another.

In the period between Nathan Bangs's first arrival in Upper Canada and the appearance of the *Christian Advocate* twenty-eight years later, the Methodist Book Concern's market strategies had become too fixed – and were frankly too successful in the United States – to be replaced by alternate and more politically benign approaches that might safeguard its market in Upper Canada. Thus, the growing tensions between the needs of Upper Canadian Methodists, who increasingly wished to exonerate themselves from charges of political disloyalty, and the intractability of the Concern's decidedly denominational market, were bound to come to a head sooner or later. Egerton Ryerson, that young preacher who possessed a natural talent for throwing fuel on the fires of religious and political controversy in the province, played a major role in complicating these tensions. Those complications began to multiply with the surprising appearance of an insolent and anonymous rebuke of John Strachan's calumnies in William Lyon Mackenzie's upstart newspaper, the *Colonial Advocate.* That rebuke, authored by Ryerson, set off a series of events that catapulted him to the forefront of his denomination and prepared the ground for unprecedented religious upheaval. Methodism, and the Methodist Book Concern's market in Upper Canada, would never be the same.

Chapter Three

"Rancorous Calumnies and Abuse": Contending for Methodism in Print

In the spring of 1826, Anson Green and Franklin Metcalf, Methodist preachers on Upper Canada's Augusta circuit, sat down in a field behind a parsonage and began to read aloud to one another. As the men read, they also wept. A casual observer familiar with Methodism might not have remarked anything unusual in this at first. After all, John Wesley had taught his followers to read the Bible as though it had been written especially for them. But these men were not reading the Bible. Nor were they reading one of the popular fire-and-brimstone harangues authored by William Law or Joseph Alleine. Instead, spread out on the grass between them, was the latest issue of William Lyon Mackenzie's reformist – not to say mudslinging – newspaper, the *Colonial Advocate*. In its pages was an adroitly argued rebuttal of John Strachan's latest anti-Methodist rant published as part of a eulogy delivered on the occasion of Bishop Jacob Mountain's funeral. But as Green and Metcalf sat poring over their tear-stained copy of the *Advocate*, neither they nor the majority of their fellow preachers in the colony knew the identity of the daring writer who had simply signed the article "A Methodist Preacher." What they did know was that their cause had finally been taken out into the open. The publication of Egerton Ryerson's Methodist apology – for it was he, that young and still untried preacher, who had penned it – marked the most dramatic entry yet of a Methodist author into Upper Canada's emergent public sphere.[1]

Ryerson's intervention had intended as well as unintended consequences. That it set Strachan and his coterie of supporters back on their heels is undoubted. But it also threatened to attract unwanted attention to the Methodist Book Concern's enormous but still denominationally sequestered market for books and periodicals in Upper Canada. In Ryerson's eagerness to gain the upper hand, he rashly delineated in detail – and thereby invited members of the public to scrutinize – the kinds of books that aspiring preachers were required to read as part of the Canada Conference's newly adopted and American-inspired course of study. Although this was meant to serve as a kind of antidote to Strachan's usual calumnies about the so-called extensive ignorance of Methodist preachers, it also threatened to provoke additional questions on the part of Upper Canadians about where these books had come from, who apart from preachers might have access to them, and especially to what degree they might undermine the political loyalties of those who learned from them – in the menacing words of the *Montreal Herald* – to hate the government they ought to support "and to think that there is nothing great or good, generous or brave, anywhere to be found but in the United States."[2]

Although unprecedented in its boldness – one contemporary characterized its publication as "the commencement of the war for religious liberty" in Upper Canada – Egerton Ryerson's polemic was not the only thing complicating the Methodist Book Concern's access to its Canadian market. Several years before, Methodists had succeeded in attracting unwelcome attention from the colonial government for injudiciously attempting to convert a tribe of Mohawks living along the Grand River, who were widely known to have had long-standing ties to the Church of England. Strachan responded to this and other Methodist incursions by promising to increase state funding to these and other Natives on condition that they all foreswore Methodism forever. Possessing no comparable political leverage, Methodists appealed to public opinion by issuing gushing missionary reports as well as a growing body of their own Native translations – tellingly printed not by the Concern in New York but by local printers in Upper Canada – for widespread non-denominational consumption.[3]

This slow bifurcation of the market for Methodist texts – one strictly denominational in character and supplied by the Methodist Book Concern, and another aimed at the colony's non-denominational reading public supplied entirely by Upper Canadian printers – is strong evidence that Methodists knew what they were doing and well understood the risks associated with continuing to rely on the Methodist Book Concern for the bulk of their books and periodicals. When Ryerson brought the fight with Strachan out into the open, he became particularly vulnerable to any attack that might point to the extent of this more established and much larger denominational market served by an American publisher – particularly one that awkwardly insisted on connecting every purchase in Upper Canada with the interests of the Methodist Episcopal Church in the United States. Eventually, preachers like the young Egerton Ryerson could deny those risks no longer: severing the Methodist Book Concern's access to its denominational market in Canada became second in importance only to suspending direct episcopal oversight by bishops residing in the United States. Nothing less would prepare the ground for the eventual achievement of full religious equality with the Church of England.

I

Before the 1820s, Strachan and his fellow clergymen confined their efforts to discredit itinerant preachers to the expression of establishmentarian sentiments in private correspondence addressed to one another and to a handful of government officials with the power to effect changes in policy. After 1820, as it became only too evident that Anglicanism would never become Upper Canada's religious centre of gravity despite the colony's growing number of clergymen, Strachan, following the lead of Bishop Jacob Mountain, began to disseminate his views more widely. And yet, the rising clergyman had no interest in initiating a public controversy or stirring up any real debate. His plan was to slowly boil his frogs alive by imperceptibly raising the temperature and the stakes around these questions. "I will," he explained to Bishop Mountain in a letter outlining his plan for starting his own periodical, "gradually lead my readers in favour of the Church taking care to insert nothing particularly offensive to Dissenters; as the work gains ground, we can be more explicit, but caution is necessary as the whole of the population not of our Church is ready to join against us."[4]

Quiet assent, not debate, to the principles of church establishment and religious homogeneity was Strachan's desired outcome. When he later delivered his sermon on the death of Bishop Mountain, in July 1825, his aim remained unchanged. His choice of audience is particularly suggestive. On this occasion, the faces looking up to his pulpit were those of prominent colonists and government officials who might have it in their power to bring about, or at least profitably advocate for, an increase in the emoluments to which the Church of England in Upper Canada was entitled. When Strachan went to James Macfarlane in Kingston in the early spring of 1826 to have his sermon printed, moreover, he did so not to disseminate his arguments to an Upper Canadian reading public, but in order to have an adequate number of copies on hand to distribute to government officials during a trip to England while he sought a university charter and higher levels of ecclesiastical financial support. Strachan's purpose, then, was not to turn public opinion in his favour, much less initiate a debate with those who might oppose his views, but to seek favourable action from Parliament, the Colonial Office, and the colonial secretary. Unfortunately for Strachan, however, that sermon almost immediately fell into the wrong hands.[5]

In April 1826, when Strachan was already in the middle of his transatlantic crossing, Ryerson's young brow grew dark as he listened to the clergyman's latest offending words read aloud in York's wooden Methodist meeting house. "Even when [Anglican] churches are erected," the attack ran, "the persons who give regular attendance are so few as greatly to discourage the minister, and his influence is frequently broken or injured by numbers of uneducated itinerant preachers, who, leaving their steady employment, betake themselves to preaching the Gospel from idleness, or a zeal without knowledge, by which they are induced without any preparation, to teach what they do not know, and which from their pride, they disdain to learn."

Although he did not mention the Methodists by name, no one at the meeting had any doubt about the intended target of his barbs. After all, even though Strachan could hardly stand Mountain as a man when he was alive, he had to find someone to blame for his failures as a bishop now that he was dead. He did not have to look far. Who else but those preachers "from the republican states of America" could be at fault? "If the Imperial Government does not immediately step forward with efficient help," warned Strachan, "the mass of the population will be nurtured and instructed in hostility to our parent church." Worse still, the colony itself would soon be in danger as Upper Canadians indiscriminately "imbibe[d] opinions anything but favourable to the political institutions of England."[6]

It is hard to know which of Strachan's two charges – political disloyalty or religious ignorance – would have stung Ryerson more. Although Methodists in Upper Canada were routinely suspected of sedition, particularly in the period after the War of 1812, members of Ryerson's own family had repeatedly proven themselves willing to bleed for the Crown. Joseph Ryerson, Egerton's father, was a Loyalist veteran of the Revolutionary War, and he had fought again for the British in the War of 1812 – this time alongside his three eldest sons George, William, and John. The trials of war stirred something in Egerton's older brothers that caused them all to become "deeply religious" after the hostilities had ended. Despite their father's staunch attachment to the Church of England – an attachment so strong that it threatened to undo the bonds of kinship between Joseph and his five sons – all but one found his way into the Methodist itinerancy to become part of a growing complement of Canadian preachers. As members of a United Empire Loyalist family, however, Ryerson and his brothers enjoyed all the cultural and intellectual benefits that an education in the province's government-supported grammar schools could afford. Indeed, not only did Ryerson attend his local grammar school, fortunately located only a short walk from his childhood home in Vittoria (in Norfolk County), but his brother-in-law James Mitchell taught at the school. Ryerson's father and his uncle Colonel Talbot were also school trustees.[7]

Egerton Ryerson was more driven by a spirit of intellectual acquisitiveness than were most of his brothers, and in the early 1820s, he took up the post of usher, or teaching assistant, at the London district grammar school where he styled himself "both teacher and student." During this time, he "took great delight" in John Locke's foundational Enlightenment text *Essay Concerning Human Understanding* and William Paley's *The Principles of Moral and Political Philosophy*, as well as William Blackstone's massive *Commentaries on the Laws of England*. Locke had been a staple among Methodists since Wesley's day, and Paley was highly recommended by Nathan Bangs in his *Letters to Young Ministers of the Gospel*. Deep familiarity with Blackstone, however, would have been a rare thing indeed for a North American Episcopal Methodist. After August 1824, Ryerson also enjoyed unrestricted access to the library owned by John Law, the head of the Gore district grammar school, with whom he undertook an intensive course of study in classical literature. By the mid-1820s, Egerton Ryerson had much more in common with the intellectual habits of men like John Strachan and John Beverley Robinson than with William Case, Henry Ryan, and other Upper Canadian Methodist preachers. As such, he was probably better prepared than any other North American Methodist to engage the province's conservative elites in public debate according to the norms of a common British intellectual tradition.[8]

William Case, Ryerson's presiding elder at the time, was not alone in recognizing the young preacher as "as one of the best educated men of the connexion." Almost as soon as the Methodists at York had finished listening to Strachan's screed against them, fingers began to be pointed in Ryerson's direction. Hesitant at first, Ryerson reluctantly agreed to compose a response when his circuit's supervising preacher, James Richardson, agreed to do the same. By the time of the next meeting, however, only Ryerson had anything to show. "The reading of my paper," recalled Ryerson, "was attended with alternate laughter and tears on the part of the social party, all of whom insisted that it should be printed." Ryerson demurred, but the manuscript was snatched away from him before he could throw it on the fire. Thus thwarted, the young preacher relented, agreed to make a few editorial adjustments, and finally returned it to his congregation for publication. "Two of the senior brethren took the manuscript to the printer, and its publication produced a sensation scarcely less violent and general than a Fenian invasion. It is said that before every house in Toronto might be seen groups reading and discussing the paper on the evening of its publication in June; and the excitement spread throughout the country." However reluctant Ryerson may have been to go down this road, then, the reach of William Lyon Mackenzie's *Colonial Advocate* ensured that there would be no turning back.[9]

II

By the time Mackenzie published Ryerson's rebuttal, that quarrelsome Scottish immigrant had already earned a reputation for poking the bear that was John Strachan and his clique of like-minded conservatives. Indeed, Mackenzie had established the *Colonial Advocate* for the express purpose of afflicting those influential statesmen. "I had long seen the country in the hands of a few shrewd, crafty, covetous men," he fumed, "under whose management one of the most lovely and desirable sections of America remained a comparative desert." Politics was just the beginning. Religion in the province also needed a major overhaul. "The Church of England, the adherents of which were few, monopolized as much of the lands of the colony as all the religious houses and dignitaries of the Roman Catholic Church had had the control of in Scotland at the era of the Reformation; other sects were treated with contempt and scarcely tolerated." As far as Mackenzie was concerned, John Strachan, Peregrine Maitland, John Beverley Robinson, and their supporters were at the root of all these problems. Denouncing them as a "family compact," Mackenzie characterized them as "the avowed enemies of common schools, of civil and religious liberty, of all legislative or other checks to their own will."[10]

Mackenzie was determined that his little weekly would constitute one such "other check" to the will of these men who undeniably constituted a kind of political oligarchy in Upper Canada. At first his campaign went well. Candidates he supported in elections often found seats as the popularity of his newspaper increased. In November, Mackenzie relocated his press to York, where he deliberately targeted taverns, often sending out free copies, in an effort to transform them into informal distribution centres. This did not always net him very large profits, but Mackenzie's aggressive methods and his entertainingly poisonous invective helped to ensure that his paper was among the most widely read in Upper Canada. Despite the paper's growing popularity, however, by July, Mackenzie was mired in serious financial difficulties and was forced to suspend the *Colonial Advocate* for a number of months.[11]

With competitors springing up on all sides, Mackenzie needed the Methodists every bit as much as they needed him. So certain was Mackenzie that Ryerson's rebuttal would not only boost circulation, but bring in a little extra lucre as well, he took on the added trouble of advertising a forthcoming "Review" by "A Methodist Preacher" two weeks before its appearance. When Ryerson's anonymous "Review of a Sermon, Preached by the Honourable and Reverend John Strachan" finally appeared, in May 1826, Mackenzie breathed a sigh of relief. His efforts had not been in vain. "It was," in Ryerson's own words, "the sole topic of conversation, and the subject of universal excitement in town and country."[12]

The appearance of Egerton Ryerson's anonymous "Review" in the *Colonial Advocate* did more than complicate Strachan's ecclesiastical and political plans. It also openly associated Methodism with the forces of reform active in the province's oppositionist press – an alliance that carried considerable risk for the Methodists as they tried to move into the colony's political and religious mainstream. For the time being, however, Ryerson's anonymity sheltered him at least from those who had shown an unsettling readiness in the past to take up the law, arms, or both, to defend their entitlements. More importantly, it also allowed a reading public to evaluate the merit of Ryerson's arguments without comparing Strachan's elevated social standing to Ryerson's own far less impressive status.

Early Methodist historians often described these events by comparing Ryerson to the biblical David with "sling and stone" and Strachan to the much more formidable – but soon to be felled – Philistine Goliath. It is an apt comparison. Strachan, by the mid-1820s, was a respected ordained Anglican clergyman, a member of Upper Canada's Executive and Legislative councils, a former periodical publisher and the author of several books, chairman of the Board of Education of Upper Canada, a leading member of the Clergy Reserves Corporation, a principal shareholder and director of the York Joint-Stock Bank, and a missionary for the Society for Promoting Christian Knowledge. Strachan was also regarded as a hero for saving York from destruction by fire. Next to a man like Strachan, Ryerson looked like little more than an inexperienced upstart. After all, as yet he had no real public service record, no publications, and only tentative standing as a Methodist preacher since he remained on trial at the time of writing. While Ryersons's education and his status as the son of a United Empire Loyalist was certainly worth something, it counted for little when set alongside Strachan's own reputation as wartime hero and a distinguished schoolmaster with a Doctor of Divinity degree. Without the use of Mackenzie's press to render Ryerson's "Review" anonymous and impersonal, then, it is highly doubtful that his contention – as a spoken set of arguments – would have had nearly as significant an impact on the Upper Canadian public.[13]

When Ryerson's piece appeared in the spring of 1826, the *Colonial Advocate* remained in such serious financial trouble that Mackenzie was able to remain in the province only long enough to publish one more issue before fleeing across the US border to avoid arrest for debt. That final issue, probably in a last-ditch effort to increase circulation, contained as scathing an attack on the province's ruling elite as Mackenzie had ever published. Had he remained in the province, he might well have found himself the recipient of a public horsewhipping – something that had actually happened to reformist Robert Gourlay after testing Strachan's patience a decade earlier. With Mackenzie himself out of harm's way for the time being, a cabal of fifteen young reactionaries decided to raid his York office and, under cover of darkness, smashed his printing press and threw it and his type into Lake Ontario. This turned out to be just the defeat Mackenzie needed.[14]

In the immediate wake of this vandalism, Hugh Thomson, a more moderate voice for reform and a man not likely to suffer a similar fate, published an article in Kingston's *Upper Canada Herald* advocating for freedom of the press. Mackenzie, meanwhile, with the help of his former subscription agent and member of the Legislative Assembly of Upper Canada, Marshall Spring Bidwell, took the young miscreants to court and won an astonishing £625 in damages. Thus was Mackenzie not only vindicated, but his financial woes were eliminated at a single stroke. The province's Methodists were stunned and heartened by the outcome. Although, as one preacher remarked, the settlement would furnish Mackenzie "with the sinews of war, [for] lashing the Family Compact in fine style," the court of public opinion proved to be far less expedient in Ryerson's case. The "newspaper altercation" – as Strachan derisively called it – that Ryerson's "Review" had provoked the week before Mackenzie's press was destroyed was still only midway through its life by the time Mackenzie received his money.[15]

Even the casual reader could not have failed to see that when Ryerson took up his pen against Strachan he was angry. Very angry. Strachan's sermon was, Ryerson contended, an attack not merely on Methodists and other dissenters, but on Christianity itself and the Church writ large – and an attack, moreover, authored by the Church's most dangerous kind of enemy, "one who lurks within her borders, shelters himself under her canopy, and [who] feeds upon her benevolence." Egerton Ryerson accused Strachan not once but three times of "ignorance" – ignorance of "religion and church history," ignorance of the "gracious power" of Jesus, and ignorance of the flagrant incompetence of his fellow clergymen. The pews of the Church of England sit empty each Sunday not because Methodist preachers have stolen their worshippers, but because the clergymen responsible for them "are constantly dabbling in politics" – so much so that they have become "a disgrace to the church and a pestilence to their parishioners." Until the Church of England realizes that its calling is to religion and not politics, "the Doctor's mournful cries of Sectarianism! Schism! Republicanism! will still be screeching in our ears; and the response of the 'Imperial Parliament' will continue to be disturbed by the desponding exclamations, 'The church is in danger – money! power!'" As for those "religious teachers of the other denominations" Strachan triumphantly condemned as closet republicans – they "do not talk or think quite so much about politics as the Doctor does. They have something else to do."[16]

All of this no doubt would have been gratifying in the extreme to readers of Mackenzie's *Colonial Advocate*. But to open a real debate in the province's emergent public sphere, Ryerson's "Review" had to do more than cut Strachan down to size while appealing to democratic forms of sociability. That, for Methodists, was the easy part. After all, Wesley's brand of Arminian theology was spiritually egalitarian, and Methodist polity, particularly in the United States, was founded on the principle of religious voluntarism. But as a member of a denomination that also made claims about the importance of "experimental religion," and that was regularly accused of fanaticism by those who had witnessed the wild circus of demonic exorcisms, miraculous healings, and dramatic conversions that accompanied revival camp meetings across the province, most Methodists would have found it very difficult indeed to limit their polemics to purely rational arguments that could be evaluated by a reading public without recourse to privately held supernatural convictions.

It might be guessed that Egerton Ryerson's involvement as a student and teacher in several of the province's district grammar schools, his upbringing in a respectable Loyalist family, and his early involvement in the staid Church of England would all have combined to purge him of beliefs about the importance of direct revelations and supernatural epiphanies. But such was not the case. In his private journal, for example, Ryerson often described having "a conscious Divine strength according to [his] need." And in a biographical sketch prepared for publication, Ryerson even recounted in vivid detail a moment in which Jesus appeared both to his mind and to his "bodily eye." It was experiences like these – no matter how profound they had been from a subjective point of view – that Ryerson had to avoid completely if he hoped to sway a broader audience of non-Methodist readers in Upper Canada. Remarkably, he did avoid them. Methodists seem to have reacted to the "Review" with just the sort of emotionalism they were often accused of – laughing and crying by turns. Ryerson himself, however, understood what his wider non-denominational audience expected of him when he made his appeal to the only locus of authority – a rational reading public – that was open to him outside the colony's conservative government.[17]

Ryerson's "Review" had two aims as a polemic: to destabilize the principle of church establishment, on the one hand, and to deflate Strachan's dual accusation that Methodist preachers were ignorant and disloyal nobodies who preached "what they do not know," and who came, "almost universally from the republican states of America, where they gather their knowledge and form their sentiments," on the other. No other Methodist in Upper Canada could have managed it quite as well. As it turned out, however, arguing against ongoing ties between church and state was the easy part. Ryerson cited dozens of biblical passages, the works of the early church fathers, as well as eighteenth-century clergyman William Paley, who argued that a church could not be properly established without enjoying the support of the majority of a nation's inhabitants. By adopting this approach, Ryerson managed to open the way for a rational dialogue with his readers in precisely the same way that any public polemicist might have done by appealing to authoritative secular documents in support of political or legal positions. Ryerson left his readers to judge for themselves whether his interpretation of his source material was reasonable or unreasonable based on dispassionate exegetical principles rather than supernatural insight. But when it came to disproving Strachan's claims about Methodist preachers, Ryerson's task was considerably more complicated – and not just because he took Strachan's slights against the intellectual abilities of Methodist preachers much more personally.[18]

Egerton Ryerson had an abundance of material to draw on. But not all of it was suitable for Upper Canada's non-denominational reading public. He began, of course, with reference to John and Charles Wesley, their status as authors and university graduates, and their place in society as ordained clergymen. He made reference to those passages in the Methodist *Discipline* that outlined the number of hours preachers were expected to devote to reading and study on a daily basis. Somewhat more tediously, and as it turned out more dangerously, Ryerson also reproduced in full – a title-by-title listing – the entire course of study that the Canada Conference had adopted at its meeting in September

1825. What he did not reveal, however, was that the Canada Conference's course of study had been closely modelled on the American template provided by Nathan Bangs in his *Letters to Young Ministers of the Gospel*. Nor did he mention that Canadian preachers enjoyed easy and inexpensive access to that entire catalogue of books through an extensive book distribution network supplied by Methodism's own massive denominational publisher in New York. Although this latter fact, in particular, would have powerfully undermined Strachan's claims about the ignorance of Methodists, admitting to Methodism's almost complete reliance on a publisher based in New York might easily have been reframed as proof that Canadian Methodists continued to "gather their knowledge and form their sentiments" in ways that dangerously compromised their loyalty. Even worse, information of this sort might have provoked one of Strachan's supporters to look more deeply into the Methodist Book Concern's market in Upper Canada and to discover that it was sustained by a rhetoric that made powerful transnational claims on the denominational identities of all its customers.[19]

Thus, Ryerson could go so far, and only so far, in adducing evidence to counter the first part of Strachan's accusation without inadvertently proving the second. Egerton Ryerson's remarkably adroit skirting of this boundary suggests that he was well aware of its existence and of the difficulties that would continue to accompany the work of exculpating Methodism from charges of disloyalty as long as the province's Methodists continued to purchase books from a foreign publisher determined to link acts of patronage to the religious identities of readers.

In the weeks following the publication of Ryerson's "Review," four responses appeared in three of the province's leading newspapers – the *Kingston Chronicle*, the *Upper Canada Herald*, and the *Brockville Recorder*. Three were authored by Church of England clergymen and one by an Anglican layperson. No public reply had been or ever would be written by Strachan. But Ryerson did not need Strachan's participation to carry on a debate with other conservatives who shared Strachan's political and religious views but who were less circumspect about where such democratic modes of exchange would inevitably lead. In the end, Strachan's refusal to stoop to participate in a "newspaper altercation" probably only hurt his cause by leaving it in the hands of less capable writers.

Even under these circumstances, however, Ryerson had to remain especially careful, as he had in his original "Review," not to shine any light on the Methodist Book Concern's continually expanding Upper Canadian market and the increasingly entrenched rhetorical strategies the book agents used to promote the sale of the *Christian Advocate* after 1826. This was made more difficult because Ryerson's interlocutors took up Strachan's original attack on the educational qualifications of Methodist preachers with the utmost vigour. One writer speculated, for example, that the "Review" was too accomplished to have been the work of any Methodist, while another attacked the apology for being insufficiently rigorous. A third accused Ryerson of citing "authors whom he had never read," while others charged him with deliberately taking the words of various authorities out of context to support obvious misinterpretations in the furtherance of his own position. All recognized, however, that Ryerson's "Review" had been written in a purposeful effort "to sway the public mind."[20]

Questions of authorship and intellectual integrity aside, it was the arguments around what Methodists did and did not read that had the greatest potential to expose the Methodist Book Concern's market in Upper Canada. One of Ryerson's critics took particular issue with the course of study on the grounds that it included many titles that had no obvious connection to theological training but instead had the appearance of serving only as remedial textbooks for illiterate preachers. "Will [Church of England clergymen]," he wrote, "who have trodden the enchanted paths of science – who can call up and combine the varieties of nature – who can search out and bring forth the treasured stores of philosophy to fortify and adorn the excellencies of religion – will *they* suffer by comparison with those who admit amongst their systematic studies in theology so strange a classification as that of 'Murray's Grammar' and Morse's Geography? Why not annex to that dazzling catalogue the perhaps necessary appendages of the 'New England Primer,' 'Entick's Dictionary,' and the 'Ready Reckoner?'"[21]

This back and forth did not finally exhaust itself until February 1827. "During the past year," Ryerson confided to his diary a month later, "my principal attention has been called to controversial labours. If the Lord will, may this cup pass by in my future life." It is plain to see from this brief entry that Ryerson's remarkable persistence flowed not from any enjoyment he derived from it, but rather from William Case's insistence that he "devote himself" to the public defence of Methodism in the Upper Canadian periodical press for as long as he could. Years later, Egerton Ryerson seems to have thought it was worth the effort. "I believe this was the first article of the kind ever published in Upper Canada," he mused in 1832, "and, while from that time to this a powerful combination of talent, learning, indignation, and interest has been arrayed in a vain attempt to support by the weapons of reason, Scripture, and argument, a union between the Church and the world – between the earth and heaven; talents, truth, reason, and justice have alike been arrayed in the defense of insulted and infringed rights, and the maintenance of the system of public, religious, and educational instruction, accordant with public rights and interests, the principles of sound policy, the economy of Providence, and the institutions and usages of the New Testament." For Ryerson, then, that public contest was one that had been waged on both sides using the "weapons" of reason and argument to assert a right interpretation of Scripture for the sake of "public rights and interests."[22]

John Strachan saw things differently. The debate and its outcome did nothing to alter his view about the inability of a reading public to adjudicate religious and political disputes. "Having gotten into an interminable paper war," he confided in a letter to a friend, "I have abstained for some time from corresponding, in the hope of its being brought to a close [...] The flood-gates of the most licentious press were opened upon me; newspapers in both Provinces, day after day and week after week, poured out the most rancorous calumnies and abuse against me. Having very good nerves, I permitted them to rail on; and, conscious of my integrity, I maintained an invariable silence. I am, indeed, so situated, that I cannot, with propriety, enter into a newspaper controversy; nor can I descend to the language made use of in such publications." For Strachan, then, the "paper war" was nothing if not intensely personal. Even though Ryerson omitted any mention of the clergyman by name in his own later reflection – taking instead the institutional bulwark of a political church as the object of the contention – Strachan persisted in reminding those around him that he, and not his ideas only, had been the target of the press's "rancorous calumnies and abuse."[23]

III

The publication of Egerton Ryerson's "Review" in the *Colonial Advocate* marked the first step in what would eventually become a major shift in attitudes towards church establishment in Upper Canada. Still, the pressure that it placed on the Methodist Book Concern's access to its market was incremental rather than revolutionary. Nor was it, as Ryerson himself claimed, "the first publication put forth by the Methodists in Upper Canada in their own defense." Between six and eight months before the appearance of Ryerson's "Review," Methodists in Upper Canada had already made use of the local press to publish the first annual report of their newly established Missionary Society. Vastly different in tone and rarely mentioned by historians, this report served the same rhetorical purpose as Ryerson's polemic: to influence public opinion about Methodist religious rights and practices in Upper Canada. As such, this report was also aimed at a community of readers outside the Methodist Book Concern's Upper Canadian market, a market comprised of non-partisan members of the reading public who, although interested in religious issues, were not necessarily affiliated with Methodism. The emergence of this distinct secondary market – one where the Concern's imprint would have served as a profoundly counterproductive reminder of precisely the sort of American cultural hegemony Strachan so darkly condemned in his religious rivals – was linked to the protracted struggle that Methodists waged with the Church of England as their missionary work among Natives gained momentum.[24]

In the early 1820s, Alvin Torry became the first Methodist preacher to exert himself in a serious and sustained way among Native groups in Upper Canada. Many of the Natives he encountered were nominal Anglicans, but Torry was convinced that their Christian beliefs were superficial. "I was accustomed to cross the Grand River," he wrote, "within a few miles of the Mohawk tribe, and frequently met with groups of them here and there, and not unfrequently saw them lying drunk around hucksters' shops, kept by white people for the purpose of getting the Indians drunk, and then robbing them of all that was of use to them." Sights like these convinced Torry that "the Gospel of Christ could be the power of God to the salvation of the Indians." At the time of writing, and despite the obvious need, Torry had hoped to return to the United States. William Case, however, the district's presiding elder, persuaded him otherwise, and Torry soon resumed his preaching along a new and separate circuit by the Grand River. It was a bold move and one that Case knew carried risks. By stationing Torry among these Mohawks, Case was placing that missionary, and by extension the whole of the Methodist Episcopal Church, in direct and dangerous competition with the Church of England.[25]

William Case believed that the Church of England's commitment to the colony's Natives was tepid at best. "The only religious services performed among these Indians," he reported in the *Methodist Magazine*, "is at the Mohawk Village, 50 miles from the mouth of the river. Here they have a Meeting-House, here Divine Service is performed occasionally, by a Minister of the Church of England, and where the church service is read in Mohawk, by one of the natives every Sabbath day." Torry's assessment was much more pointed: "It was easy to see," he complained, "what the Church of England had done, and was doing in the way of religious instruction. Instead of reforming and bettering their condition, they were likely to provide their ruin, both body and soul." Worse still, Torry had discovered in the course of his missionary work that the Natives had already been warned away from Methodist preachers on the grounds that their religious fanaticism meant that they did not permit "drinking rum and playing cards and horse racing."[26]

Yet, for all that, not even Torry could deny that the Church of England had done more than simply smooth the way for white abuses and warn the Natives away from the spiritual excesses of Methodist preaching. Liturgical texts that had been translated into Mohawk and put to use among Natives were evidence of that. Torry admitted as much, noting that Joseph Brant had been employed by the Church of England in the late eighteenth century to "translate into Mohawk portions of the Holy Scriptures, some part of their prayer-book, and also the ten commandments." Indeed, without any translations of their own, Torry and other Methodist missionaries were obliged to rely on Brant's work as they devoted more and more resources to their missionary efforts.[27]

When the Canada Conference was first established 1824 – four years before the General Conference of the Methodist Episcopal Church formally and finally granted Canadians ecclesiastical independence – Methodists in the colony created an auxiliary Missionary Society to ensure that the work among Upper Canadian Natives would not slacken. By the autumn of that year, William Case noted again in the pages of the *Methodist Magazine* that a separate building had been erected "for the double purpose of schools and meetings" where "twenty-five Indian children are daily taught the rudiments of reading." With a growing emphasis on reading and writing, the need for translations into Mohawk became more pressing, particularly in the mind of Case who insisted, contrary to others, that Natives "were capable of comprehending the complexities of Christianity even before they were transformed by secular European civilization."[28]

Soon, new translations of the Gospels into Mohawk were being prepared by Joseph Brant's son-in-law Henry Aaron Hill – a man Torry described as "an intelligent Mohawk chief." Torry and Case considered these translations to be denominational in character since they were largely devotional and intended for circulation only among Native converts and potential Native converts associated with the Grand River Methodist Mission. For this reason, economy of time and money superseded political considerations in their production, and they were accordingly sent to the Methodist Book Concern in New York for publication. "He [Henry Aaron Hill]," Torry observed, "entered upon his work with much spirit and ambition, for we had promised him a compensation if he succeeded in his work. He first translated the Gospel according to St Matthew and St Luke, and having corrected a former translation of St Mark and St John, he soon finished the collection of hymns, and they were immediately sent on to New York, where our

Missionary Society printed them, and sent us back a neat hymnbook, containing the English and Indian on opposite pages."[29]

Hill was not the only Native working on translations in Upper Canada. Several years earlier, in June 1823, at a camp meeting organized in Ancaster by Torry and Case, a young Mississauga chief later known as Peter Jones was converted to Methodism. Jones's father was a Welsh Loyalist and his mother the daughter of a Mississauga chief. Peter and his brother John were raised by their mother and in their mid-teens joined their father's household where they were taught to read, write, and farm. Thus, Peter had learned to be at home in both Native and white settings. Case was convinced that this upbringing would allow Jones to explain with unique insight "one society to the other." Two years later, Jones was appointed an exhorter and within months set about the work of translating texts into Ojibway. In an article published in the newly established weekly *Christian Advocate*, William Case explained to readers how such translations were proving useful even before they were printed. "While we are employed out," he wrote, "Peter Jones, (besides superintending the cookery) is engaged in the wigwam, in translating portions of the Scriptures into the Chipawa [*sic*]. During the evenings, these portions are taught to the Indians, Peter pronouncing the sentence thus, – '*ing-ke-chu-Hoo-se-non Esh-pe-ming a-ya-gun*, (Our Great Father who in Heaven resides).'"[30]

All this progress among the Natives did not go unnoticed by colonial partisans of the Church of England. Thomas Webster, in his history of the Methodist Episcopal Church in Canada, observed that it was not long before "very high-handed measures had been attempted by those high in authority, in order to coerce the Indians into coming to their terms, with regard to their adherence to the Church of England." John Strachan, in particular, took a serious and sustained interest in Peter Jones after his conversion to Methodism in the hope he might convince the young Mississauga to shift his denominational loyalty towards Anglicanism.[31]

In mid-June 1825, less than two weeks after denouncing Methodists in his funeral sermon for Bishop Jacob Mountain, Strachan arrived at the Credit River with his wife and Colonel Givins, the government's Indian agent, to make the annual distribution of "gifts" to the Natives. Jones, who had met with Colonel Givins in York several days earlier, was also in attendance. Strachan singled Jones out for special attention by presenting him with three books and asking him to "assemble the Christian Indians together by themselves, that he might hear some of the children sing and read." Strachan then urged Jones to consider settling his entire community on the Credit River where, he suggested, the government would provide assistance for the erection of a permanent village. Strachan met privately with Jones the following day to provide further "advice as to the way he had better proceed to obtain assistance from Government in our proposed undertaking to settle at the Credit." Methodist suspicions were already aroused even though Strachan did not finally reveal his purely sectarian motives until several years later when he informed Jones, after the latter's unyielding refusal to convert to the Church of England, that "the Governor did not feel disposed to assist the Indians so long as they remained under the instruction of their present teachers, who were not responsible to Government for any of their proceedings and instructions."[32]

At the annual meeting of the Canada Conference, held in mid-September 1825, little was discussed – or at least recorded – in this connection. Nevertheless, evidence suggests that William Case regarded the danger Strachan and his government money posed to Methodist interests with growing seriousness. This was reflected in a sharp increase in the care Case took over ensuring that accurate records of Native missionary work were maintained and preserved. The very next month, on 5 October 1825, William Case carefully instructed Peter Jones to keep detailed accounts of Native converts, including their "Indian name, then the name by which they were baptized, and of what tribe." He concluded his letter by urging Jones to "see that the Book is deposited in safe keeping, free from wet and other injury."[33]

As evidence of Strachan's interest in Methodist missionary activities continued to mount on behalf of church and state – Jones informed Case in a subsequent letter that Lieutenant Governor Peregrine Maitland had promised to "build twenty dwelling houses, and a school house for us, between this and next spring" on the Credit River – Case appears to have determined to incur the costs involved in setting before the Upper Canadian public a printed record of Methodist progress among the Natives. Doubtless Case hoped that such a public record might help to minimize the efficacy with which Strachan, Maitland, and others could exercise an undue interference over Methodist missions. Had Case wished merely to preserve the report and to inform his fellow Methodists in Upper Canada about progress among the Natives, he could have done so much more easily – and saved himself and the Canada Conference £10 12s 6d in the bargain – by submitting the report for free publication in the *Methodist Magazine*. Indeed, such reports continued to appear in the pages of that periodical throughout these months – Alvin Torry's 1825 four-page report describing his ongoing efforts along the Grand River being the latest – suggesting that Case had another audience in mind. This audience, a second and distinct market for Methodist texts in Upper Canada, was public in character and thus beyond the reach of the Methodist Book Concern's denominational distribution infrastructure. Accordingly, when Case visited Kingston later that month, he hired Hugh Thomson, the publisher of Kingston's *Upper Canada Herald*, to print a thousand copies of the first annual report of the Missionary Society.[34]

Initially, these two markets – the Methodist Book Concern's denominational market and the broader public market for Methodist texts – remained distinct. Materials of a devotional nature for use within denominational settings such as Henry Aaron Hill's translations of the Gospels into Mohawk continued to be produced in the United States on the presses of the Methodist Book Concern. Documents with a political purpose, however, such as these annual reports in 1826 and 1827, were entrusted to local printers for distribution to Upper Canadians outside the denominational boundaries of the Concern's market. At the same time, those within that denominational market continued to be able to read about Methodist advances among the Natives in the pages of the *Methodist Magazine*, and later the *Christian Advocate*, where Case persisted in publishing regular and more detailed accounts. Indeed, apart from Mackenzie's printing of Ryerson's original "Review," in pamphlet form in April 1826, the annual reports of the Missionary Society remained the only Methodist texts produced on local presses before the last few months of 1828. For reasons of economy, convenience, efficiency, and denominational loyalty, William Case seems to have resolved that wherever missions remained sufficiently marked by denominational insularity to permit an American imprint, he and his preachers would continue to rely on the Methodist Book Concern for all their publishing needs.[35]

In the spring of 1827, shortly after establishing a new mission and "Indian school" on Grape Island, William Case set out for New York to arrange for the publication of several translated texts by the Methodist Book Concern. While there, he wrote to Egerton Ryerson – then serving as the first permanent Methodist missionary to the Natives on the Credit River while continuing to debate his ecclesiastical opponents in the colonial press – to indicate that when he returned from the United States he would bring a newly printed "Indian book, containing the Decalogue, the creed, hymns, and our Lord's Sermon on the Mount." Although unidentified by its title, this book was probably the Concern's first edition of Peter Jones's sixteen-page translation *Tracts in the Chippeway and English comprising seven hymns, the Decalogue, the Lord's prayer, the Apostles' creed, and the fifth chapter of*

St Matthew. A short notice also appeared in the *Christian Advocate* describing "the visit of the Rev. William Case to this city, for the purpose of [...] the printing of the gospel of St Luke, and a collection of hymns, in the Indian tongue, for the use of the native Christians in Upper Canada."[36]

IV

Stress on the Methodist Book Concern's continued access to this portion of the denominational market in Upper Canada entered a new phase when, in August 1827, John Strachan returned to the colony from overseas bearing a Royal Charter for an Anglican university, as well as the elevated ecclesiastical rank of archdeacon. Egerton Ryerson's initial public contention with the proponents of the Anglican establishment had wound down by this time. William Lyon Mackenzie, however, rekindled the dispute with the publication, in the 20 September 1827 issue of the *Colonial Advocate*, of Strachan's inflammatory and anti-Methodist "Ecclesiastical Chart" – drawn up the previous April and delivered in May to convince the incoming colonial secretary, Lord Goderich, of the merit of the Church of England's continued claim to state monies. Not surprisingly, especially considering that it was never intended to become a public document, the Chart contained the same anti-American slurs Strachan had earlier directed against the Methodists in his 1825 funeral sermon and that had provoked Egerton Ryerson to write his original "Review."[37]

William Case was incensed and immediately wrote to Ryerson to urge a public response. Public protests that followed the appearance of the Ecclesiastical Chart in Upper Canada soon prompted Strachan to issue a second pamphlet that contained a more nuanced, yet still unambiguous condemnation of his religious adversaries. As might have been expected, this second pamphlet did little to assuage public outrage. Finally, Strachan appeared in person at the Legislative Council in York, on 6 March 1828, to argue that he should be cleared of all charges of religious intolerance. Emboldened by the warm reception he received in that partisan setting, Strachan ordered Robert Stanton, the King's printer, to publish his speech to the Council the following month. Like so many of Strachan's earlier attempts, however, that document also failed to have the desired effect on the general public.[38]

Egerton Ryerson received a letter from his brother William the following month encouraging him to respond to Strachan through the press, pointing out that the publications Strachan issued after his Ecclesiastical Chart became public did not effectively address any of the criticisms made against that original document. "Should you pursue this course," the older brother concluded, "you had better endeavor to write in a candid, mild, and sweet stile [*sic*]. It will have a much more powerfull [*sic*] effect on the mind of the public." Egerton reluctantly followed this advice and threw himself once more into the fray. In June, a series of eight letters systematically refuting all of Strachan's contentions, signed by Egerton Ryerson, appeared in Hugh Thomson's *Upper Canada Herald* and William Lyon Mackenzie's *Colonial Advocate*. Ryerson was probably grateful when, once again, Strachan declined to publish a response. A year later, Ryerson had Thomson print the collected letters as a separate pamphlet to be sold for 1s 6d "at different Book Stores in Upper and Lower Canada."[39]

While Ryerson thus engaged for a second time in crossing swords with Strachan, Peter Jones was in the midst of preparing another of his translations for publication. This time, however, Case made arrangements for its publication with Mackenzie rather than with the Methodist Book Concern in New York. It seems probable that Case had determined, in the shadow of yet another quarrel between Ryerson and Strachan, that the religious temperature in Upper Canada was simply becoming too hot to take any further risks. Although Jones's translation was devotional rather than polemical in character, by this time Methodist missions among the colony's Natives had become an area of major contention. Case well knew that an American imprint on Jones's latest translation would have only added fuel to the fire and opened the way for Strachan to renew his anti-Methodist slurs. And yet, for all that, it seems Case remained somewhat conflicted. In a letter published in the New York *Christian Advocate* dated 17 June 1828, mere days before Jones delivered his completed manuscript to Mackenzie, Case enthused about Canadian plans for teaching "the Indians to read, in a sabbath [*sic*] school which they have instituted on their account." Yet, he said nothing about Jones's latest translation for the instruction of these young converts. Perhaps, as a man who had imbibed the Concern's rhetoric his entire life as a preacher, William Case was worried that by taking his business to Mackenzie he and his Canadian brethren were in some way robbing the Concern of its rightful due.[40]

Case probably felt rather less compunction about doing much the same thing when he used a local shop to rush into print the minutes of the Canada Conference later in the autumn of 1828. This time he had a very compelling reason to do so: Henry Ryan's political attacks against his own brethren had reached such a fever pitch that there could be no delay in putting them down. Ryan, playing right into Strachan's hands, had been a thorn in the side of Upper Canadian Methodism ever since the Genesee Conference, of which Upper Canada remained a part until May 1824, had refused to elect him as a delegate to the General Conference of the Methodist Episcopal Church. Ryan's dissatisfaction finally erupted into the open when, in 1826, he published a mud-slinging pamphlet denouncing Canadian Methodists as hypocrites for claiming to be loyal subjects of the British Crown while continuing to subject themselves to the authority of American bishops. The pamphlet appeared anonymously, but Egerton Ryerson reported that "*no one* had any doubt that to Mr Ryan belonged both the authorship and the circulation." The following year, Ryan published another pamphlet even "more insolent and libelous than its predecessor." Finally, at the annual Canada Conference of 1827, Case at last grasped the nettle and openly accused Ryan of publishing both documents. Ryan confirmed his guilt by storming out of the assembly without answering the charge.[41]

In the autumn of 1828, Canadian Methodists moved decisively to put an end to their troubles with Henry Ryan. At their annual conference, they struck a committee of five, William Case and Egerton Ryerson among its leading members, to pass sentence on the dissident preacher. Naturally, Case was extremely anxious to set the committee's findings before the public both to discredit Ryan and to brush aside any perception that Methodism was beset by internal dissent. The audience for these minutes, therefore, like the annual Missionary Society reports, was comprised of a reading public outside the Methodist Book Concern's denominational market. Methodists themselves, of course, would have needed no confirmation of the committee's verdict since that news would have travelled to them much more quickly through the ministrations of the province's travelling preachers. But the public also needed to be alerted to the hollowness of Ryan's continued accusations before Strachan and his coterie could seize on them to their own advantage. Case urged for quick action in a letter to Ryerson and others dated 17 November 1828. "As Bro. Egerton is one of the Committee for publishing the proceedings of Conference relative to Mr Ryan," he wrote, "I hope he will assist Bro. Richardson to complete it without delay, & have it published & circulated as soon as may be. Perhaps the printing of McKenzie [*sic*] under the inspection of Bro. Metcalf." Although not identified in the final document, Mackenzie was almost certainly the printer.[42]

By the time Case instructed Ryerson to print the committee's findings on Mackenzie's press, he had obviously learned to appreciate the usefulness of local printers for reaching a public audience in Upper Canada, and even producing the occasional short publication of a denominational character for the colony's Native missions.

Although his loyalty to the Methodist Book Concern undoubtedly persisted, even Case was beginning to realize that it was increasingly important that Methodists in Upper Canada not appear to be labouring under any domineering cultural or ecclesiastical influences emanating from the United States if the political progress they had already begun to make – in 1828, Methodists were authorized to hold land for the purpose of building churches, but they had not yet been given authority to perform marriage ceremonies – was to continue.

The same year that Canadian Methodists became formally independent of the Methodist Episcopal Church in the United States, the contours of the colony's political environment also began to change. Sir John Colborne replaced Strachan's long-time supporter Peregrine Maitland as Upper Canada's lieutenant governor, and the province's first reform majority had been returned in the most recent Legislative Assembly elections – an outcome one Methodist preacher described as "very much to our liking." Just as importantly, the British House of Commons had by the end of the year issued a report against Strachan's "exclusive theories" and also censured "the inaccuracies of his statements." For all these reasons, the colony's new lieutenant governor, although certainly a partisan of the Church of England, did not so easily fall under Strachan's sway. Nor was he able to proceed quite as openly against the Methodists as his predecessor had. In this delicately calibrated political context, Colborne was appointed head of the colony's Indian Department in March 1829 and began to take a keen interest in the translation and production of texts for use in mission schools. Colborne's attention, and the attention of ministers from other religious bodies to these texts, began slowly to divest Peter Jones's translations of their denominational character as they attracted first public interest and later state funding.[43]

A month before Colborne's appointment as head of the Indian Department, William Case and Peter Jones crossed the St Lawrence River to tour Methodist missions in New England, raise money for their own missions in Upper Canada, and oversee the production of more translations. By the middle of March, Jones and Case had reached New York – an arrival noted in the *Christian Advocate* – but their plans were interrupted when a package of letters arrived from Canada announcing that "His Excellency Sir John Colborne had been appointed by the British Government to be the head of the Indian department in Upper Canada" and that, as a result, Colborne wished Jones to "return to Canada" so that he could have his translation "printed at his own expense in the town of York."[44]

At first, Case ignored the summons. Instead, he wrote two days later to Ryerson to inform him that "the Gospel of Mark is now in the press, as also a Hymn Book & spelling book in Mohawk, & a Hymn Book in the Chipeway." By the following day, perhaps with some reluctance, Case had made up his mind. "We shall not get Peter's translation of the Scriptures printed till we return to Canada," he admitted in a letter to George Ryerson, "but the Hymn Books are now in press, and must be done here, as they are wanted immediately, and beside, the numerous accents cannot be furnished at any printing establishment in Canada. We hope the Bible Society of York will soon be able to provide for the further printing of the Mohawk translation now preparing of the Gospels & Epistles." Signalling his awareness of the political context at home, Case added, "We are very grateful for the kind offers of his Excellency, Sir John Colborne, and that he feels desirous to promote the welfare of the Indians on the most liberal principles in matters of religion." With Colborne's eye on them, printing Native translations in New York was becoming increasingly difficult.[45]

On 4 June 1829, after a second fundraising tour, Case and Jones returned to New York and finally "began to make preparations for our return to Canada" after attending a meeting of the "Parent Missionary Society" and having Nathan Bangs – since Methodists were still not authorized to perform marriages in Upper Canada – officiate at the marriage ceremony of William Case to Hetty Hubbard, a teacher employed in one of the Upper Canadian missions. When Case finally returned to Upper Canada, he wrote to thank his brethren in New York for their work producing the translations he was now putting to work. "The Mohawks are very much pleased," he began, "and will be very much profited by the new edition of the Mohawk Scriptures [...] as also with the new edition of the Mohawk hymn book and spelling book. The 2,000 Chipeway hymnbooks lately printed by your [New York District Methodist Bible] society are also highly valued by our Mississauga brethren, and it will give a new impulse to the children, and even to many of the older people, to learn to read."[46]

The two thousand copies of Peter Jones's translation of the Gospel according to Matthew into "the Chippewa tongue" printed by Robert Stanton later that year were never mentioned by Case, or by any other Upper Canadian Methodist, in letters addressed for publication in the *Christian Advocate*. On 8 June 1829, two months after Colborne refused the bill that would have authorized the province's Methodists to perform marriage ceremonies, Jones met the lieutenant governor in his residence at York to discuss the printing of his translations at the "Government press." Two weeks later, Jones also met with a Baptist and a

Presbyterian who, perhaps because of growing public interest in Native missions, had learned of his translations and offered to contribute to pay costs associated with their printing as well. Jones declined these offers, but it is clear that his translations were fast losing their denominational character as both the colony's administrators and members of rival denominations took an increasingly lively interest in their availability. Finally, on 26 June 1829, Jones met one last time with Colborne, who officially placed an order with Robert Stanton for two thousand copies of Jones's first seven chapters of Matthew with English and Chippewa (or Ojibway) on facing pages. Strachan also met with Jones later that same day to make yet another attempt to draw him away from the Methodists by arguing that camp meetings were unscriptural.[47]

In the following years, interest in the production of Jones's, and later James Evans's translations, would only increase. The attention they attracted from Strachan, Colborne, and even ministers of other religious denominations, all helped to draw them out of the Methodist Book Concern's denominational market and into a public market for Methodist texts in Upper Canada. Case's reluctant willingness to accept this fact, and the inconveniences that sometimes resulted in the material production of these texts, are evident in his disinclination to sever relations with the Methodist Book Concern, even after Methodists achieved ecclesiastical independence in the autumn of 1828. Ryerson, on the other hand, although certainly aware of Case's continued patronage of the Methodist Book Concern through the letters he regularly received as well as the reports that appeared in the *Christian Advocate*, had become highly sensitized by his public conflicts with Strachan to the cultural factors that differentiated the Methodist Book Concern's existing denominational market from an emergent and growing public market for Methodist texts in Upper Canada.

V

When Egerton Ryerson decided to publish in a single volume the documents that comprised his public debate with proponents of establishmentarianism, he was under considerably more pressure to be attentive to the implications of its material production than any Methodist before him. Until then, William Case and Peter Jones had made only selective use of the local press for a very specific set of reasons. The Missionary Society reports had been published, first by Hugh Thomson in 1825 and subsequently through William Lyon Mackenzie, to meet both logistical and cultural demands. Such reports were published quickly and made available to a market of public readers in Upper Canada in order to counter Strachan's political efforts to reassert his denominational hold over Upper Canada's Native communities. Given Strachan's tendency to denounce Methodists for their connections to the United States, it was equally important that such reports, although not overtly polemical in nature, not carry the imprint of a denominational publisher operating within the United States. Similar considerations governed the publication of the Canada Conference committee's findings on Henry Ryan in early 1829. That document, moreover, had to be rushed into print before Henry Ryan's contagion could spread any further. Decisions about publishing translations for use in the colony's Native missions, meanwhile, had largely been taken out of Methodist hands by the lieutenant governor.

Months before Colborne's appointment as head of the Indian Department, Egerton Ryerson was looking for a printer to produce his own book. Like the Canada Conference committee's report against Ryan, a document that Case ordered Ryerson to publish with Mackenzie around this time, Ryerson understood that his publication would be closely scrutinized as both a material and a cultural artefact. But Ryerson's book was even more vulnerable to attack because it was a direct and very public assault on the colony's powerful forces of establishmentarianism. Thus, Ryerson had to be careful not only to choose a printer within the colony, but one whose political associations would not leave him open to any criticism by association. By the time he set about making the final arrangements with Mackenzie to print the committee's report on Ryan, Ryerson had already determined to turn his manuscript over to Hugh Thomson for publication.

Ryerson knew that William Case had deliberately moved business away from Thomson after 1825 and clearly preferred Mackenzie on grounds of cost and efficiency. But Ryerson also knew that Thomson was a far better choice when it came to insulating his own book from the political and nationalist calumnies that might be hurled against it by Methodism's detractors. Although a reformer, Thomson was far more moderate than Mackenzie in his criticisms of the colony's government. He was a member of the Church of England and a part of his local Freemasonry Society. He had also been elected to the Legislative Assembly in 1824 and was credited with helping to bring about, through the advocacy of Kingston's *Upper Canada Herald*, a reform victory in the province's 1828 elections. So, while Thomson's membership in the Church of England helped to place him above any facile accusations of clandestine republicanism, his prominent but measured participation in the reform movement also prevented anyone from accusing Ryerson of outright hypocrisy in his choice of printer.[48]

Although he was undoubtedly a perfect political choice, Thomson soon proved to be a very inconvenient one from a practical perspective. While Ryerson read about the ease, speed, economy, and accuracy with which the Methodist Book Concern fulfilled orders for the province's mission schools in Case's letters to him, Ryerson's own relationship with Thomson was characterized by frustrating delays, unforeseen costs, and inferior composition. On 27 October 1828, Thomson wrote to Ryerson to apologize "for the delay which has taken place in the publication of the Controversy." He offered the excuse that one of his employees had "absconded" and another was "seized with an illness." In a shop as tiny as Thomson's, apparently difficulties with just two employees were enough to bring projects to a grinding halt. More than a month elapsed before Thomson wrote again to say that he was "really ashamed" that he could not provide Ryerson with "more satisfactory information regarding the Book." It wasn't until late March 1829 that Thomson finally wrote to Ryerson to inform him that he had forwarded the first seven hundred copies of *Claims of the Churchmen and Dissenters of Upper Canada Brought to the Test*. Thomson also appended a bill for a total of twelve hundred copies that included forty-five reams of paper as well as composition, press work, and binding. The total charge amounted to just over £115.[49]

Ryerson found all this to be anything but satisfactory, and he seems to have seriously considered moving his business elsewhere despite the political advantages Thomson's press offered. In what appears to be a response to a direct question, William Case, in a letter to Ryerson dated 7 April 1829, wrote, "Such to the printers of U. Canada. I don't know of one who can be depended on for doing anything promptly, except it may be Mackenzie." Whatever Mackenzie's other merits, for Ryerson he had simply become too strident an opponent of the colony's administration to be considered a practicable substitute. The Methodist Book Concern was also utterly out of the question for producing a book expressly written to demonstrate that Canadian Methodist preachers were not guilty of "gathering their knowledge" from the "republican states of America." Thus, Ryerson probably felt he had little choice but to put up with Thomson's high prices, slow work, inaccurate composition, and refusal to accept responsibility for mistakes.[50]

Despite the degree to which these concerns so completely occupied Ryerson's thoughts and dictated his choices as an author, shipping records nevertheless indicate that the Concern's reach in Upper Canada continued to expand in the quietude of its denominationally sequestered market – even after Methodist missionary activities had begun to attract the attention of both the colony's lieutenant governor and the wider reading public. William Case and two of his fellow presiding elders, John Ryerson and Thomas Madden, for example, all received shipments of books during this time. Separate orders were dispatched from the Methodist Book Concern in New York to Case in 1827 – on 5 October, and 2, 16, and 23 November. John Ryerson and Anson Green were also sent separate shipments of books by the Concern on 2 November. "The people very much depend on us for their books," one preacher observed, "The agents in New York send them on sale to the Presiding Elder, and we get them from him and supply our people as best we can."[51]

In the three or four years before Methodists in Upper Canada acquired their own press in the fall of 1829, William Case and Egerton Ryerson emerged as the most prominent figures in growing Methodist efforts to produce texts by and for Upper Canadians. For a variety of reasons, Case clearly continued to prefer using the Methodist Book Concern to supply Upper Canada's sequestered denominational market wherever he could. Although Case understood the importance of a developing secondary market composed of Upper Canada's wider reading public and encouraged Ryerson's efforts to counter Strachan in the periodical press at every opportunity, he remained committed to publishing intimate accounts of his own work and the work of other Upper Canadian Methodists in the Methodist Book Concern's periodicals with remarkable regularity. As someone born in the United States and who had first been received on trial there, perhaps Case felt more than just a religious affiliation with his American brethren. He was also reluctant to deprive the Concern of revenues that would be returned to Canadian Methodists in the form of dividends. But as Methodist activities, particularly among Upper Canada's Natives, continued to attract attention from the colony's political figures, Case was practical enough to know that the market for Methodist books would inevitably have to adapt to meet the cultural demands being imposed on his denomination as a whole.

Egerton Ryerson's inclinations ran another way. There can be little doubt that as his protracted public contention for Methodism played itself out in the colonial press, he became acutely aware of the willingness of his detractors to fasten upon any available evidence that might help them to smear a denomination planted in the colony by American itinerants after the Revolutionary War. Ryerson's consistent reliance on printers in Upper Canada to publish his own writings, and his politically astute choice of Hugh Thomson as the publisher of his first book, are evidence of his attentiveness to the cultural weight a book's imprint carried. Indeed, in the entire time that Ryerson employed his pen in the defence of Canadian Methodism, on no occasion did he submit any of his work to the Methodist Book Concern for publication in any of its periodicals. His focus, as the son of a United Empire Loyalist and a former student of the province's best grammar schools, was instead directed entirely towards members of Upper Canada's wider reading public. For Egerton Ryerson, Methodism would never achieve its goals of religious equality until it had successfully moved into the province's mainstream. Publishing in the New York *Christian Advocate* would never achieve that end.

As the years passed, Egerton Ryerson's status continued to grow while the influence of older preachers, including William Case, waned. The situation reached a breaking point when Ryerson opened the Methodist Book Room to the public in the provincial capital in late 1829. That new business marked a powerful and irrevocable shift away from the Concern's denominationally sequestered market for books and periodicals and rendered its rhetorical strategies for equating patronage with membership in a foreign church finally and utterly untenable north of the border. As the public and denominational markets for Methodist books and periodicals thus collapsed into a single whole, all that was left for the Canadians to do was to disentangle themselves once and for all from the Concern's sprawling transnational market. Ironically, it was the interference of the British Wesleyans that prevented them from doing so.

Chapter Four

"Schemes and Evils of Divisions": Denominational Identities and the Public Market for Print

When delegates to the Canada Conference in 1829 elected Egerton Ryerson founding editor of the *Christian Guardian*, his earlier contention for Methodism in the colony's public sphere must not have been far from their minds. Anson Green, who served on the committee that recommended the establishment of the newspaper, later reflected, "We had long felt the need of a *Press* at our command, not only to explain our doctrines and polity, but more especially to fight the battles in which we were engaged for equal rights and for religious equality." As a platform soon identified with reform interests, the *Christian Guardian* quickly became one of Upper Canada's most widely read papers. But publishing a popular newspaper was, as William Lyon Mackenzie could well attest, often a better way to lose money than make it. For this reason, many Upper Canadian publishers resorted to bookselling to fill the gap. The editor of the *Guardian* was no different. One of the earliest indications of Egerton Ryerson's activities as a bookseller can be found in a curiously worded advertisement that appeared in the *Guardian* towards the end of the summer in 1830. "FOR SALE AT THIS OFFICE," the text ran, "Excellent Bibles and Testaments, printed by the British and Foreign Bible Society, at very low prices; Methodist Hymn Books and Watt's Psalms and Hymns, of different qualities and sizes; also Sunday School Hymn Books of different kinds, and a small assortment of Sabbath School Books. We hope to obtain a larger supply shortly."[1]

Attentive readers, those who knew that the British and Foreign Bible Society dealt only in Bibles "without note or comment," might have wondered from whom Ryerson had acquired his supply of hymn and Sunday school books. It seems probable, however, that most casual readers would have inferred from the prominence given to the British and Foreign Bible Society in Ryerson's advertisement that the whole of his stock, from whatever supplier, was of British manufacture. Such an inference – one that Ryerson appears to have deliberately encouraged by his careful choice and arrangement of words – would have been very wide of the mark. Around the same time that the type for this issue of the *Christian Guardian* was being set in York, its new editor was quietly dispatching a large order to the Methodist Book Concern in New York. The *Christian Advocate* noted the arrival of that order several weeks later, and soon shipped two boxes of books to Ryerson at his newspaper office "care S. M'Afee, opposite Black Rock."[2]

Perhaps more than any of his coreligionists, Egerton Ryerson would have learned, from his joint experiences as Methodism's first advocate in Upper Canada's public sphere and as its first permanent missionary among Natives on the Credit River, to recognize the liabilities associated with openly selling books rhetorically linked by the Methodist Book Concern to membership in a foreign church. As the *Christian Guardian* became more popular among the colony's non-Methodists, moreover, these liabilities would compound as the books advertised in its pages fell under growing scrutiny in Upper Canada's public market for such goods. In one highly publicized incident, Ryerson was even openly scolded for the far more minor sin of importing paper from the United States. That incident, disdainfully referred to by Ryerson as "The Paper Affair," was yet another reminder for Ryerson of how closely his actions were being watched for even the smallest sign of undue American influence.[3]

The awkward situation that Ryerson found himself in, as both the editor of a popular newspaper and the public bookseller of denominational books tainted both by the location of their manufacture as well as the circumstances of their cultural production, flowed in large part from the complicated terms under which Upper Canadians achieved ecclesiastical independence from the Methodist Episcopal Church in the United States, in 1828. As this chapter will show, that independence did nothing to sever the Concern's access to its Canadian market or lessen the financial dependence of Canadian Methodists on their American brethren. Indeed, it was that very dependence on the Methodist Book Concern for both books and money that ruled out the possibility of Canadians declaring themselves independent without first obtaining the permission of the Americans.

I

Upper Canadians achieved their first taste of being an independent polity in May 1824, when the American General Conference agreed to set them apart as an annual conference in their own right. Under that new arrangement, Canadian Methodists began receiving their own annual dividend paid out of the profits earned by the Methodist Book Concern over the previous year. Accordingly, when delegates gathered for their annual conference in Hallowell, a town in Prince Edward County, that spring, they did so with permission from Nathan Bangs to draw a dividend against the Methodist Book Concern in the amount of $150. That figure remained constant for the following two years before being increased to $200 in 1827. Such dividends were paid in recognition that the purchase of the Concern's books and periodicals were important markers of membership in and commitment to the Methodist Episcopal Church. From a practical point of view, they also helped pay for Methodism's missionary activities in Canada. All this was in addition to the commissions that were routinely paid to individual preachers for selling the Concern's books. Thus, with their single largest source of revenue at stake, it is not surprising that when Canadian preachers petitioned their American brethren for independence, they asked for more than a mere severing of episcopal oversight. They also requested "an outlet from the Book Concern, and the Chartered Fund, to enable us to carry on the great work before us, in this new Country."[4]

As the Canadian petition circulated in the United States, members of Canada's new annual conference were obliged to wait patiently until the next quadrennial General Conference of the Methodist Episcopal Church for anything to be done. It was a difficult four years. Anti-Americanism was reaching new heights in British North America, and Methodists faced scrutiny from within and without. John Strachan's attacks on Methodism were becoming more strident as the Church of England attempted to use government monies to lure the province's Native Methodists – so dear to William Case's heart – away from the Canada Conference. At the same time, Henry Ryan redoubled his own efforts to sow internal discord by printing incendiary pamphlets and touring Upper Canada to denounce "Republican domination, the tyranny of Yankee Bishops, [and] the fallen state and corrupt character of the preachers in Canada."[5]

In spite of these considerable pressures, Methodists in Upper Canada continued to choose to wait for the next General Conference of the Methodist Episcopal Church to press their case for a negotiated settlement rather than declare unilateral independence. Such a declaration would undoubtedly have silenced Ryan and his fellow detractors – but it would have also altered the way American Methodists perceived their Canadian brethren. By refashioning their religious identities in this way, their patronage of the Methodist Book Concern might have become so emptied of its cultural significance that the rhetorical links binding Canadian and American Methodists together in a common market would have been broken. That would have deprived the Canadians not only of discounted books and periodicals, but of all the financial proceeds in the form of dividends and commissions that attended their distribution in Canada. Even more importantly, the enormous financial investment Canadians had accumulated in the Methodist Book Concern's capital worth over three decades of almost exclusive patronage would have been placed in jeopardy.

Apparently, these consequences were even less palatable to Upper Canadians than the prospect of a disgruntled Henry Ryan at the head of a noisy and schismatic body loudly denouncing his former coreligionists as disloyal republicans. Until Canadian Methodists could find a way to achieve financial independence – together with an alternative source of inexpensive books and periodicals in order to put money in the pockets of its preachers – the American General Conference would maintain its ability, however indirect, to govern key cultural and financial aspects of Canadian Methodism through the Book Concern. By the time Canadians sent delegates to the General Conference of 1828, they had reformulated their petition to seek something more than simply an "outlet from the Book Concern." This time they sought complete ecclesiastical and cultural independence from both the Methodist Episcopal Church and the Methodist Book Concern. They did not get it.

On 5 May 1828, William and John Ryerson presented a formal petition on behalf of the Canada Conference to delegates gathered in Pittsburgh for the Methodist Episcopal Church's General Conference. "Our political relations," it ran, "and the political feelings of a great part of the community, are such that we labour under many very serious embarrassments on account of our union with the United States; from which embarrassments we would, in all probability, be relieved by separation." The general argument remained essentially what it had been in 1824, but this new petition also requested that "the General Conference will, together with an independent establishment, be pleased to grant your petitioners a portion of the Book Concern, of the Chartered Fund, and a portion of the fund of the Missionary Society."[6]

Willing to sympathize with their Canadian brethren "in their present state of perplexity," the American struck a special committee to consider these requests. To the surprise of the Canadians, however, that committee concluded that it was "unconstitutional" for the General Conference to grant them "a separate Church establishment." Although a devastating blow to their cause, the Ryersons were clever enough to see that what lay at the heart of the objection was not a constitutional problem at all: it was the money tied up in the Methodist Book Concern's market. A hasty severing of the Concern's access to its growing market in British North America, all at a time when the Concern remained $100,000 in debt after years of capital expansion under Nathan Bangs's direction, was quite simply insupportable to the Americans. Several days later, William Ryerson presented an alternative proposal that, although it did nothing to obviate the constitutional difficulties, deferred the Canadian claims against the Methodist Book Concern by specifying that such claims "shall be left open for future negotiation and adjustment between the two connexions."[7]

With the Methodist Book Concern thus off the table, a way around the constitutional difficulties was, as the Ryersons no doubt had suspected, miraculously found. A committee was struck immediately to formulate terms under which a mutual and amicable ecclesiastical separation might be effected. With the interests of the Methodist Book Concern no longer threatened, the committee concluded, adopting an idea proposed by none other than John Emory, that ecclesiastical independence for Canada was perfectly constitutional on the grounds that Methodist preachers had been sent to serve north of the border strictly on a voluntary basis. Thus, the committee argued, Upper Canadians had "a perfect right to request us to withdraw our services."[8]

Importantly, the last of three clauses of the committee's report made the analogous right of Canadians to request the Methodist Book Concern to withdraw its products from their market an entirely different matter. Instead, the Concern was guaranteed uninterrupted access to its Canadian customers for the foreseeable future. Canadians would be provided with the Concern's books "on the same terms by which our agents are regulated in furnishing them in the United States," the report stated. Canadians would also be entitled to the annual payment of dividends provided that the "Canada Church ... may continue to support and patronize our Book Concern as in the past." That the Canadian delegates agreed to that final clause would be much regretted in four years' time.[9]

II

For all its purported importance, the relationship that Methodists bore to other actors in Upper Canada's political drama was not much altered by the achievement of ecclesiastical independence. The bludgeon of republicanism and perfidy was too convenient an instrument to abandon so easily. John Strachan and the new lieutenant governor, Sir John Colborne, if never as united in sentiment as Strachan had been with

Maitland, continued to harbour a common suspicion about the lingering influences that American Methodists exerted over their Canadian coreligionists. With the exception of being granted the legal right to hold land corporately for the erection of churches, Methodists remained far from realizing their goal of religious equality with the Church of England. Marriages performed by their preachers continued to be unrecognized in law, and Strachan remained at liberty to carry on his own affairs as though the Church of England's claims to establishment were largely uncontested.[10]

By 1829, Canadian Methodists became convinced that a newspaper under their own control might be an essential means for advancing the cause of religious equality. Perhaps by this time Upper Canada's Methodists feared that, after the attention their Native translations had already begun to attract from outsiders, the ongoing widespread distribution of the *Christian Advocate* among the colony's supposedly "independent" Methodists would provide their critics with all the evidence they needed to prove that the influence of American Methodism in Canada was as pervasive as ever. "One imperative want," wrote Thomas Webster, "which the Church had long felt, was that of a connexional paper." In an apparent reference to the colony's existing newspapers, Webster added, "No merely secular paper could fully understand the wants, or enter into the interests of the religious community, nor could it so ably defend the Church from the ungenerous and untruthful assaults of its enemies."[11]

That the printers in Upper Canada were unsuitable cannot be doubted. William Lyon Mackenzie was far too radical to be seriously considered. Other printers were too conservative, either to accept Methodist business, or to publish Methodist opinions in their own newspapers. The rest, including moderate reformer Hugh Thomson, were simply too inefficient or too expensive to be relied on. William Case, writing to Egerton Ryerson from Philadelphia in the spring of 1829, where he and Peter Jones were raising money for Native missions in the province, sweepingly dismissed all Upper Canadian printers, apart from Mackenzie, as incapable of "doing anything promptly." Case added, presciently, that he could return to Upper Canada from the United States bringing a full "printing establishment" without much difficulty. Although that did not happen quite yet, Case was undoubtedly right about one thing: Canadians needed more than their own newspaper. They needed their own printing press.[12]

With no clear sense of how best to procure their own press, or how much money would be necessary to finance the endeavour, Canadian Methodists looked south for support and advice, relying especially on

Francis Hall, a leading New York Methodist who published the *New York Commercial Advertiser*. William Case and Peter Jones had often stayed with Hall while they oversaw the printing of Native translations at the Methodist Book Concern. Anson Green, a member of the Canada Conference committee appointed to superintend the establishment of the newspaper, either knew Hall himself or had been referred to him by Case and Jones. As Green set about discovering what was required to establish their own paper, he noted that he was "favoured with a long conversation concerning the probable expense of a press, type, paper, &c., with Francis Hall, Esq., Editor of a New York paper, and we saw that by advancing liberally from our own pockets, and asking some of our laymen to aid us in this matter, we could accomplish our object." Accordingly, after being elected editor and "appointed an agent to procure the apparatus and materials for commencing the paper," Egerton Ryerson travelled to New York to make arrangements for an American press to be shipped to him at the new offices of the *Christian Guardian* in York.[13]

With a printing press now under his own command, Ryerson lost no time appropriating the Methodist Book Concern's rhetorical strategies for increasing the denominational appeal of the new *Christian Guardian*, regularly claiming in a space above his weekly editorial that "the proceeds of this paper will be applied to the support of superannuated or worn out Preachers of the M.E. Church in Canada; and of widows and orphans of those who have died in the work; and to the general spreading of the Gospel." Almost identical to the wording employed by the Concern's own book agents, Ryerson's rhetoric proposed a politically acceptable relationship between patronage and denominational identity in an ecclesiastically independent Methodist Episcopal Church in Upper Canada. But by defining the boundaries of his market in terms that were both denominational *and* national in character, Ryerson also placed the *Christian Guardian* in direct competition with the *Christian Advocate*. Thus, the more successful the *Guardian* became, the more it threatened to weaken Canadian claims to a portion of the Methodist Book Concern's stock and worth at ensuing General conferences. This was all the more unfortunate since the denominational rhetoric Ryerson repurposed for the *Christian Guardian* ultimately had little to do with its eventual commercial success. That success began with the defeat of Upper Canada's reformers in the elections of October 1830 and marked a critical turning point for both Ryerson and the *Guardian*. In a move that he believed to be consistent with developments overseas, Ryerson resolved after that election to harden the *Guardian*'s editorial stance in favour of reform.[14]

"The posture of affairs in England," he wrote to his brother George in the following month, "appears upon the whole more favourable to Reform than in U. Canada. We are resolved to double our diligence." By thus shifting his editorial slant, Egerton Ryerson transformed the *Christian Guardian* from a newspaper whose appeal was primarily denominational in character, into a political weekly whose readership was no longer coterminous with the boundaries of Methodism. In early 1830, William Bell, a Presbyterian minister, was one of many people who wrote to Ryerson to convey that, although he differed with the editor "in many particulars, yet in some we agree." The particulars on which they disagreed were denominational. But, as Bell elaborated, the new reader he represented wholeheartedly supported Ryerson's attempts to promote civil and religious liberty. Politics, not religion, is what drew these readers to Ryerson's banner. Unfortunately, the change placed yet further stress on the Concern's market in Upper Canada by attracting the eye of a wider circle of readers who did not share Ryerson's denominational convictions, and who would therefore view the public sale of the books linked to membership in a foreign church as evidence of continued American cultural hegemony.[15]

Without a financial settlement from the Methodist Book Concern to draw on, Ryerson had no choice but to continue to underwrite the *Christian Guardian*'s expenses – by 1832 the newspaper was encumbered by more than $5,000 in unpaid subscriptions – by selling books. To minimize the political risks to interests that remained intensely denominational in nature, Ryerson supplied himself, where possible, with books that were not encumbered with the denominational rhetoric that the Methodist Book Concern continued to use to insulate its own market from competitors in the United States. As already noted, he sold bibles printed by the British and Foreign Bible Society rather than bibles printed by the Methodist Book Concern. Moreover, in addition to taking on contract printing jobs where he could, as early as 1830 Ryerson also began to advertise the availability of his own denominational titles, most significantly a Canadian edition of one of the Concern's most lucrative titles, namely, *The Doctrine and Discipline of the Methodist Episcopal Church.*[16]

Canadian Methodists urgently needed their own edition of the *Discipline* in part to excise from it declarations about the virtues of republicanism in the United States. They also hoped it might generate a small profit that could be used to defray the costs of publishing the *Christian Guardian.* The Canada Conference minutes indicate that Methodists were aware that printing such a large document on their own press might result in financial losses; nevertheless, they preferred this gamble to the cultural risks associated with printing a Canadian edition of the *Discipline* on the presses of the Methodist Book Concern. Fortunately, it paid off, and Ryerson was able to report that a profit of £37.10.11½ had been realized by the time of the Canada Conference met in 1831.[17]

But while Canadians held out their hands to receive yet another annual dividend payment from the Methodist Book Concern at that same meeting, it seems not to have occurred to Egerton Ryerson or any other Methodist that the profits earned from the sale of the Canadian *Discipline* and the *Christian Guardian* ought to have been similarly shared with the Americans. That would, after all, have violated the logic of the Concern's own rhetoric since payments were the consequence of patronage. For obvious reasons, the Americans had shown no interest in buying copies of Ryerson's edition of the *Discipline*. By the same token, however, the Methodist Book Concern had probably not shipped a single copy of its own 1829 edition of the *Discipline* to Upper Canada. Thus, a cleavage in the transnational market for Methodist books began to grow wider as Canadians, at least for now, enjoyed both the annual dividend payments from the Methodist Book Concern as well as the profits they earned from the sale of their own books "to aid in paying the debts of the printing establishment." John Emory and Nathan Bangs, meanwhile, who continued to receive the *Christian Guardian* in New York and who would have long before noted a decrease in the number of *Christian Advocate* subscribers in Upper Canada, no doubt found in every advertisement Ryerson ran for Canadian editions of the *Discipline*, minutes of conference, British and Foreign Bible Society bibles, and other such commodities, additional evidence to explain why the volume of American books being shipped to Canada was also beginning to decrease.[18]

John Emory and Nathan Bangs were not the only Methodists outside the colony reading the *Christian Guardian* with dissatisfaction. In London, the British Wesleyans found themselves increasingly embarrassed by Ryerson's political strivings on behalf of a denomination they believed should be far more acquiescent to the claims of the Church of England in British North America. The editorial stance of the *Christian Guardian* after October 1830 – an irritant they attributed to the latent influence of the Methodist Episcopal Church in the United States – was among the reasons British Wesleyans would later cite for their return to Upper Canada. Their patience with the *Guardian* finally ran out when Ryerson took it upon himself to challenge not only Strachan and the proponents of colonial Church establishment, but also the lieutenant governor himself over his handling of the colony's Native missions.[19]

This conflict was long in the making and one in which John Colborne and other conservative members of the government of Upper Canada had long sought the help of the politically congenial British Wesleyans. And although decreasing levels of patronage certainly diminished the degree to which Upper Canadians could claim to support the Methodist Book Concern as members of a single transnational religious body – however configured ecclesiastically – it was ultimately the arrival of British Wesleyans in the province that had the greatest potential to subvert the Canadian claim against the Concern by altering the religious identity of Canadian Methodists so thoroughly that it threatened to reframe their acts of patronage as straightforward economic transactions rather than acts of denominational solidarity. Unlike the adoption of a more mainstream print culture, however, the return of the British Wesleyans was something that Canadian Methodists, at least at first, had little control over and vigorously resisted.

When, in 1827, John Strachan finally accepted that Anglicanism would never have the strength to defeat Methodism on its own, he quietly set about encouraging the Wesleyans to resume their preaching stations in Upper Canada. Peregrine Maitland, Colborne's immediate predecessor, had also promised the Wesleyans the support of his administration if they sent preachers west of the Ottawa River. Little happened as a result of these efforts. Then Robert Alder, a prominent British Wesleyan who had worked for several years as a missionary in both the Maritimes and Lower Canada before returning to England in 1827, openly expressed a desire on the part of his brethren to return to Upper Canada in the summer of 1828. As one of the witnesses called by the Imperial Parliament's Select Committee on the Civil Government of Canada, Alder was asked whether Methodists in the province fell under the direct supervision of British Wesleyans. Admitting that they did not, Alder added that, since they were no longer under the direction of the American General Conference, he expected "that an arrangement will soon be made, by which the Methodists of Upper Canada will be brought to act under the direction of the British Conference, as the Methodists of Lower Canada have done for several years."[20]

III

In May 1832, Canadian preachers William Case, Franklin Metcalf, and William Ryerson arrived at the General Conference of the Methodist Episcopal Church in Philadelphia to seek a full financial settlement against the Methodist Book Concern on behalf of their Canadian brethren. That same month, John Ryerson, chair of the Canada Missionary

Board, received an ominous letter from Robert Alder informing him that a British Wesleyan return to the colony was now imminent. Alder's letter struck Ryerson and his fellow Methodists in the province "like thunder-claps." "Oh!" opined John Ryerson with more than a touch of drama, "the darkness! What a cloud seemed to spread over the whole Methodist family in Upper Canada!" Despite Ryerson's evident astonishment, every preacher in the province knew the Wesleyans had long had their eye on Upper Canada. Meanwhile, back in Philadelphia, Case, Metcalf, and William Ryerson already had their hands full convincing American delegates – and that without the confusion a British Wesleyan presence in Upper Canada might mean for Methodist religious identity in the province – that the Methodist Book Concern's declining colonial market did not in itself invalidate the Canadian claim against the stock and worth of the Concern.[21]

The formal claim of the Methodist Episcopal Church in Canada against the New York Methodist Book Concern was submitted at the beginning of May 1832. On motion, the claim was referred for consideration to the General Conference's Committee on the Book Concern. This committee was large and extraordinarily diverse, consisting of one delegate from each of the Church's nineteen annual conferences, but the Canadians had at least one committed advocate among its members in the person of Wilbur Fisk. President of Wesleyan University, Fisk had been one of the most outspoken supporters of Canadian independence in 1828, and had only recently declined an offer to become Canada's first Methodist bishop. Before the committee was able to report back to the General Conference, however, John Emory used his report as senior book agent to raise serious doubts in the minds of delegates about the validity of the Canadian claim. Emory, it will be remembered, had been instrumental in finding a way around the supposed constitutional obstacle to Canadian independence four years earlier when he proposed that preachers had always been sent to Canada strictly on a voluntary basis. He was also a part of the committee that had proposed the ongoing payment of annual dividends to the Canadians "so long as they may continue to support & patronize our Book Concern." But the Canadians, according to Emory, had not entirely lived up to that condition.[22]

"Under the resolution of the last General Conference," Emory complained in his report, "we have continued to pay an equal dividend to the conference of the Methodist Episcopal Church in Canada, yet not without some doubt, to say the least, whether the condition annexed by the General Conference has been complied with on the part of our brethren in Canada." Perhaps the most obvious problem for Emory was that Canadian subscriptions to the *Christian Advocate* had declined precipitously since Ryerson began publishing the *Christian Guardian* in York. "In consequence of the establishment of a separate weekly paper, under the control, and for the exclusive benefit of the Canada annual conference, the subscriptions for the Christian Advocate and Journal, which were once respectable within the bounds of that conference, have been almost wholly discontinued; nor, indeed," he continued, "has the patronage extended to the General Book Concern, on the part of that conference, been anything like equal in amount to what it formerly was, although the numbers of its ministers and members have been increased, and also the dividends from the Book Concern."[23]

That Canadians might be said to justly have an enduring claim against the Methodist Book Concern hinged for John Emory and the majority of the General Conference delegates on the continued existence of a common religious identity that was defined by a shared market. Between 1828 and 1832, the number of Methodists in Canada had grown from ten thousand to just under fifteen thousand. Emory, who understood the Methodist Book Concern's domestic market in terms that were exclusively denominational, expected growth in ecclesiastical membership to be accompanied by an inevitable and proportionate increase in the sale of the Concern's wares. Indeed, the payment of annual dividends was wholly premised on this belief. Although this logic continued to hold in the United States, where the Methodist Book Concern's books and periodicals functioned as unproblematic denominational status objects, in Upper Canada this was simply no longer true.[24]

Emory put his finger on the cause of the problem when he singled out the *Christian Guardian* in his report. The substance of his objection to the introduction of this newspaper flowed not from its contents – which often declared with force the ecclesiastical autonomy of Upper Canadian Methodists – but its very existence as a commodity aimed solely at benefiting only Methodists living in the province. Unlike the New York *Christian Advocate*, the *Christian Guardian* was a product with no transnational appeal. Methodists in the United States, even if they did subscribe to the *Christian Guardian*, would not thereby confer any financial benefit on their own Church. Because it was not part of a common market, the *Guardian* could not be tied to a common religious identity that spanned the border with the United States. Thus, the very existence of this newspaper signalled a new division in what had been until that time a single North American market – and a single transnational religious identity predicated on that market – uniting Upper Canadian Methodists, irrespective of their local polity, with their American brethren in a common community of religious interest. For these reasons, the introduction of a newspaper "for the exclusive benefit of the Canada annual conference" did much to undermine the grounds on which Canadians might make a claim against the Methodist Book Concern. For Emory, it demonstrated the willingness of Canadian Methodists to set themselves apart from their American brethren by misappropriating what had been a shared rhetorical framework to further interests that were as much political as they were denominational in character.

Egerton Ryerson and the *Christian Guardian* were also largely to blame for the fact that the Methodist Book Concern was selling fewer books in Upper Canada relative to its expanding Methodist population. Emory's report implied that Canadians, by eschewing the Concern's offerings in order to avoid accusations that they continued to exist under the shadow of American cultural influences, failed to properly acknowledge the claims the Methodist Book Concern made about its denominational exceptionality in the market. This further subverted the bonds of a common religious identity founded on the uniquely privileged and exclusive relationship that the Methodist Book Concern insisted on maintaining with its customers.

In comparison with the continued vitality of this shared market, the independence Canadians achieved at the American General Conference in 1828 was largely abstract in character. American Methodists did not take it personally because they were persuaded that it was undertaken entirely in order to assuage political pressures in Upper Canada. Indeed, from a cultural and financial perspective, it would remain perfectly superficial – and therefore unproblematic – as long as Canadians maintained their "union" with the Methodist Episcopal Church by participating in the Methodist Book Concern's undivided North American market.

As Emory argued, however, things had changed since 1828. Every time Egerton Ryerson sold a book or a newspaper that had not been printed on the Concern's presses, he steadily eroded, one purchase at a time, a shared religious identity that was founded not on the oversight of a common episcopacy but on the far more tangible exchange of denominational goods in a rhetorically charged and highly circumscribed market for books and periodicals. The only question that remained, in May 1832, was whether that erosion had advanced so far as to invalidate utterly the Canadian claim against the Methodist Book Concern by negating their status as members within a market that burdened purchasers as well as sellers with responsibilities. Since the Canadians were no longer meeting their responsibilities, their whole case hung on whether or not the Americans would be willing to recognize their historical patronage by effectively buying them out. More bluntly, would the Americans allow Canadian Methodists to take the money and run? The answer to that question turned out to be yes – and no.

The report of the General Conference committee on the Canada claim was finally called up just after the middle of May 1832. Initially, assurances were demanded by Conference delegates that any funds the Canadians received from the Methodist Book Concern would not, according to the logic of the Concern's rhetoric, be applied to any other purpose "than for the benefit of the travelling, supernumerary, superannuated, and worn-our preachers, their wives, widows, and orphans." This, however, was withdrawn – perhaps in recognition that different, less denominationally bound, rhetorical strategies were already being used in Upper Canada. The following day, John Emory and William Ryerson, undoubtedly representing widely different perspectives, addressed the delegates for some time. Despite Ryerson's efforts, Emory's contention that declining levels of patronage in the colony complicated the Canadian claim appears to have hit its mark. An indication that things were not progressing as the Canadians hoped came two days later when William Case asked Wilbur Fisk to address the delegates. His remarks appear to have been unavailing.[25]

When a vote was finally called on the subject, Conference delegates rejected the Canadian claim by a wide margin: 75 in favour, with 130 against. John Emory then suggested that the report of the General Conference committee be revised, and it was submitted to a much smaller committee for examination. Canadians were doubtless worried that the committee included Emory but not Fisk. When the new committee's report was read on 23 May 1832, Emory, William Case, William Ryerson, and several others addressed delegates at the General Conference. Joshua Soule, founder of the *Methodist Magazine* and now a bishop, also spoke to the matter at hand. It is not known precisely what happened to the proposals of the Canadians as they underwent the scrutiny first of the large Book Committee of the General Conference, and then the smaller committee on which Emory was the leading voice; there can be little doubt, however, that they failed to receive all that they had hoped for. When a vote was called on the revised report and terms, it passed 152 in favour and 34 against. This cleared the first hurdle. However, delegates also raised an objection on constitutional grounds. "Though it was generally agreed by the members of the conference that the Canada brethren had a just claim upon a portion of the Book Concern," Nathan Bangs observed several years later, "yet, after a full examination of the subject, the conclusion was drawn that the General Conference had no constitutional authority to make the apportionment without first obtaining the concurrence of the annual conferences."[26]

To overcome this objection, a majority comprising "three-fourths of all the members of the several annual conferences" was required to ratify the terms of the agreement. Only then would the Methodist Book Concern's agents be authorized to divide its assets, including "a full proportion of the unsaleable and saleable stock, as of the bad as well as good debts," in proportion to the "number of travelling preachers in the Canada Conference" relative to the number of "travelling preachers in the Methodist Episcopal Church in the United States." The total amount to be divided, although enormous, was calculated beyond the last penny: $413,455.93½. Case, Metcalf, and Ryerson were probably disappointed by a number of factors – the delay a vote by the annual conferences would entail; the necessity of accepting one last large shipment of the Concern's commodities in Upper Canada; and the fastidious, even penurious, way in which the worth of the Methodist Book Concern was calculated beyond the last penny. Yet, the amount of the final settlement was considerable enough to assuage these irritants. Anson Green estimated that Canadians expected to receive from New York some $27,000 after ratification by the annual conferences – an amount so large it would have been enough to purchase a new press for every printer operating in Upper Canada at that time. Such a settlement would have conferred an almost incalculable advantage on Methodist interests in Canada, allowing Egerton Ryerson not only to underwrite the costs associated with selling British books to the Upper Canadian public through the *Christian Guardian*, but also to expand his own publishing enterprise at a rate far faster than the province's market conditions would otherwise have allowed. It would take almost a year, however, before the votes from the Methodist Episcopal Church's nineteen annual conferences could be tabulated. Until then, the Canadians were entitled to continue receiving "the same equal annual dividend of the profits of the Book Concern as heretofore." Despite the importance of these negotiations, affairs with the British Wesleyans back in Upper Canada were not standing still. Indeed, John and Egerton Ryerson were about to have a dramatic change of heart.[27]

IV

"One day, while walking along Bay Street," John Ryerson wrote later, reflecting on these tumultuous times, "pondering in my mind what would be the result of pending matters, and that if there was any possible way by which the impending evil could be averted, it came into my mind suddenly, as though some supernatural power had suggested it, whether or not some arrangement could not be entered into by which the Two Conferences could be united, and thus mutually help and strengthen each other, instead of devouring one another, as the enemies of Methodism were seeking that they should do, and thus prevent the further schemes and evils of divisions." Read in isolation, this passage has been interpreted by most historians to mean that fear was the chief factor motivating John and Egerton Ryerson, as well as other Methodists, to drop their opposition to the British Wesleyans in the face of Robert Alder's unyielding resolve. When viewed against the context of wider religious and political developments then unfolding in North America, however, it becomes clear that fear had little to do with the decision.[28]

As far as Egerton Ryerson was concerned, when Alder arrived in Canada, Methodism had never been stronger. "The circulation and influence of the *Christian Guardian* (then the leading newspaper in Upper Canada)," he observed, "increased daily; the number and power of the Methodist Church grew more and more every year; so that the greedy few felt that their prey was in great danger of being lost." Those "greedy few," whom William Lyon Mackenzie had dubbed "the Family Compact," although not moribund, had become steadily less influential since Peregrine Maitland left the colony in 1828. Whig forces in Britain, moreover, were stronger than ever, and the Reform Act was on the verge of being passed into law. At the same time, the financial support that Canadian Methodists received from the United States had grown considerably in recent years. Monies the American Methodists provided for the support of Native missions in Upper Canada had more than doubled from $700 to $1,500 per year. Canadian preachers and presiding elders continued to receive the same bookselling commissions they had before 1828, and the annual dividend paid by the Methodist Book Concern to the Canada Conference was boosted from $500 to $800 between 1831 and 1832 – an increase of 60 per cent in just one year.[29]

As if that were not enough, at precisely the moment when John and Egerton Ryerson began to entertain seriously the possibility of a cooperative effort with the British Wesleyans, they stood on the verge of receiving a financial settlement from the Methodist Book Concern large enough to eliminate all financial worries for years to come. So confident, in fact, was Ryerson in the successful outcome of that claim that he publicly mentioned it in the *Christian Guardian* for the first and only time in the middle of May 1832. In response to a call for more books and the establishment of a "general depository [...] under the direction of the Editors" on the part of the Sabbath School Union, Ryerson attributed the lack of such a depository to the "unsettled state of the Financial affairs of the Methodist Conference, in respect to the Book Establishment" and suggested that the "inconvenience and evil" associated with a lack of suitable books would be "remedied at our ensuing Annual Conference, to be held in August."[30]

That settlement was not quite yet in hand, however. No doubt Ryerson understood that any formal association with the British Wesleyans, particularly before the General Conference of 1832, would likely endanger the Canadian claim against the Methodist Book Concern by altering the religious identity of Canadian Methodists and thereby weaken the legitimacy with which Canadians could continue to claim to be members of a single transnational market bound by common religious and financial interests. His bookselling activities had also taught Egerton Ryerson that, as long as the claim against the Methodist Book Concern remained unsettled, the establishment of a "general depository" would be too politically dangerous to be undertaken with any vigour. But once they secured the money they sought from the Americans at the General Conference outright, there would be no reason not to merge with the Wesleyans and begin selling books imported from the Wesleyan Book Room in London in a public market without fear of political censure.

Until now, the editor of the *Christian Guardian* had maintained an unyielding opposition to British Wesleyan advances, even writing a letter of protest to leading British Wesleyan Richard Watson on behalf of his Canadian Methodists. Yet, the timing of events occurring south of the border help to explain why John was able to convince his brother to reverse his entrenched opposition with such apparent ease. No record survives of the private conversations that took place between them that May. Nevertheless, John Ryerson later wrote, "After several interviews and conversations on the subject, we agreed upon the outlines of a plan of pacification, or one to *prevent* strife." To "*prevent* strife" the plan not only called for a possible merger with the British Wesleyans, but also left the door open to accepting British Wesleyan leadership in Upper Canada, turning over control of Native missions to Wesleyans missionaries, and beginning to import books and periodicals from the London Book Room.[31]

What neither man could have known, as they prepared to convince their fellow Methodists of the merits of their plan, was that negotiations in Philadelphia were not moving along as smoothly as Ryerson's confident remark in the *Christian Guardian* indicates he believed they would. Had the American General Conference not referred the Canadian claim against the Methodist Book Concern to the annual conferences for ratification, a return of the British Wesleyans to Upper Canada at this time would have had no material implications. Ties to the Methodist

Book Concern could have been neatly severed, and the monies realized from the settlement used to establish a "general depository" furnished with shelves filled with locally produced texts and subsidized books and periodicals imported from overseas. The golden moment to move Methodism ever closer to the colonial mainstream by shedding lingering suspicions about disloyalty finally seemed at hand. This plan would have been perfectly executed had not the British Wesleyans moved too quickly – or the annual conferences voted too slowly – to permit the eventual ratification of the Canadian claim Egerton Ryerson's brother William and others had argued for with such difficulty in Philadelphia. Meanwhile, Robert Alder was already making his way across the Atlantic.

V

On 7 June 1832, Alder and a dozen other British Wesleyan missionaries arrived in Lower Canada. Three days earlier, the New England Annual Conference, the first annual conference to meet and vote on the Canadian claim, overwhelmingly approved the terms recommended by the General Conference, with 73 in favour and 1 against. Alder almost certainly knew little and cared less about the progress of the voting then moving through the Methodist annual conferences in the United States. He was equally in the dark about John Ryerson's recent epiphany about the importance of cooperation – even union – between the two bodies. Thus, almost as soon as his feet touched the soil, Alder dispatched two British Wesleyan missionaries to begin the competition along two preaching circuits already occupied by Methodists in Upper Canada. The Americans, meanwhile, who knew as little of Alder as he knew of them, continued to vote on the Canadian claim at their annual conferences.[32]

That claim appears to have been contested with the greatest animation at the proceedings of the annual New York Conference held early that June. That only made sense: New York was the home of the Methodist Book Concern, and its Conference delegates included among their number the current as well as many former book agents. Although the vote was not close – 142 in favour and 13 against – it passed only after two hours of debate, accompanied by an ambiguous resolution that cast a moral shadow over the legitimacy of the entire claim. "That this Conference," the resolution read, "concur in the resolutions recommended by the late General Conference in the negotiation with the Delegates from the Canada Conference respecting their claims on the Book Concern, provided, that nothing here is to be construed as an admission or denial of a claim founded in right." Reservations of the sort expressed in this resolution underscored that, even in view of the General Conference's recommendations, the approval of the Canadian claim was still far from assured. Alder's presence, meanwhile, placed the relationship between patronage of the Methodist Book Concern and denominational identity in Upper Canada, a relationship that remained essential to the achievement of a successful outcome, under further stress.[33]

About two weeks after the New York vote, Alder and his missionaries arrived in the capital of Upper Canada. That arrival was marked by a powerful demonstration, observed with envy by Egerton Ryerson and his Methodist brethren, of how dramatically a closer association with the British Wesleyans might literally open doors in the colony that had been until then impassable. No less a figure than John Strachan was on hand to welcome the new missionaries and to invite them to make use of the district grammar school for their religious services. "No instance had ever occurred of any Methodist minister preaching in one of these school houses" John Carroll groused, "and no one believes that they would have been granted, if asked, to any Canadian preacher; but now the Metropolitan school-house, under the direction of the Archdeacon of York himself, is thrown open to two newly arrived Wesleyan ministers."[34]

Egerton Ryerson saw in this spectacle an opening for change. He moved quickly to take advantage of it – and perhaps to signal to Strachan as well that his plan to set the Wesleyans and the Methodists at one another's throats would not be quite so easy to effect. No doubt turning over in his mind the conversations he had had with his brother John, Ryerson used the *Christian Guardian* to float the idea of a "union of Wesleyan Methodism throughout the British Empire, as far as circumstances will justify … upon a common principle and under a common management." This was a bold proposal and Ryerson knew it. No one in any party – not the Canadians, not the Wesleyans, and certainly not the Americans – was very keen on the idea, at first. Ryerson seems to have been particularly concerned about the possible resentment such a course might invite in the United States. In an effort to assuage the possibly bruised feelings – not to say outright displeasure – of the Americans, Ryerson, with more than a little audacity, suggested that the whole thing had been their idea in the first place. "It is an event," he ventured, "which was anticipated by even American preachers, (particularly Dr Fisk,) who advocated the separation of the Canada Connexion from the United States, at the Methodist General Conference in 1828, and which constituted a strong argument for that measure. It is an event to which we have often adverted, publicly and privately, with a feeling of strong desire, during the last four years; an event which will afford a practical illustration of that glorious principle, that the Wesleyan Methodists are one in every part of the world."[35]

Calculated to steer a middle way between the widely divergent and often competing interests of three distinct religious communities, the whole piece no doubt caused many readers to shake their heads in bewilderment. The Americans, of course, had never "advocated" for separation at all and had, in fact, only grudgingly agreed to it on the grounds of extreme political necessity. Ryerson's claim, moreover, that he and other Canadian Methodists had "adverted" to a potential union with the Wesleyans both in public and in private over the previous four years was patently false. At this early stage, however, Ryerson's proposal appears to have been merely aspirational. This remained the one and only reference to a possible union – at least before that union was suddenly and formally approved at the Canada Conference later that year – to appear in the *Christian Guardian*. Perhaps Ryerson meant merely to test the waters. If so, no evidence followed its publication to indicate that violent protests would erupt – as they later did – among rank-and-file Methodists across Upper Canada.[36]

Yet, to say even this much in public was dangerous – especially for Methodist religious identity in the province and the voting then taking place in the American annual conferences to ratify the Canadian claim against the Methodist Book Concern. Ryerson's attentiveness to his American readers, and his invocation of Fisk by name, betrays his awareness of the delicacy of the situation. But Ryerson's suggestion that the Americans had, in granting separation in 1828, foreseen an eventual union between Canadian Methodists and British Wesleyans was particularly fraught. No doubt John Emory, Nathan Bangs, and other Americans reading this would have remembered with justifiable resentment that when John Ryerson negotiated the terms of separation at the General Conference of 1828, he expressed a consistent and pointed desire, in both his original and revised proposals, that British Wesleyans should remain outside the colony according to the terms of the 1820 agreement with the Methodist Episcopal Church.[37]

The voting in the United States proceeded, and Ryerson probably breathed a little easier as it became clear that the Americans had decided not to take his public musings as a prophetic utterances. When the Annual Maine Conference voted on the claim about a month later – enough time for at least some American Methodists to have read Ryerson's editorial – the vote carried easily with 71 in favour and none against. The Genesee Conference met the same month with a similar outcome: 69 in favour and 1 against. Finally, in early August, the Annual New Hampshire Conference met and voted to approve the Canada claim with 71 in favour and none against. Did Ryerson imagine for a moment that perhaps a union would not imperil the Canadian claim? If so, he would have been badly mistaken. Yet, by the time these votes were being counted, Ryerson and his collaborators had already set in motion a series of events that would set Canadian Methodism on a path to union – a path that would alter Methodist religious identity in Upper Canada so thoroughly that Methodists north of the border were rendered no longer recognizable to their American brethren.

VI

Robert Alder attended his first meeting of the Canada Missionary Board sometime towards the end of June 1832. Although it began tempestuously enough, the Ryersons worked to calm the anxieties of their brethren, and in the end an invitation was extended to Alder to attend the upcoming Canada Conference. Meanwhile, the board, under John Ryerson's direction, left no ambiguity about its position and prepared "a memorial for the Conference itself, requesting it to take the matter of an organic union of the two sections of Methodism in the Province into its earnest consideration." Alder, for his part, continued to maintain a close correspondence with Lieutenant Governor John Colborne, probably without the knowledge of the Ryersons.[38]

On 5 July 1832, the day after the opening of a new Wesleyan Chapel in York, Colborne expressed his confidence that the Wesleyans would soon, through competition and not cooperation, have matters under control. "The Rev'd Mr Alder," he wrote, "the Minister sent out by the British Conference, informs me that in future they will supply the Province with Missionaries qualified to take charge of the congregations which may be established in every district." Uppermost in Alder's mind, whether through cooperation or competition, was his goal to diminish the "Yankee influence" that American Methodists, he believed, continued to exert over the colony through the Canada Conference. In letters written to the Wesleyan Methodist Missionary Society in London that July, he expressed his anxiety about securing adequate financial resources to proceed, conjecturing, "If we are to do anything with the Yankees, we must be Lords of the Treasury."[39]

Although he made no mention of it in his letter, it is probable that Alder had heard whisperings about the enormous amount of money Canadians continued to hope they would receive for their interest in the Methodist Book Concern, and he was worried that, if union did not proceed, the Wesleyans might well end up being the poorer Methodists in the colony. Had events unfolded differently, had Egerton Ryerson not been so keen on finding an alternative source for books to offer to the public through the *Christian Guardian* office, that might have turned out to be the case. Alder's presence in the colony, and his close connection with Colborne, however, only further complicated the Concern's access to its denominational market in Upper Canada because Alder was both an insider and an outsider. Unlike any conservative before him, Alder would be in a position to discern the implications of the Methodist Book Concern's rhetorical claims on the religious identities of Methodists in Upper Canada. In reference to the upcoming conference to be held that August, he wrote to Colborne, "I don't like Yankeeism. There will be no *oxygen* at the Conference but I mean to prepare a little to improve the atmosphere." If a union with the British Wesleyans ended up proving to be impossible, the Methodist Book Concern's market in Upper Canada would become more dangerous to Methodist interests than at any time before.[40]

When the Canada Conference met in Hallowell on 8 August 1832, John and Egerton Ryerson persuaded their brethren to accept a formal union between "the English and the Canada conferences." Concurring "with the Board of Missions on the inexpedience of establishing two distinct Methodist Connexions in Upper Canada," delegates passed a series of twelve resolutions designed to bring about a formal union between themselves and the British Wesleyans in the form of a new Wesleyan Methodist Church in Canada. The last of these resolutions declared that "a Representative be sent home to England, to negotiate with the Wesleyan Committee and Conference on the several subjects embraced in these resolutions." Not surprisingly, Egerton Ryerson was appointed to be that representative.[41]

But the Ryersons were not able to persuade everyone. It is significant that among the three dissenting voices – William Case, Franklin Metcalf, and Thomas Whitehead – two had represented the Canadian claim against the Methodist Book Concern in Philadelphia that past May. Only William Ryerson, who had also attended the General Conference with Case and Metcalf, yielded to the combined suasion of his brothers. After witnessing how John Emory's observations about declining levels of patronage in Upper Canada threatened the foundation of the Canadian claim, it seems Case and Metcalf were better situated than most to understand the risk the Canadians were taking. The annual conferences had not yet finished voting on the Canadian claim and, if word of a union with the British Wesleyans got out, things could quickly go sideways. Yet, it is just possible that these preachers were also taking a principled stand against these proceedings on the grounds that it would have been fundamentally disingenuous on the part of their colonial brethren to accept a large financial settlement from the Methodist Episcopal Church with one hand while surreptitiously embracing British Wesleyanism with the other. Their discomfort was doubtless increased when a letter from Beverley Waugh, John Emory's successor as senior book agent, was read aloud at the conference authorizing Canadian Methodists to draw yet another annual dividend of $800 from the Methodist Book Concern.[42]

Whatever qualms Case and Metcalf may have felt about the legitimacy with which Canadian Methodists could continue to claim a settlement in recognition of "undivided patronage" – and the damage Canadian duplicity might inflict on their own reputations in the United States as the preachers who had represented that claim only three months earlier – did not in the end dissuade their brethren either from proceeding with the "union" or from incorporating into its fabric a means for supplying themselves with books and periodicals from the London Book Room. On this latter point, John Carroll notes, "Minute 'instructions' were drawn up for the guidance of the representative, which were approved by the Conference." Thus was Ryerson "authorized to negotiate with the Wesleyan Committee and Conference respecting a Book Concern and the establishment of a depository in this province with special reference to the interests of Sabbath Schools." With this alternative source of stock at his disposal, Egerton Ryerson would at long last be at liberty to openly sell Methodist books and periodicals in a public market without fear of political censure.[43]

Yet, Ryerson knew – as he attempted to accommodate the Wesleyans, appease the Canadians, and forestall the Americans – that he was sailing closer to the wind than he ought. As his gaze remained fixed on events unfolding in the United States, he was very careful to ensure that not a word about the union – with the one noted exception – made its way into the pages of the *Christian Guardian*. His caution was borne out when the annual conferences abruptly turned against the Canadian claim when that news finally spread into the United States. Perhaps feeling he could delay it no longer, Ryerson at last announced the union in the *Christian Guardian* at the end of August 1832 – ten full days after the Canada Conference had concluded its momentous deliberations. John Durbin, Nathan Bangs's successor as editor of the *Christian Advocate* in New York, rushed an announcement into the *Advocate* as soon as he received the issue – devoting almost an entire page to Methodist affairs in Upper Canada.[44]

Keenly aware that the annual conferences across the United States were then conducting voting on the Canada claim, Durbin called the attention of "the members of our annual conferences" to the "Union of Methodists in Canada and Great Britain" and reprinted from the *Christian Guardian* all twelve resolutions passed by the Canada Conference on that matter from the previous August. The effect of the announcement, as Egerton Ryerson no doubt feared, was devastating. Every conference that voted after the appearance of the twelve resolutions overwhelmingly rejected the Canadian claim. Although many of these were southern conferences, whose members may have been less inclined from the outset, they also included both the Philadelphia and Baltimore conferences. The first of these rejected the claim on 24 April 1833 with a vote of 89 against and 1 in favour, while the second, voting the very next day, unanimously rejected the Canada claim with 90 votes against. In the end, far from achieving the required three-fourths majority, the total number of votes against the claim amounted to 758 with only 599 in favour. The part Durbin's announcement played in bringing about this outcome was not lost on Canadian Methodists. "Every Conference before which it was laid by the Bishops, voted yea," Anson Green noted bitterly, "until the *Advocate* called their attention to our proposed union with the British Conference; after that significant hint, they all voted nay."[45]

Meanwhile, back in Upper Canada, Ryerson's strategy of keeping word out of the *Christian Guardian* to prevent an American backlash against the Canadian claim was having negative repercussions of its own. Chief among the complaints raised by dissenters was that the Canada Conference had refused to consult Methodist societies across the province before acting. Some even called the legality of the resolutions into question on these grounds. "The matter had not been laid before the societies ... and therefore ... the preachers composing this Conference had merely legislated themselves." The proposed union "was therefore not binding upon any excepting those who chose to accept it." This reversal had come about primarily because, back in May, when Egerton Ryerson and his brother first began to lay plans that would lead to eventual union, they had had no reason to suspect that the Canadian claim would take so long to be ratified. As Ryerson's notice in the *Guardian* suggests, he fully expected the Canadian delegates to the General Conference to return from Philadelphia with money in hand. Instead, with a protracted vote among annual conferences taking place over the course of an entire year, Ryerson had found himself inconveniently obliged to remain silent on the matter of a proposed union with the British Wesleyans for as long as possible – failing not only to notify rank-and-file Methodists of what was transpiring, but also passing up an opportunity to proclaim his denomination's loyalty to British institutions from the rooftops. In the end, Egerton Ryerson's failure to prepare his denominational readers for what was coming set the stage for a schism so far-reaching that it would endure beyond his own lifetime.[46]

Doubtless disappointed with their reversals in the United States, Canadian Methodists lost no time making alternative arrangements to supply themselves with books and periodicals from overseas. As Ryerson explained in a letter written to Alder that November, he was already, albeit with difficulty, raising money to pay for his passage to England, where he would negotiate terms for the importation of books with the London Book Room. In the meantime, even William Case, whom Ryerson criticized in his letter to Alder, began urging Peter Jones and James Evans to make arrangements with the British and Foreign Bible Society, rather than the Methodist Book Concern, to print their Native translations of the books of the New Testament.[47]

As the year 1832 moved towards its close, Canadian preachers did what they could to contend with opposition to the union on their own circuits, together with growing fears that the loss of financial support from the Methodist Episcopal Church and the Methodist Book Concern might permanently damage Methodist fortunes in Upper Canada. Most of these concerns were reflected in a letter written in October to both William Case and William Ryerson in which a local preacher, Justus Williams, decried the lack of consultation not only with lay Methodists, but also with quarterly and district meetings – a "courtesy at least required in a matter fraught with such mighty consequences as the contemplated union." Among the many dangers of union, Williams cited a suspension of "further payment of funds from the American Church" as well as "hazard to the ownership of church property" flowing from changes in polity attending the union. Both concerns proved prescient. Meanwhile, south of the border, two more annual conferences unanimously rejected the Canada claim against the Methodist Book Concern: Indiana in a vote of 36 to 0 and Kentucky in a vote of 66 to 0.[48]

However disastrous things may have looked to those on the ground, it seemed that leading British Wesleyan Richard Watson's promise to the colonial secretary, Lord Goderich, was now all but assured. "The influence of the United States," he wrote in November, "will therefore be utterly shut out and the whole of the Methodists in Upper Canada become integral parts of our general body and subject to its general rules." This "shutting out" of American influence, especially for Egerton Ryerson, applied as much to the press as it did to the pulpit.[49]

VII

The following March, Egerton Ryerson finally left York for England by way of Kingston and New York. Somewhat surprisingly, and perhaps a little disingenuously, Ryerson reported a "friendly" meeting between himself, Nathan Bangs, Wilbur Fisk, and others. "I have conversed with them all," he wrote to his brother John, "and they seem to approve of the proceedings of our conference in the affair." Durbin even asked Ryerson to provide him with regular reports of his work in England for publication in the *Christian Advocate*. Ryerson, who agreed but did not comply, must have known that the approval Bangs, Durbin, and even Fisk, expressed about the union was contingent on the rejection of the Canadian claim against the Methodist Book Concern then underway. Indeed, as Ryerson prepared to disembark, the annual Virginia Conference met and, like those before it, unanimously rejected the claim in a vote of 84 to 0. A week after Ryerson disembarked for London, Durbin reminded his readers once again about the proposed union between the British Wesleyans and the Canada Conference and published a letter written by Robert Alder on that controversial subject.[50]

By the time Egerton Ryerson met with the Missionary Committee in London, later in June 1833, at least five more annual conferences had met and rejected the Canadian claim. Later that summer, the British Wesleyans in England wrote to the Canada Conference to supply them with formal Articles of Union. Among other things, they insisted, presumably with Ryerson's agreement, that "the *Christian Guardian* become strictly a religious newspaper like the New York *Christian Advocate* and that it shall not attack the principle of receiving aid from Government for the extension of religion." That he was willing to agree to such a condition indicates how eager Egerton Ryerson was to see the union get off the ground. When he finally returned home later that summer by way of New York, he did so not only with his treasured Articles of Union but accompanied by two more British Wesleyan missionaries: incoming president George Marsden and the peaceable Joseph Stinson.[51]

In September 1833, a notice describing the successful outcome of Ryerson's negotiations in England appeared in the *Christian Advocate*. "It is a matter of much joy," the Americans managed between clenched teeth, "that we learn from all parties, that there is reasonable prospect of adjusting this important matter to the satisfaction and mutual advantage of all ... These English brethren have been in our city for a few days, and are now proceeding to Canada. May heaven guide and protect them, and send success to their good and excellent mission." That the Americans disapproved of the union can hardly be doubted. But they put a smile on the whole affair and thereby reminded their readers – especially annual conference delegates – that they had indeed done the right thing when they rejected the claim of the Canadians. After all, what may have been an agreement for the "mutual advantage" of the Upper Canadians and the British Wesleyans was most certainly not for the advantage of the Methodist Episcopal Church in the United States. As Ryerson worked to nudge Methodist print culture out into the open and further towards the religious mainstream by filling his shelves with the wares of the London Book Room, the Methodist Book Concern's colonial market threatened to dwindle away to almost nothing.[52]

Yet, for all that successful manoeuvring on Ryerson's part, the cost that he and his fellow Methodists also paid for severing a culturally inconvenient relationship with the Methodist Book Concern turned out to be much higher than originally thought. The amount of money Canadian Methodists forfeited when their claim against the Concern failed – some $27,000 – equalled almost seven years of full government support for British Wesleyan missions in Upper Canada. With that much money at their disposal all at once, Methodists in the colony would have been able to bolster their presence among the Natives without the interference of the Wesleyan Methodist Missionary Society, to fill their Sunday school libraries to bursting with religious books and periodicals, and to establish the Upper Canada Academy on the firmest of financial footings. Without it, they were reduced to begging the British Wesleyans, as Ryerson had done while in England to receive the Articles of Union, for financial rescue. In the following years, as enthusiasm for the union waned, it would become painfully apparent, even to the Ryersons, that the only real winners in the arrangement had been the British Wesleyans, who managed to gain both a new mission field and a new market for their books and periodicals in Upper Canada.[53]

Very little of this was clear when Egerton Ryerson first unveiled the agreement he had reached with the London Book Room at a special meeting of the Canada Conference in October 1833. It contained a detailed summation of the precise terms by which Canadian Methodists would begin to import books, periodicals, tracts, hymnbooks, stationery, and other commodities from London. Discounts on the minority of titles for which the London Book Room owned the copyright, together with Sunday school books, were set at 35 per cent. Hymnbooks and tracts were available at a 25 per cent discount. All other titles, which made up the bulk of the London Book Room's catalogue, were offered to Canadians at the much more modest discount of 17½ per cent. Payment for all books was to be made in advance or on an arranged credit system of twelve months. Returns would not be accepted under any condition.

All told, these terms were less liberal, the discount less generous, and the prices of the books markedly higher than Canadian Methodists had come to expect. For example, the Methodist Book Concern offered the classic *Pilgrim's Progress* at 25¢ while the London Book Room advertised the same title for a relatively costly 6s or approximately $1.50. Joseph Alleine's *Alarm to the Unconverted* with Richard Baxter's *Call to the Unconverted* were available bound together from the Methodist Book Concern for 50¢. The London Book Room sold these titles separately, Alleine's *Alarm* for 1s 6d and Baxter's *Call* for 1s 3d for a combined price of 2s 9d, or approximately 69¢. Another of Baxter's classics, *Saints' Everlasting Rest*, was sold by the Concern for 75¢ and the London Book Room for 3s 6d, or 87½¢.[54]

Everyone knew that the London Book Room's prices were higher. And so Ryerson had to find a way to justify that fact. "It may be remarked," he explained, "that English Editions of Books are in general sold at a higher price than American but they excell [*sic*] as much, if not more, in quality than they are higher in price. Hence those of our friends and of the public, who wish to procure the best editions of valuable books, will purchase the English; whilst those to whom the mere cheapness of a book, and not the quality and style of its execution, is the principal consideration, will purchase the American Editions." And for those who doggedly preferred economy to quality? "Upon this plan our purchases of the New York Book Room will not be materially lessened, and we shall possess the additional advantage of being able to supply the Connexion with English Editions of any Book published in England." In other words, for the time being, Ryerson would maintain a supply of books from both countries, but the English were to be preferred in all cases if only purchasers could afford them. Unfortunately, most of the province's Methodists could not afford them.[55]

Thus, even after making arrangements with the London Book Room, the supply of books from the Methodist Book Concern could not simply be cut off. The majority of Upper Canada's Methodists, particularly those who resided in many of the colony's least developed regions, would have had little money to afford such luxuries and would have been far less attentive to the social distinction promised by a British imprint than to the religious status the Concern's books had conferred on Methodist readers for decades. Consequently, the preference of such consumers for books from the United States, as Ryerson well knew from his time as an itinerant preacher and bookseller, ran much deeper than their "mere cheapness." It is interesting, however, that this early attempt on Ryerson's part to portray the Methodist Book Concern's books and periodicals as straightforward commodities, rather than denominational status objects, foreshadowed later developments that would more effectively sever linkages between the ongoing purchase of these products and Methodist religious identity in Upper Canada. Indeed, unless and until the Concern's books were stripped of their function as denominational status objects, the London Book Room's offerings would continue to be pale substitutes in the eyes of many readers.

In addition to the higher prices and less generous discounts, the system for distributing books and periodicals through preachers to the province's Methodists also changed. Before Ryerson's agreement with the London Book Room, preachers had been at liberty to place book orders either through their presiding elders or to deal directly with the Methodist Book Concern's agents on their own initiative. It was a lucrative arrangement for all concerned. Since the General Conference of 1812, the margin preachers could claim on the sale of these products hovered around 12–18 per cent. Presiding elders also received a 6 per cent commission on books sold throughout their districts. And on some occasions commissions could be much higher. In 1824, for example, Nathan Bangs noted that the difficulties in making up preachers' salaries had become so pronounced that "the conference stewards usually settle[d] with the preachers at a discount from thirty to sixty per cent." In 1828, commissions on the sale of books already in the hands of presiding elders and preachers were increased to 40 per cent in order to liquidate some of the Concern's debt. Of this, 26 per cent went to the preacher making the sale and 13 per cent to his presiding elder. Finally, books purchased by a preacher for his own use were sold at a discount of just over 33 per cent. The new terms negotiated by Ryerson were far more penurious. Now preachers were forbidden from dealing directly with either the London Book Room or the Methodist Book Concern. Instead, the Toronto Book Room was to be the sole supplier of Methodist books and periodicals across the entire colony. Worse still, under the new terms, preachers were entitled to a paltry 10 per cent discount on all books – including hymnbooks – in the Book Room's catalogue. This left the colony's preachers with more expensive commodities to sell, smaller commissions, and no recourse to supply themselves with cheaper books by placing their own orders directly with the Methodist Book Concern.[56]

Despite the obvious disadvantages to preachers and people, Ryerson seemed confident that his denomination was at last all but beyond reproach in both its transatlantic polity and its now ready supply of English books and periodicals. That autumn the *Christian Guardian* took a sharp turn to the right with the appearance of a provocative condemnation of both republicanism and British radicalism in an article

Ryerson innocuously entitled "Impressions Made by Our Late Visit to England." This article amounted to a kind of public declaration on Ryerson's part that he had largely ceased to care about what either the province's reformers or Methodists in the United States thought about him or about Canada. Equating Joseph Hume's atheistic radicalism with republicanism, Ryerson, although warning readers to be wary of all political "parties," advanced British Wesleyanism's "moderate toryism" as the best antidote for these terrible excesses. Ryerson's obvious aim in publishing this piece was to please the British Wesleyans. But he missed that mark by a wide margin. Indeed, Ryerson managed to please absolutely no one but himself.[57]

As far as the likes of Robert Alder were concerned, Ryerson's "Impressions" amounted to a violation of the principle that the *Christian Guardian* would avoid political controversy altogether. Almost immediately, Alder wrote to Joseph Stinson to complain that the *Guardian* should either be discontinued entirely or devoted exclusively to religious subjects from that point onward. Although the Americans did not go quite as far as William Lyon Mackenzie did in his condemnation – the *Colonial Advocate* denounced Ryerson for having "gone over to the enemy" and "hoisted the colours of a cruel, vindictive tory priesthood" – their disapproval was equally unambiguous. A month after Ryerson's "Impressions" appeared in Upper Canada, John Durbin at the New York *Christian Advocate* effectively disowned him, reprinting from his "Impressions" "such paragraphs as are relevant to our purpose" and declaring that "the American reader will bear in mind that Mr R. is a British subject writing of British affairs." Had they said, with Mackenzie, that Ryerson had simply "gone over to the enemy" the verdict could not have been clearer: Ryerson had made himself a foreigner. Thus, the bonds that had once linked Upper Canadian Methodism with its parent in the United States through a common market for books and periodicals seemed at last to be well and truly severed.[58]

Ryerson, who continued to receive the *Christian Advocate* at the *Guardian* office, no doubt read Durbin's response, but shrugged it off as largely inconsequential. With an alternative supply of books arranged from the London Book Room, and the border fortified against the products of the Methodist Book Concern, Ryerson appears to have believed that the Concern's role in supplying Canadian Methodists with books and periodicals had entered a period of irrevocable decline even without a financial settlement. In any event, he had more than enough to worry about simply dealing with the fallout his declaration of conservatism caused in Upper Canada. William Ryerson wrote immediately to complain that publication of Ryerson's "Impressions" had noticeably diminished the *Christian Guardian*'s popularity in the province. "I should much regret its appearance," John Ryerson also admitted, were it not for the fact that it helped set Methodism apart from radicalism in the colony. Ryerson's youngest brother, Edwy, complained that the article had made it difficult not only to collect money owed on existing subscriptions, but impossible to solicit new ones. Edwy even added his signature to a letter written by four other preachers protesting the *Christian Guardian*'s abrupt change in editorial policy. "Our political views," these men insisted, "are decidedly the same which they were previous to the visit of the Editor of the *Guardian* to England; and we believe that the views of our brethren in the ministry are unchanged"[59]

As subscription money dried up, the high cost of the books that Egerton Ryerson hoped to import from overseas and sell through the *Christian Guardian* office and along the province's preaching circuits began to weigh more heavily in the balance. Soon even Ryerson's denominational market – a market whose needs he had neglected in his rush to acquire books more suited to Upper Canada's wider reading public – began to shrink under the political pressures that flowed from his efforts to distance colonial Methodism from reformism. In the years immediately following, a large proportion of Canadian Methodists responded by not only abandoning their subscriptions to the *Christian Guardian*, but by forswearing their membership in the new Wesleyan Methodist Church in Canada altogether. Indeed, the new Wesleyan Methodist Church in Canada recorded Methodism's largest membership decline since the War of 1812. Even more seriously, in June 1834, an entirely separate Methodist Episcopal Church in Canada was formed.[60]

All of this confusion and discontent was made worse by the province's now unstable denominational market for books and periodicals. The London Book Room's offerings, unlike those of the Methodist Book Concern, had never been framed as denominational status objects, and their sale did little to consolidate Methodists into a single community of common religious interest across the province. In addition, individual preachers had lost much of their incentive to operate as enterprising colporteurs when their commissions on book sales had been so dramatically reduced. Indeed, it would have been hard to determine whether the sellers or the buyers were less satisfied with Ryerson's new arrangement.

Despite Ryerson's determined hopes and expectations, his dealings and the dealings of Upper Canadian Methodists with the New York Methodist Book Concern were far from concluded. Although the London Book Room's books were certainly suited to the cultural demands of Upper Canada's public market, these relatively expensive offerings remained stubbornly beyond the reach of many of the province's poorer Methodists. Subsequent efforts to publish their own books for denominational consumption, moreover, despite Ryerson's early success with a Canadian edition of the *Discipline*, did little to remedy this problem. Unable to rely either on their own books or books imported from London, Canadian Methodists found themselves at a loss. With nowhere else to turn, they began to develop a new strategy for decoupling the material and cultural aspects of the Concern's books with an eye to reinvigorating their relationship with the Methodist Book Concern while at the same time preserving the political gains they had achieved in the colony through union with the British Wesleyans. This was a strategy that would leave a lasting mark not only on Methodism, but also on Upper Canada's wider literary culture throughout the nineteenth century and beyond.

Chapter Five

"We Saw That All Was Gone": A Failed Claim and a Failing Union

"I was awakened about four o'clock A.M. by a ringing at my door and a voice which apprised me that the Book Room was on fire!" wrote Nathan Bangs one bleak winter day in February 1836, "I sprung from my bed, dressed, called my two sons, and repaired with all possible speed to the scene of the conflagration. I hoped, at least, to save the library. But the smoke was already issuing from the windows of my office, and the flames from other parts of the house! Here I found the agents, who were on the spot before me. The hydrants were frozen, and the waters were thrown but feebly, though all exerted themselves to their utmost. We saw that all was gone." This was a devastating loss. The buildings and the Methodist Book Concern's entire stock were destroyed in the flames. A single burned page of the Bible was recovered about three miles from the blaze. On it was printed a fateful passage from Isaiah: "Our holy and our beautiful house, where our fathers praised thee, is burned up with fire; and all our pleasant things are laid waste."[1]

When Egerton Ryerson returned to Upper Canada in 1833 with the Articles of Union in hand, he and his fellow Methodists still held out some slight hope that they might appeal one last time for a financial settlement against the New York Methodist Book Concern. Those hopes disappeared finally and forever in the smoke and the flames that consumed the Concern a few months before the meeting of the American General Conference in 1836. Because the Concern's buildings and stock were inadequately insured, American Methodists were left to gather on their own whatever funds would be needed to rebuild the publishing house from the ashes – and that in the wake of a financial panic then sweeping the nation. To raise the enormous sums required, the book agents underscored at every turn the vital importance of an ongoing link between support for the Concern and membership in the Methodist Episcopal Church. The denominational publisher and the denomination itself were framed as indivisible: the survival and success of the one drove and depended on the success of the other. At that very time then, when these rhetorical connections were being emphasized as never before by the book agents in the United States, they were in the midst of being utterly and completely severed in Canada. By finally and fully rejecting the claim of the Canadians in 1836, American Methodists set firm geopolitical limits on that pervasive denominational rhetoric that had defined the Methodist Book Concern's market since the late eighteenth century. That market, at least in denominational terms, could no longer be said to extend beyond the borders of the United States. Yet, for all that, that same market, understood in purely commercial terms, was on the precipice of undergoing an unprecedented revival of fortunes in Upper Canada.

Despite the continued struggles that these years witnessed between Canadian and American interests related to the Methodist Book Concern, recent historians have focused their narratives all but exclusively on relations between British Wesleyan missionaries and their colonial brethren. This is hardly surprising given how tumultuous those relations were. In 1833, the Ryersons were more than willing – indeed, they were fiercely eager – to accept Wesleyan leadership at every level of institutional Methodism. Accordingly, British Wesleyans assumed all but complete control of the workings of the Canada Conference, direct oversight of missionary work among Native peoples, and authority over the affairs of the Upper Canada Academy. They also managed to exert an increasingly profound influence over the daily operations of the Methodist Book Room in Toronto and the *Christian Guardian*. As subsequent events would show, however, Canadian acquiescence was not quite as unswerving as this suggests. Small but stubborn pockets of resistance marred the ecclesiastical union almost from its first breath. The most serious of these evolved into a rival ecclesiastical entity in its own right – the Methodist Episcopal Church in Canada – and soon Canada's Methodists were fighting each other for control and ownership of property and chapels. To make matters worse, an embarrassing and very public fallout erupted between Canadian Methodists and the British Wesleyans over the province's treatment of those who had taken part in the Upper Canada Rebellion. All the while, and despite this growing rift, scholars have intimated that whatever lingering sway American Methodists had continued to wield in Upper Canada before the union had long since withered away completely under the heat of British Wesleyan influences.[2]

This, however, is only part of the picture. By shifting focus away from polity – where American influence was undeniably in sharp decline – and towards the post-union revival of North American Methodism's shared market for books and periodicals, this chapter will explore how American Methodists continued to exert, through the New York Methodist Book Concern, an indirect yet consequential influence over cultural developments in Upper Canada for some decades to come. Even though Egerton Ryerson made undoubted efforts after 1833 to displace the Concern's market in Upper Canada by selling books imported from the Wesleyan Book Room in London, it soon became clear that unyielding logistical complications and higher costs set this end beyond practicable reach. Around the same time, the failure of the Canadian claim against the Methodist Book Concern had an ironically galvanizing effect on the Concern's market in Upper Canada. When, for the last time in 1836, the Americans refused payment, suddenly the commercial boundaries of that market were no longer coterminous with the rhetorical boundaries of American Methodism itself. Canadians were now free to redefine their participation in that market in terms that were commercial rather than denominational in character: they could now buy and sell the Concern's books openly without complicating their religious identities or risking their political standing in the colony. As just another publisher, patronage of the Methodist Book Concern would be rooted in economy rather than loyalty and its offerings valued for their quality of manufacture, cost, and availability rather than their significance as denominational status objects. As Canadian Methodists became steadily less dependent on the London Book Room for the maintenance of their denominational economy, and as they shunted aside Wesleyan priorities by reviving the Methodist Book Concern's market in Canada, it became clear that these developments ominously foreshadowed what was to become of the union itself as transatlantic relations continued to deteriorate.

I

At that very moment in 1833 when Egerton Ryerson was sitting down with his Wesleyan counterparts in London to negotiate terms for the importation of books and periodicals to Upper Canada, agents of the New York Methodist Book Concern were busy filling a flurry of orders they had received from preachers stationed across the province. In the last week of May, the Concern dispatched a box of books to Methodist preacher Ephraim Evans on the Stamford circuit in Niagara. One week later, another three boxes of books left the Concern bound for Canadian preacher David Wright on Yonge Street. The following week saw yet another shipment of books bound for Upper Canada, this time to Thomas Bevitt on the Belleville circuit near the Bay of Quinte.[3]

After Ryerson returned to the province and instituted new rules to prevent preachers from ordering books directly from New York, notices of this kind, with one or two exceptions, ceased altogether. About a month later, Ryerson ran a short but nondescript book catalogue in the *Christian Guardian* advertising "Hymn-Books of different sizes," a small selection of works by John Wesley, several titles by leading British Methodist authors Adam Clarke and Richard Watson, and a few other items. Books of this sort regularly appeared in catalogues issued by both the Methodist Book Concern and the London Book Room and were just the kind of titles that Egerton Ryerson might have been expected to keep on hand. Despite his otherwise enthusiastic embrace of books manufactured in Britain, evidence suggests that these books were probably the products of the Methodist Book Concern. Even if Ryerson had dispatched an order immediately after receiving the approval of the Canada Conference for his new terms with the London Book Room, that order could have hardly reached the British Wesleyan book steward by late November, much less been fulfilled by that time. Instead, these short catalogues probably indicate that Ryerson was quietly clearing his shelves of the Concern's wares while awaiting new stock to arrive from London.

A newly reset catalogue did not appear in the *Christian Guardian* until early March 1834. Although this delay suggests that Ryerson may have had some trouble securing his first order from the London Book Room, its text leaves no doubt that he was as eager to proclaim the British manufacture of these titles as he had earlier been reluctant to admit his dependence on the Methodist Book Concern in New York. "BEAUTIFUL ENGLISH EDITIONS," it began in capital letters, "of the following BOOKS are on sale at the Guardian Office, *at the London Prices*," adding in smaller type, "with a variety of others, both American and English." Listed below were seventeen items in various sizes bound in cloth or in stiff covers together with an expensive fourteen-volume set of Richard Watson's works "*in cambric; gilt lettered*." Apparently Ryerson's customers were rather less enthusiastic about these books than he was: this same catalogue ran unaltered in almost every issue of the *Guardian* until the middle of November that year. Ryerson probably anticipated that selling British books at higher prices would be difficult at first and no doubt planned for that eventuality. What he could not have prepared for was an unexpected and rapid contraction in his overall denominational market.[4]

In the spring of 1834, Wesleyan Joseph Stinson wrote several letters to Robert Alder to inform him that significant numbers of Canadian Methodists – or, as he described them, "half-starved Yankees" – remained unacceptably radical in their politics. Stinson also noted that James Richardson, the same preacher who had served alongside Ryerson a decade earlier when that fledgling preacher had published his anonymous rebuke of Strachan in the *Colonial Advocate*, had become their unofficial spokesman. By contrast, Ryerson's own public support of the union between British Wesleyans and Canadian Methodists remained loud and insistent. The result was a sharp polarization among Methodists around these two men. Although some of their differences were papered over after the intervention of William Case in the spring of 1834, by the time the Canada Conference met in June an appalling loss of members – 1,109 in all – was recorded in the minutes. To make matters worse, Richardson was elected to replace Ryerson at the Book Room and at the helm of the *Christian Guardian* – posts that Ryerson was able to retain only when Richardson subsequently declined them. Hardly had the ink dried on the Conference minutes when a group of disgruntled Methodists, comprised of those who had never accepted the legitimacy of the union, formed an independent Methodist Episcopal Church in Canada with 1,200 members and 25 preachers.[5]

Ryerson's problems continued to multiply when, contrary to his expectations, reformers led by William Lyon Mackenzie, a man who had become a vocal critic of Methodism since the *Christian Guardian* repudiated his brand of reformism, won a decisive victory in the province's elections and took control of the Legislative Assembly. John Ryerson, meanwhile, who had been so instrumental in convincing his brother of the importance of embracing union with the British Wesleyans in the first place, was beginning to sour on the whole business. Referring to the work of Joseph Stinson and other Wesleyans, John wrote, "I have not time nor patience to mention one half of the trickory [*sic*] & abomination of their proceedings." Perhaps in part with reference to the miserly terms the London Book Room continued to insist on, he further observed that the entire union had been "dizastrous [*sic*] and gloomy without a single *iota* of anything growing out of it that is beneficial to us."[6]

Around the same time, William Case took it into his own hands to do something more than put about idle complaints. From his location on the Credit River, and in open defiance of Ryerson's rules against it, Case placed an order for books directly with the Methodist Book Concern's agents in New York. Although not repeated, it was a bold act. Case must have known that his order would be noticed by anyone in the province, including Egerton Ryerson at the *Christian Guardian* office, where the *Christian Advocate* continued to be delivered. Indeed, Case's action may have even helped to prompt a subsequent change in

Ryerson's approach to his own market – a market that was resuming a more denominational character as many non-Methodists in the province cancelled their *Guardian* subscriptions in response to Ryerson's increasingly conservative editorial policies. Just about the time Case might have been opening his first large shipment of books from the Methodist Book Concern in almost two years, Ryerson was preparing to replace his "BEAUTIFUL ENGLISH EDITIONS" with a new catalogue that William Case, James Richardson, and doubtless many other Canadian Methodists, would have almost certainly found more to their liking.[7]

II

In the autumn of 1834, the British Wesleyans had their hands full shoring up their interests in Upper Canada. In response to the deteriorating health of the union and the rise of the schismatic Methodist Episcopal Church in Canada, they dispatched William Lord from London, a man of two-decades' experience "admirably adapted to win the confidence of the Canadians." By sending a man as proficient as Lord, the Missionary Committee in London demonstrated the importance Wesleyans continued to place on preserving the union and holding their ground in Upper Canada. Lord was charged with several overlapping objectives. First, he was to find a way to reconcile the colony's British Wesleyans and Canadian Methodists despite their widening political differences. Second, he was to blunt the fractious influence of the schismatic Methodist Episcopal Church in Canada. Third, he was to put a stop to the *Christian Guardian*'s continued calls for the secularization of the Clergy Reserves – the only significant reformist thread that had survived Ryerson's earlier political reorientation of the newspaper. But if Lord was also expected to reinforce Egerton Ryerson's commitment to the London Book Room, he was already too late.[8]

At around the same time Lord set foot in Upper Canada, Ryerson ran his "BEAUTIFUL ENGLISH EDITIONS" catalogue for the last time. No further advertisements appeared for almost a month when, in the middle of December 1834, Ryerson's first newly reset catalogue in almost an entire year appeared on the last page of the *Christian Guardian*. Its content strongly suggests that even Egerton Ryerson was at last beginning to reconcile himself to the fact that English editions would never be as saleable as he had originally hoped. Of the thirty-six separate titles in this catalogue, Ryerson identified sixteen as English and seventeen as American in manufacture. Although Ryerson left no record to document what was behind his new approach, there can be little doubt that he was attempting to respond to the changing contours of a volatile market. The emergence of a rival Methodist Church in the colony, together with a resurgent reform movement under Mackenzie's leadership, had diminished both the size of his denominational market and Ryerson's ability to reach members of a wider reading public. The appearance of this catalogue suggests that, among those who remained within the ecclesiastical fold, or who at least continued to subscribe to the *Christian Guardian*, too few had reconciled themselves to the higher prices Ryerson was charging for the London Book Room's wares. However reluctant he may have been to publish it, the juxtaposition of rival British and American editions in this catalogue marked the first sincere attempt on Ryerson's part to offer those readers who preferred the less expensive American editions a real choice. Ryerson may have also concluded that this was the only practicable way to keep the Toronto Book Room in business. Had he continued to offer for sale only the relatively expensive books he imported from the London Book Room, Ryerson knew he would be running a serious risk that preachers might be tempted to follow William Case's extraordinary example by dealing directly with the Methodist Book Concern themselves.[9]

Sometime in the next two weeks, Egerton Ryerson abruptly decided to step aside from his role at the *Guardian* office. This decision has never been fully explained. Historians have generally argued that it had much to do with the mounting difficulties Ryerson was encountering in his role as editor of the newspaper. That makes some sense. After all, by his own admission, Ryerson had always found contending for Methodism in the public sphere wearisome. With Mackenzie now organizing a Select Committee on Grievances in the reform-dominated Legislative Assembly, it would have been easy to see that new storm clouds were gathering on the horizon. But Ryerson's decision to resign was not just about the *Christian Guardian*. It was also about removing himself from oversight of the Toronto Book Room. The timing of this decision, coming as it did on the heels of the appearance of Ryerson's new catalogue advertising both American as well as British books, suggests that his attempt to steer a middle course between the London Book Room and the Methodist Book Concern may have provoked serious displeasure among the Wesleyans. Indeed, as subsequent events will show, Ryerson may well have heard whispers that the Wesleyans intended to replace him at the upcoming conference in June whether he liked it or not.[10]

In whatever proportion Ryerson may have suddenly found his dual roles as editor and bookseller no longer tolerable, it was everything his brother John could do to talk him out of resigning both positions immediately. "The more I think of your leaving the office, the more unfavourable I think of it ... you had better stop until conference," he wrote at the end of January 1835. One of John Ryerson's chief concerns was that the business might fall into the hands of James Richardson who, although he continued to oppose the union, had not yet joined the schismatic Methodist Episcopal Church in Canada. Thus, while John Ryerson may have found himself reluctantly ambivalent about the continued expediency of union, he was not quite prepared to see his denomination's newspaper and the Toronto Book Room fall to the control of one as decidedly antagonistic to the Wesleyans as Richardson. He need not have worried. It was the British Wesleyans, and not the schismatic Methodists, who stepped into the breach at the Book Room. The Wesleyans also managed to ensure that the highly conservative Ephraim Evans took over at the helm of the *Christian Guardian*. It must have looked very much like the Wesleyans had things well in hand. In fact, these appointments turned out to be the beginning of the end for the union.[11]

Egerton Ryerson's last catalogue appeared on 1 April 1835, just two months before the annual meeting of the Canada Conference. Consisting of 101 items – 74 new items plus the 27 items listed in his December 1834 catalogue – its length suggests it may have been a final effort to salvage the business. Marking a return to an earlier advertising strategy, it also appears to have been deliberately constructed in a way not to offend British Wesleyan sensibilities. Like the short catalogue Ryerson ran in November 1833 before receiving his first large shipment of books from the London Book Room, the new items in this catalogue were identified by title only and included no prices or physical descriptions. That a significant proportion of these books were American in manufacture is suggested both by the terseness of the entries and that, quietly inserted among the 27 items listed in Ryerson's earlier December catalogue, is a single new title that was available only through the Methodist Book Concern in New York: a three-volume edition of Francis Asbury's *Journal*.

All this is enough to suggest that, despite what appears to have been a sincere and sustained effort on his part, Egerton Ryerson had learned in the twenty months since his return from England, that displacing the Methodist Book Concern's products from the Upper Canadian market would require more than the mere availability of rival English editions. What is worse, because his efforts to centralize the distribution of books and periodicals through the office of the *Christian Guardian* appear to have been largely successful, he had only himself to blame for failing to understand the extent to which high prices would influence the ability and the willingness of Canadian Methodists to participate in the market. Moreover, because the Canadian claim against the Methodist Book Concern remained outstanding during these months, the sale of the Concern's books in Canada took place in the fading shadow of a rhetorical framework that continued to characterize them in the United States as religious status objects within a decidedly denominational market. Thus, despite Ryerson's efforts to portray these offerings as nothing more than cheap alternatives to superior British editions, the religious identities of Canadian Methodists continued to be complicated by their participation in what remained, at least partially, a transnational as well as a transatlantic market.

Until some kind of settlement was finally reached with the General Conference of the Methodist Episcopal Church, no amount of discretion on Ryerson's part could wholly obscure this aspect of their cultural production – particularly among those who had converted to Methodism before November 1829 when both the *Methodist Magazine* and the *Christian Advocate,* periodicals that regularly stressed the relationship between patronage and denominational identity, continued to be widely read throughout Upper Canada. Although British Wesleyans were far less attentive to these rhetorical subtleties than their North American counterparts, they appear to have remained as committed to severing the Concern's access to the colonial market as ever. They would soon find themselves in a much better position to do so.

III

William Lord, described by the British Conference as "our long-tried and highly esteemed brother," officially assumed his new role as president when the Conference of the Wesleyan Methodist Church in Canada met in Hamilton in June 1835. When the Address of the British Conference to the Canadians was read aloud it turned out to be, as usual, an exercise in tactful diplomacy that contained both words of straightforward encouragement and steady admonition to greater zeal. The British Wesleyans clearly thought that more could be done for the "many thousands of Indians on your borders who yet require assistance," and that insufficient effort had been expended to establish and promote "Sunday and week-day Schools." It was also clear that the Wesleyans were disappointed with the lacklustre reception that the London Book Room's offerings had received in the colony. "It is very desirable that, in your rapidly increasing population, the standard writings of our body should be extensively circulated," they finessed. "In the solitary and retired parts of the country, where families connected with you reside, they should be furnished with suitable books, that the young people may be trained up in Christian knowledge. And in the small villages and towns also, it is important that our members should be well acquainted with the writing of Mr Wesley, and with our other works, with a view to increase in piety."[12]

With this urging in view, conference delegates quickly accepted Egerton Ryerson's resignation and divided his former duties at the *Guardian* office between two separate positions. Ephraim Evans became editor of the weekly newspaper and Matthew Lang was appointed to superintend the Toronto Book Room as its first official book steward. Interestingly enough, there is no record that these men were actually elected to these posts as would have been expected under normal circumstances. Instead, it appears William Lord may have appointed them directly on his own authority. By whatever means they found themselves in these roles, however, both men were counted on by Lord to steer a course that British Wesleyans overseas would approve. Although not a Wesleyan himself, Ephraim Evans was British by birth, conservative by inclination, and could be trusted as the *Guardian*'s new editor to sidestep any and all political controversy. Matthew Lang, born in Ireland in 1798, was received on trial by the British Wesleyans in 1823 and served for several years in Lower Canada before being transferred west of the Ottawa River after the union of Canada's Methodists with the British Wesleyans. He was well acquainted with Robert Alder and could be relied on to make every effort to supply Canadian Methodists with "the standard writings" of British Wesleyans from the London Book Room.[13]

These appointments were significant: together they placed control of the province's Methodist print culture directly, or in Evans's case indirectly, in the hands of British Wesleyans for the first time since union. Some of the challenges facing Lang, however, were different from those that had faced his predecessor. Unlike Ryerson, Lang was not obliged to divide his energies between editorial work and bookselling while stubbornly continuing to advocate for Methodist interests in the colony's public sphere. Nor was he as concerned as Ryerson had been with warding off accusations of disloyalty from readers in the public market. As the address of the British Conference made clear, Lang's primary task was to supply "families connected with [Methodism]" with books and periodicals.[14]

As the editorial focus of the *Christian Guardian* shifted further and further away from colonial politics in accordance with Wesleyan preferences, whatever waning interest Upper Canada's wider reading public may have continued to have in the newspaper declined yet further. In this way, Ephraim Evans's ostensibly apolitical outlook at the helm of the *Christian Guardian* would further hasten the return of the market to its former denominational homogeneity. That, in turn, meant that whatever book catalogues Lang chose to run in the pages of the *Christian Guardian* would reach the eyes of fewer and fewer non-Methodists. Yet, for all that, this reorientation towards a denominational market posed ironic challenges of its own. Although the Canada Conference reported a modest increase in numbers in 1835, for example, Lang must have known that the vast majority of those who now subscribed to the *Christian Guardian* were colonial Methodists who had long become accustomed to buying books at relatively inexpensive prices through channels supplied almost exclusively by the Methodist Book Concern in New York. To succeed where Ryerson failed, then, Lang would have to convince these Methodists to place an increasingly high value on British books for purely cultural reasons in order to justify the London Book Room's higher prices. That such readers would be willing to pay these higher prices, however, remained as doubtful a proposition under Lang as it had been under Ryerson.

Despite these challenges, Lang undoubtedly enjoyed the continued support of many Canada Conference delegates to stay the course and redouble Ryerson's earlier efforts to displace the Methodist Book Concern's books from the Upper Canadian market. Such support is particularly evident in the resolutions passed that concerned the supply of books and periodicals to the colony's Sunday schools. In partial response to the British Conference's urging that "young people be trained up in Christian knowledge," a general resolution was passed requiring that "the Members of this Conference pledge themselves *individually* to pay increased and special attention to Sabbath Schools, and to the instruction of the children and youth of our congregations, as directed in the Discipline." Recognizing that little could be accomplished without a ready supply of literature to support such instruction, the Sabbath School Committee also complained of an "*immense deficiency* in the number of books in the schools" – a deficiency so acute that "in some schools there is not a solitary volume."[15]

A denominational census of such schools taken the previous year numbered a total of 3,973 Sunday school students and 1,944 Sunday school books across the province – or approximately two readers for every book. To augment the holdings of these tiny libraries, the Sabbath School Committee implied a strong preference for books of British manufacture, noting, with emphasis, that, "*as we understand that a large quantity of books is expected from England* the present year, we recommend that the Superintendents of Circuits as far as possible, see that an early supply be obtained."[16]

The Committee on the Improvement of Singing appears to have been equally keen to find alternatives to the Methodist Book Concern's hymnbooks, but recommended another course. Rather than import large quantities of such books from the Wesleyan Book Room in London, the committee authorized Lang to publish at the *Guardian* office, "a small Pocket Edition of the best tunes, suited to the various meters of our hymns, and familiar to the Methodists, particularly from Europe." This was an important step for the Canada Conference since hymnbooks occupied a central place in communal worship as well as denominational identity formation. But because there was no standard transatlantic canon of hymns in use among Methodists in North America and Britain, and because hymns were typically called out by number rather than by title in public worship, the displacement of any hymnbook that had already found a wide audience would be particularly difficult to effect. Unless a sufficiently large number of worshippers were willing to bear the costs of individually replacing their own hymnbooks to shift communal practice, resolutions adopted by the Conference would be largely unavailing.[17]

A commercially viable Canadian Methodist hymnbook was still several years away. Nevertheless, there is in this resolution a tacit but unmistakable admission that, while the London Book Room's hymnbooks might be culturally superior, their relatively high cost would continue to place them beyond the reach of a large enough number of Canadians as to render them an impracticable choice. It also indicates that Ryerson's earlier attempts to promote the use of Mark Burnham's Port Hope *Colonial Harmonist* among Methodists had fallen short of the mark. By the time Matthew Lang assumed control of the Toronto Book Room, then, the lack of an official Methodist hymnbook in Canada, and the uneven sale of American, British, as well as Canadian hymnbooks, must have resulted in considerable confusion. For example, congregations consisting of mixed numbers of British Wesleyans and Canadian Methodists would have been obliged to call out one set of hymn numbers for those possessing the Methodist Book Concern's hymnbook, another set for those owning the London Book Room's hymnbook, and perhaps even a third set for those who had recently purchased Burnham's *Colonial Harmonist* from Ryerson.

In addition to remedying this confusion by providing a common body of hymns around which public worship could be conducted, the Committee on the Improvement of Singing was probably quite aware of the potential economic benefits the production of their own hymnbook might yield. If sufficiently inexpensive, it would almost certainly be a bestseller. Any surplus revenue realized from its sale might thus help to defray ancillary costs in the form of duties and fees associated with continuing to stock Lang's shelves with titles imported from the London Book Room.

Yet, even if Lang's hymnbook turned out to be a bestseller, the way before him remained far from clear. Even with a "large quantity of books" on hand from London, Matthew Lang would be hard-pressed to convince Methodists, particularly those within the denomination's Sunday schools sprinkled across the colony's remotest settlements, that a British imprint was truly worth the higher price. Costs associated with producing or even superintending the production of a Canadian hymnbook, moreover, might not be so easily controlled that Lang could guarantee the availability of a local alternative that would be as comparatively inexpensive as the Methodist Book Concern's wildly popular rival editions.

A way forward through these stubborn financial difficulties might yet be at hand not in spite of – but because of – those wildly popular rival editions published by the Methodist Book Concern. Although the annual conferences had undoubtedly turned wholly against the Canadian claim after the union in 1833, there yet remained a small hope that the General Conference meeting in May 1836 might finally relent and offer the Canadians at least a portion of what they had originally hoped to collect in compensation for their erstwhile patronage of the Methodist Book Concern. With this end in view, the Canada Conference selected incoming president William Lord and its secretary Egerton Ryerson "to attend the American General Conference, to be held in Cincinnati, May, 1836, in order to negotiate on the claims of this conference upon the New-York Book Concern." Ephraim Evans took the bold step of printing this notice in the *Christian Guardian* shortly after proceedings concluded in the middle of June. The agents of the Methodist Book Concern, who continued to receive the *Christian Guardian* in New York, printed their own notice of this development in the *Christian Advocate* a month later. William Lord, identified as a member of the "British Conference," was named as one of two delegates, together with Egerton Ryerson, to negotiate the claim against the "Book Concern of the Methodist Episcopal Church." The notice concludes with the statement that this information was derived "from the *Christian Guardian*, of June 17; a religious paper published under the direction of the Wesleyan church at Toronto, U.C."[18]

Although subtle, the wording of the notice as it appeared in the *Christian Advocate* was obviously formulated to reinforce American prejudices against the claim. Its reference to the denominational publishing house as the "Book Concern of the Methodist Episcopal Church" rather than simply the "Methodist Book Concern," as it was all but invariably identified, combined with the repetitive use of the word "Wesleyan" strongly suggest a deliberate effort to foreground denominational differences and to signal to American readers that the earlier rejection of the claim was right and just. Moreover, although Egerton Ryerson assuredly had a clear grasp of the issues at play around the Concern's market and religious identity, William Lord could not possibly have understood these foreign subtleties. John Carroll, writing twenty-five years later, hinted at this when he observed that "Mr Lord was an Englishman," and that he, "knew nothing of the arrangement." Nevertheless, with delegates selected to represent the Canadian claim at the 1836 General Conference, and British Wesleyans firmly in control of the denominational newspaper and the Toronto Book Room, the stage was set for major changes in the nature of Canadian Methodism's cultural and commercial relationship with the Methodist Book Concern. Although this led to a critical turning point in Upper Canadian Methodist culture, the subsequent changes turned out to be a very far cry from what either Lord or Lang had hoped they might be.[19]

IV

After the Conference of the newly formed Wesleyan Methodist Church in Canada had concluded, Egerton Ryerson relocated to Kingston, where William Lord hoped he might be able to persuade a significant body of dissenting British Wesleyans to accept the union with the Canadian Methodists. During the first six months of his absence from Toronto, Ryerson exchanged several letters with Samuel Junkin, his former clerk at the *Guardian* office. In the first, Junkin noted that he and Lang were "getting on in the old way in the office" – that is, he and Lang continued to have difficulty securing an adequate supply of books from the London Book Room to stock their shelves and supply itinerant preachers. Apparently William Lord had paid a visit to the Toronto Book Room sometime in early July to inquire why Lang had not run any book advertisements in the *Christian Guardian* since taking over in June. "The reason," Junkin explained, "is we are not likely to [have] any to advertise before long. Mr Lang has sent off an order for about £400 worth, which we hope, tho' late, to get this Fall coming."[20]

A large part of Lang's problem flowed from the fact that Ryerson, after returning from England, had never bothered to set up a reliable system for making regular payments to the London Book Room.

Apparently there was little trust on either side of this relationship, and complications arising from the receipt of payment in London meant that shipments were often late. Money was also a constant problem for Lang. "We have got no books from Mr Mason yet," Junkin grumbled in another letter, "I suppose because we had not paid the first invoice." This time the problem was with the missionary treasurer, Joseph Stinson. Although they had managed to transfer £90 to Stinson in September, apparently the money had still not reached Mason at the London Book Room two months later. As a result, it was now too late to hope that anything would arrive from London before "*early* in the spring."[21]

Egerton Ryerson, however, had more to worry about than how things were getting on back at the Methodist Book Room in Toronto. The Upper Canada Academy was also in dire financial straits – so much so that William Lord had asked Ryerson to undertake an emergency overseas fundraising mission on its behalf. Although he claimed that the request came as a surprise, Ryerson well knew that things had been going downhill at the Academy for some time. In his valedictory editorial published in the *Christian Guardian* the previous June, Ryerson had scolded his readers, asserting that, although between £7,000 and £8,000 had been pledged by Upper Canadians for the Academy, less than half of that amount had actually been collected. Indeed, as Canadian Methodists became increasingly disenchanted with Wesleyan views of what the Academy should be, they withheld their support, and Ryerson was forced to assume personal responsibility for some of the debt. To make matters worse, the schismatic Methodist Episcopal Church in Canada was by then in the process of staking a claim of ownership over several chapels across the province.[22]

Amid all these financial pressures, Junkin took the trouble to remind his old boss how great a difference a successful claim – yet still possible – against the Methodist Book Concern would make for Canadian Methodists. In a letter written just before Ryerson disembarked on his overseas mission, Junkin urged him to remember that "however important the success of the Academy may be, it is still more important that you return in time to attend the General Conference on the Book Room business. Indeed, I consider the success of the mission will depend on you. Let nothing prevent you from attending the General Conference." It was yet another reminder of how remarkably inept the Wesleyans were proving themselves to be in Upper Canada. They could not negotiate a reliable and affordable supply of books from London. They could not properly oversee the Upper Canada Academy. They could not serve as effective fundraisers. And now it seemed they also could not competently represent the Canadian claim against the Methodist Book Concern at the American General Conference. Yet, despite Junkin's prudent adjuration, Ryerson allowed himself to be kept away from the colony until June 1837 – more than an entire year too long for him to attend the General Conference at which the fate of the Canadian claim was to be decided. As a result, the whole of that heavy burden would fall on William Lord – a man Anson Green incidentally described as possessing "little imagination" – and his very uncertain knowledge of the stridently denominational character of the Methodist Book Concern's market. Ryerson's lengthy absence also meant that whatever shadow he may have continued to cast over the affairs of the Toronto Book Room from his station in the eastern reaches of the province was at last lifted. Matthew Lang now had a completely free hand.[23]

V

Partly in response to the difficulties he and Junkin were encountering in securing books from the London Book Room, together with the fact that those books remained prohibitively expensive, Lang, towards the end of 1835, took the bold step of publishing his own edition of James Everett's venerated book *The Village Blacksmith* – a didactic memoir of the pious life of Yorkshire local preacher Samuel Hick. This was a surprising move if only because *The Village Blacksmith*, unlike anything Ryerson had published at the *Guardian* office before, was already available in a variety of British editions, including one published by the London Book Room itself. Indeed, only a small handful of printers in Upper Canada had tried anything like this before. Henry Chapman's fledgling attempt to turn a profit with his own edition of a few volumes from *Murray's Family Library* in the early 1830s met with agonizingly slow sales. Around the same time, Joseph Wilson appears to have made a somewhat better wager when he published a Canadian edition of Susanna Rowson's colossally popular novel *Charlotte Temple*; having already gone through more than seventy separate editions by the early 1830s, it must have seemed like a sure bet. Yet, however successful Wilson's *Charlotte Temple* may (or may not) have been, neither he, nor Chapman, nor anyone else, took a similar risk until Lang decided to gamble with money he did not have on the marketability of an Upper Canadian edition of Everett's moralizing biography of Hick.[24]

Matthew Lang's first advertisement for "this excellent little work" appeared in the *Christian Guardian* on 21 October 1835. Far from concealing that the work was already widely available from other publishers,

Lang pointed out that Everett's book had already "gone through five large Editions in England in a very short time." In addition to its proven saleability, Lang's decision to publish an Upper Canadian edition of *The Village Blacksmith* may have also been influenced by the fact that the Methodist Book Concern had as yet not published its own edition on this side of the Atlantic. In the end, however, neither its popularity in Britain nor lack of a competing American edition were enough to turn Lang's gamble into a financial success. Lang's Canadian publication simply could not compete with the London Book Room's editions. And, although the Methodist Book Concern would delay for another four years before finally getting around to issuing its own edition of Everett's popular work, Lang was haunted by the constant fear that an inexpensive American edition from some other publisher would appear on the market at any moment.[25]

In the shadow of these fears, Lang raised the financial stakes even further by producing *The Village Blacksmith* in an imprudently large – some might even have said preposterously large – edition of one thousand copies. By producing so many copies at one time, the Toronto Book Room certainly realized a significant economy of scale. But that would only matter in the event that the book became a bestseller. Alas, when that did not happen Lang was left to regret that he had not taken a more cautious approach to the market. So badly had he misjudged the demand for Everett's biography in Upper Canada that the union itself would unravel in less time than it would take to finally clear the Book Room's cluttered shelves of the unwanted copies at deeply discounted prices. In the end, Lang's failure put the Toronto Book Room under further financial pressure, exacerbated difficulties associated with relying on an unpredictable transatlantic supply of books, and – to mitigate his own publishing losses – obliged him to charge the highest possible prices for the London Book Room's wares. The commercial failure of *The Village Blacksmith* also made a successful outcome of the Canadian claim against the New York Methodist Book Concern both less likely and even more important.

By the winter of 1836, the colony's supply of Methodist hymnbooks had almost run out. William Case, who continued to work closely with the province's Natives, complained that his own stock had dwindled to just two copies by the middle of January. While Matthew Lang spent that winter in Toronto waiting for what he and Samuel Junkin hoped would be a large shipment of books from the London Book Room in the early spring, William Lord was growing steadily more nervous about the upcoming General Conference of the Methodist Episcopal Church. By February, it seemed increasingly less likely that Egerton Ryerson would return to the colony in time to represent the Canadian claim in May. Fearing that the task would fall to him alone, William Lord hurried off a letter seeking Ryerson's detailed guidance on how best to represent the claim against the Methodist Book Concern to American Methodists. "I expect to be in N. York April 3rd;" he wrote, "afterward I mean to proceed to Cincinnati. If I do not hear from you before, *be sure* to write to me at Cincinnatti [*sic*]. Let your letters be long & full of Methodistical information. I am daily expecting the paper you promised respecting the Book Questions. I should like well to understand it. If any thing strikes you, write."[26]

Lord was not the only one worried. Methodists across Upper Canada were also demanding to have some influence over the choice of Ryerson's replacement. Although Lord and Ryerson seem initially to have agreed that William Case would be the best choice, John Ryerson wrote to his brother later that month to inform him that twelve or fourteen "preachers at the west are making quite a noise about *you* or Mr *Lord* attempting to appoint your successor & saying that neither of you nor boath [*sic*] of you had or have any authority to do any such thing &c." According to another letter written by John Ryerson several months later, subsequent protests over the same issue broke out right across the Niagara District. It seems that, between the writing of these two letters, Egerton Ryerson had switched his preference from William Case to John Ryerson – a move that only opened up a new occasion for dissatisfaction among those who preferred Case. Perhaps to keep the peace, John voluntarily removed himself from consideration. Although Lord ultimately ignored calls made by some preachers to hold a special session for the election of Ryerson's replacement, these controversies underscore the extent to which Upper Canadian Methodists had come to believe that a favourable outcome at the General Conference could not be left to chance.[27]

A great deal of their concern flowed from the fact that money in the colony had become desperately scarce. John Ryerson, like his brother Egerton, had assumed personal responsibility for some of the expenses of the Upper Canada Academy. By the spring, the debt was weighing very heavily on him. In a letter written at the beginning of May, John Ryerson implored his brother in terms that were almost hysterical to make every possible effort on behalf of the Academy. "Everything depends on the success of your exertions. Four thousand pounds is the least that will answer ... O!! How awfully we have got involved in this most painful & protracted business! O! if you can help us out of this mire the Lord reward you!" Indeed, so agitated had he become that he confessed to entertaining serious thoughts about fleeing to the United

States to escape his creditors. When Egerton Ryerson received this letter in England a month later, he noted in his own journal, "Although I find that collecting for the Upper Canada Academy is a wearisome task, yet I must not slacken my exertions so long as our friends in Upper Canada are in such straits for funds."[28]

VI

While the Canadians continued to look wistfully across the border in the hope of financial rescue, American Methodists found themselves suddenly confronted with a disaster so immense and unexpected that it shook their faith in God's very providence. On a bitter and cold winter morning in 1836, Nathan Bangs and a throng of Methodist onlookers stood in the street and watched helplessly as the Methodist Book Concern was reduced to ashes. The financial losses were immense. Buildings, equipment, and all the Concern's stock were lost in the flames. Even worse, the Concern's insurance policies were all but non-existent.[29]

Almost four years earlier, John Emory reported to the General Conference in 1832 – the same Conference at which Emory had done his best to cast doubts on the Canadian claim – that the Concern was debt free and that its combined operations in New York and Cincinnati were valued at nearly $450,000. In September 1833, when the Methodist Book Concern moved into new buildings at 200 Mulburry Street in New York City, the book agents maintained as many as seven separate insurance policies against loss by fire. But in mid-December 1835, just a few months before disaster struck, another fire – the "great fire" that tore through New York's Ann Street – destroyed millions of dollars of property and pushed many of the city's insurance companies into bankruptcy. When the book agents sought to renew their policy and increase their coverage, they were shocked by the runaway cost of the new premiums. Insurance companies as far away as Boston, Baltimore, and Philadelphia, once they discovered the value of the Concern's operations, refused outright to assume the risk. Unable thus to obtain insurance for what they deemed a reasonable price, the agents decided to commence "a more careful and rigid system of self protection" to prevent fires, including requiring the Concern's porter who lived on the premises to make nightly inspections of all the rooms and the stoves used to heat them. The result was that when the fire struck, the Methodist Book Concern's remaining policies would yield a mere $25,000 in compensation. The rest would have to be painstakingly recovered, if it could be recovered at all, through voluntary subscriptions and donations.[30]

Using borrowed presses, type, and office space volunteered by Harper and Brothers, the *New-York Observer*, and others, the book agents published a lengthy account of the fire, the losses incurred, and the minutes of meetings in the following days in the *Christian Advocate.* The minutes of the meetings, although not nearly as exciting as the account of the fire itself, were especially important since they allowed the agents to establish clearly and firmly that the loss of the Methodist Book Concern's property and stock was a loss sustained not by the agents as mere publishers, but by the whole of the Methodist Episcopal Church: "That in this great loss, we recognize its serious consequences upon the prosperity of the M.E. Church in general and particularly and more intimately upon the comfort and support of our superannuated and beloved brethren in the ministry, who have worn out their lives for Christ; and in the calamitous condition of the many widows and orphans of our preachers, who are also thus deprived of the ordinary provision of the conferences." Remarkably, the agents also implored their Methodist readers to refrain from purchasing any books from any other publisher until the Concern had resumed its operations. "We have only time to add that we request our friends to withhold their orders for Methodist books," they wrote, "except to the branches at Cincinnati and New-Orleans, and those persons who may have on hand books of *our former publication*, until they can be supplied from our own press."[31]

In the months following the fire, pledges and donations flowed into the Concern's coffers from Methodists across the continent. Letters accompanied many of those donations that reinforced the connection between the Methodist Book Concern and the denomination's wider interests. In a letter dated about a month after the fire, one correspondent observed, "The destruction of that great establishment must be felt as a heavy calamity throughout every part of our field of labor, and I can but fear it is destined to exert a paralyzing influence upon the Church for years to come." After acknowledging that the Book Concern's books and periodicals served in the place of schools and colleges for many, the writer dismissed the financial loss itself as insignificant when compared with the attenuation of the Concern as the Church's chief centripetal influence, "the focus where all the scattered energies of the Church were collected, and the radiating point from which a thousand salutary influences proceeded to cheer and bless our widespread congregations."[32]

As spring advanced, the book agents published a collection of letters together under the title "Every Cent Will Tell" in which various writers observed that the Concern was integral to the functioning of the Church, that its destruction amounted to "the greatest evil she could be called to suffer," and that the whole Church had a duty to rise simultaneously to its aid. A quarterly conference in Alabama wrote the following April to inform the agents that they had ordered all their preachers to collect donations on behalf of the Concern because "we think the whole Church has participated in the loss, and she should help to repair it." Samuel Luckey, a student at the Genesee Wesleyan Seminary, went even further when he accused his fellow Methodists of causing the very calamity that now beset them by neglecting to support the Concern as fully and as wholeheartedly as they ought. God, Luckey argued, permitted the fire to destroy the Concern in order to send a powerful message to Methodists about their duty to uphold an organization so central to the welfare of the Church's superannuated preachers, widows, and orphans. "And shall we now," Luckey thundered, "talk of satisfying our consciences by barely rendering the institution what it was before? This is not what our heavenly father intended by afflicting us. This admonition extends much further."[33]

All of this had devastating consequences for Canadians. Not only did it mean that the Methodist Book Concern had no ready money to pay any claim they might make at the General Conference of 1836. It also served as a powerful reminder to Methodists across the United States of the relationship between the Concern's market and the bonds of religious identity that held them together. In early March, Ephraim Evans reprinted the *Christian Advocate*'s initial announcement describing the Concern's destruction in the *Christian Guardian*. "I suppose," Samuel Junkin confided to Egerton Ryerson just as the General Conference was getting underway, "there is no probability of getting any thing at present, on account of the disastrous fire which destroyed their all at New York."[34]

Still, money had already begun flowing in from all across the United States and even from some quarters in Upper Canada. Indeed, a second notice relating to the fire appeared in the *Christian Guardian* a month before the General Conference and urged Canadian Methodists to "manifest their concurrence in the sentiment that 'Wesleyan Methodism is one throughout the world' by imitating according to their ability" the examples of William Lord and William Case, who had both made recent donations to the Methodist Book Concern in New York. The timing of those donations was no doubt calculated to further Canadian interests at the General Conference; they nevertheless demonstrated that, despite the circumstances, Lord and his newly appointed co-delegate William Case continued to believe that some kind of constructive settlement might still be within reach if only they conducted themselves with the necessary discretion. Although it ended up being not at all what either man had hoped for, the terms of settlement the Americans finally did offer, and that Lord and Case felt they had no choice but to reluctantly accept, opened a critical new phase in the cultural development of Canadian Methodism that helped prepare the ground for the Toronto Book Room to achieve unprecedented commercial success in Upper Canada's wider and non-denominational market for books and periodicals of all kinds.[35]

VII

When American Methodists arrived in Cincinnati to attend the 1836 General Conference, they had far more on their minds than the unresolved claim of the Canadians. In addition to the destruction of the Methodist Book Concern and a worrying decline in membership unprecedented since the War of 1812, delegates also mourned the recent deaths of two prominent bishops: William McKendree and John Emory. McKendree, a tried veteran of the episcopacy, had served as American Methodism's senior bishop since the death of Francis Asbury almost twenty years earlier. His death, however, would have meant little in Upper Canada. Concerned primarily with the westward expansion of Methodism, there is no evidence that McKendree even once crossed the border into British North America. John Emory was another matter. Not yet fifty years of age, and having served less than four years as a bishop, Emory's death came unexpectedly when he was accidentally thrown from a wagon in late 1835. Although he had never held a preaching appointment north of the border, Emory was widely remembered for travelling to Britain in 1820 to negotiate the surrender of Lower Canada after the War of 1812 in exchange for the permanent withdrawal of British Wesleyan missionaries from Upper Canada. William Case would also have remembered how, just four years earlier, Emory had spoken forcefully against the Canadian claim in his capacity as outgoing senior book agent of the Methodist Book Concern. William Lord, who no doubt learned of Emory's opposition through Egerton Ryerson, probably joined Case in quietly rejoicing to see the young bishop's place vacant.[36]

Yet, whatever small advantage may have flowed from Emory's death was more than compensated for by the destruction of the Methodist Book Concern just three months earlier. And, as the most recent issue of the *Christian Advocate* reported just before the General Conference got underway, only $16,047.93 had yet been recovered through voluntary donations. Case and Lord must have blanched at that figure. A mere fraction of what would be needed to rebuild the Concern's premises and replace its lost stock, that whole amount was just over half of what Canadian Methodists had claimed for themselves as their rightful portion of the Concern four years earlier. To make matters worse, delegates from the dissident Methodist Episcopal Church in Canada also arrived at the General Conference and soon set about loudly proclaiming themselves to be the true offspring of the American Methodist Episcopal Church. Although calculated chiefly to strengthen their own legal claim to church property in Canada, the embarrassing presence of these schismatics had the potential to complicate the representations of Lord and Case. Since the claim of the Canadians to a share of the Methodist Book Concern had always been premised on the notion of an earlier shared transnational religious identity founded on participation in a common market, the eruption of this rival claim threatened to weaken, and perhaps even destroy, the whole basis on which a successful claim against the Methodist Book Concern might yet rest.[37]

William Lord showed at least some understanding that the success of the Canadian claim would ultimately hinge on the question of identity. "Although a stranger in a strange land," he addressed the Americans, "I am surrounded by brethren – by those who are peculiarly members of the same family; for we bear, in addition to the common and catholic name of Christian, that of Wesleyan Methodist." This was a surprisingly good beginning. Unfortunately, things went downhill from there. After recapitulating the same basic arguments advanced by Canadian Methodists at the 1832 General Conference about the relationship between publisher and consumer on which the Concern's North American denominational market had been predicated, Lord shifted the emphasis of his address away from that relationship altogether and addressed the problem of the union directly by suggesting that the Methodist Book Concern would be nothing without Wesleyan authors. "We will only remark," lectured Lord, "that the union of the 'Canada Conference' with the 'English,' to which they were unexpectedly led by Providential Circumstances ... presents an additional security to their continuance in the Doctrine and Discipline of Methodism, and cannot weaken their claims, when it is considered that not a small portion of the profits of the Book Concern arises from the sale of works of our English Fathers and Brethren."[38]

At first glance, Lord's argument appeared to successfully link the notions of religious identity, market participation, and the disposition of profits. Unfortunately, however, it did so by making an appeal to the transatlantic cultural ownership of texts that Americans throughout much of the nineteenth century would have found untenable, and that any attentive participant in the Concern's market would have found rhetorically foreign. Since Lord could not make the argument that British Wesleyans had participated in the Concern's market and had therefore earned a right to the Concern's profits on those grounds, he instead attempted to distort the Concern's rhetorical framework by urging American Methodists to acknowledge a cultural debt to their "English Fathers and Brethren."

The argument was weak on two counts. First, it failed to recognize that the Methodist Book Concern's rhetorical strategies had nothing to do with authorship and everything to do with the production of commodities that were made to function as religious status objects through an economic – not a cultural – transaction. The place of the author in the Concern's market always occupied one of secondary importance next to that of the publisher. American Methodists were adjured in catalogues, books, and periodicals to identify not the names of authors on the titles pages of the items they purchased, but to look for the Concern's imprint as a guarantee that the purchase of that commodity would benefit the missionary and charitable interests of the wider Church. Thus, the cultural production of the Concern's commodities had more to do with linking patronage and denominational identity in a commercial transaction than in bolstering the reputation of any individual author. Purchasing a book authored by a non-Methodist reinforced the religious identities of Methodist consumers every bit as much as purchasing a book by Wesley, Fletcher, or Watson – provided that all those books bore the Concern's imprint.

Second, no publisher operating in the United States at this time, including the Methodist Book Concern, would have been willing to acknowledge any form of cultural debt to British authors that might entail attendant financial obligations in the form of payments for intellectual property. The US Federal Copyright Act had been providing Americans with a legal antidote to such arguments for nearly fifty years. That William Lord would advance such an argument betrayed not only a faulty understanding of the Concern's denominational market strategies, but also a striking ignorance of American literary and cultural practices more generally. Not surprisingly, the Methodists who were appointed to a committee to consider Lord's arguments found them unconvincing.[39]

Five days before the Committee on Canada Affairs made its report to the General Conference, John Bailey and James Powley made their own claim to a common religious identity with the Americans on behalf of the schismatic Methodist Episcopal Church in Canada by casting themselves as representatives of "the true, Original Methodist Episcopal Church of Canada" and "request[ing] to be recognized as the children of the M.E. Church." Lord and Case, who doubtless saw the danger such a pretension might pose to their own claim, lobbied vehemently against them. In a later report to the Canada Conference, Lord described the "delicate part" he and Case played "in reference to the case of the self-styled Episcopal Church." His tone was temperate and reflected Lord's pleasure with the eventual outcome. By contrast, Canadian Episcopal Methodists described the ordeal as a "bitter struggle," where Case and Lord characterized them and their religious brethren as "a set of arrogant, ambitious, dissatisfied local preachers, with a few uninformed people whom they had induced to follow them, almost too insignificant and contemptible to be noticed at all."[40]

In the end, the committee appointed to consider the matter wisely decided not to intervene. "In view of all the circumstances," their report concluded, "as far as your committee has been able to ascertain and understand them, they are unanimously of the opinion that the case required no interference of this General Conference." Although it is unclear to what extent the rival claims Bailey and Powley made to a shared religious identity with the Americans weighed against them in the balance, by the time this report was tabled, the Canadian claim against the Concern had already been rejected. As Lord later reported to the Canada Conference, "The Committee reported at length, and strongly against your claims. They considered the decisions of the Annual Conferences a final settlement of these claims, & that it was not competent for the General Conference again to interfere, and the Report concluded with a Resolution to this effect, – That the General Conference could take no further action upon this subject."[41]

With their backs now to the wall, William Lord made a final appeal to Nathan Bangs – a man who, with John Emory dead and Egerton Ryerson overseas, probably knew more about the intricate history of the Canadian claim than any other delegate attending the General Conference. Although never fully reconciled to either the ecclesiastical independence of Upper Canadians or a permanent British Wesleyan presence west of the Ottawa River, Bangs was willing to intervene on behalf of the Canadian delegates – but not without an eye to furthering his own agenda. Lord later reported that he and Case had "two interviews with Dr Bangs, and Mr Waugh, and finally a Document was drawn up." The compromise that Bangs and Waugh, the latter having served as senior book agent since the General Conference of 1832, worked out with Lord and Case appeared to have been delicately calibrated to downplay the insistence that the Canadians were owed something while still leaving open the possibility that the Methodist Book Concern's market in Canada might yet be reinvigorated on commercial rather than denominational terms. It is doubtful that Lord did not perceive this possibility, but perhaps the thought of returning to Upper Canada with absolutely no concessions from the Americans was an even less palatable alternative. In any event, two days after the committee rejected Lord's original arguments, on a motion tabled by Bangs, "the report of the Committee on Canada affairs was called up and recommitted, for the purpose of hearing a proposition from the brethren from Canada"[42]

Three days later, a final settlement showing clear signs of Bangs's influence was submitted to a vote. The document was carefully crafted both to extend a generous program of discounts to the Canadians and to place them forever beyond the Concern's emphatically denominational market of readers in the United States. The Canadians were focused primarily on financial matters, but for the Americans there was far more at stake in this agreement than mere money. Although the annual conferences had unmistakably rejected the Canadian claim against the Concern, the arguments behind that claim could not be easily brushed aside without compromising the market principles that had been used so effectively to build and protect the Concern's denominational market in North America – especially at a time when Beverley Waugh and his successor, Thomas Mason, needed to rebuild the Methodist Book Concern from the ground up. Bangs knew that the Canadians were right to point out that the payment of dividends to annual conferences implied that each conference, as an integral part of the wider ecclesiastical body, effectively owned a portion of the stock and value of the Methodist Book Concern. Moreover, since Canadians had always occupied a different geopolitical region of North America, Bangs could not counter that claim by simply pointing to differences in nationality. And while he might argue that Canadian patronage of the Concern had dropped off precipitously in recent years, nothing could void the fact that Canadians had been long and stable participants in the Concern's market for more than four decades. Finally, since the Canadians had continued to receive annual dividends after 1828, Americans could not assert that the establishment of a separate ecclesiastical entity in Upper Canada materially weakened their claim by diminishing their status as something more than straightforward consumers. The only way to sidestep the Canadian claim without compromising the Concern's rhetorical strategies, then, was to find a way to situate Canadian Methodists outside the boundaries of the Concern's denominational market altogether by redefining their religious identities relative to their American and British Wesleyan brethren.

William Lord had begun his own address to the General Conference by stressing the closeness of the connection between himself and his hearers as "members of the same family." The settlement, by contrast, attempted to widen those distances by declaring in its opening sentences that Canadian Methodists were "formerly united" to the Methodist Episcopal Church – a subtle but unmistakable framing that subverted any claim the Canadians might make to suggest they remained partakers of a common religious identity reflected in and reinforced by a common market for religious book and periodicals. That distance was widened further by the assertion that the Canadians fundamentally altered their own religious identities by not merely "uniting" with the British Wesleyans, but by becoming "part of the Wesleyan Methodist Connexion." While none of this amounted to a direct refutation of the Canadian claim, carefully chosen language of this kind weakened the Canadian position by drawing a distinguishing line between the religious identities of those who formed part "of the Methodist Episcopal Church" from those who formed part of the "Wesleyan Methodist Connexion." While these bodies may have been of the same family, as Lord asserted, they were nevertheless, as the preamble of the settlement suggested, of different households. The program of discounts that followed, then, was based not on an admission that Canadian Methodists were justly entitled to a portion of the stock and value of the Methodist Book Concern, but on the incomparably weaker "affectionate remembrance of the Canada Brethren" and a purely voluntary desire "to manifest … fraternal regards in every suitable way."[43]

Wholesalers as a rule received a discount on the Concern's products of 33 per cent. According to the terms of the settlement, the Canadians would receive a more generous (and unprecedented) discount of 40 per cent. Sunday school books and tracts, on which the Concern earned a smaller margin, would be offered at a discount of 18 per cent. And all debts incurred with the Concern, on which no interest would be charged, were to be paid within a year. Furthermore, the agreement would remain in force until the meeting of the General Conference in 1852, provided that "it is hereby mutually understood and agreed that the foregoing arrangement is considered as a full and definite satisfactory adjustment of the question which has arisen between the Canada Conference and the Methodist Episcopal Church in the subject of the Methodist Book Concern." That is, if the Canadians accepted these terms of settlement, their claim against the Methodist Book Concern would be considered forever settled.[44]

With the Concern's agents now not merely indifferent, but openly averse to making any rhetorical claims on the religious identities of

Upper Canadians, and with an offer of steep discounts on the table, the pieces were at last in place for a vigorous reopening of the Canadian market to the Methodist Book Concern's products as straightforward commodities rather than denominational status objects. Those books, moreover, would be less expensive and more readily available than any that the Canadians could obtain from either the London Book Room or any other publisher. Once the document was prepared and accepted by both the General Conference and the Canadian delegates, copies of the agreement were given to Lord and Case for removal back to Canada. It must have seemed to all concerned paultry compensation when measured against what the Canadians had hoped to obtain at the General Conference four years earlier. Not only had Lord and Case failed for the last time to secure a financial settlement sorely needed to shore up the Toronto Book Room and the Upper Canada Academy, but also they had inadvertently negotiated an agreement that, once implemented, would disrupt the London Book Room's overseas market and thereby contribute to the further destabilization of the union between British Wesleyans and Canadian Methodists. As they had in 1820, it seemed that the Americans had once again managed to get the better of their British Wesleyan counterparts in Upper Canada. "Thus," Bangs wrote several years later, "was this long-pending question brought to an amicable termination, on such terms as to preserve and perpetuate the harmony and brotherly affection heretofore subsisting between the two connections."[45]

VIII

At the end of May 1836, after William Lord had returned to Toronto, he dispatched an urgent letter to Egerton Ryerson overseas. In it he lamented that, despite an inconvenient journey with William Case to the General Conference, their efforts to secure a cash settlement had failed. In the meantime, the debt owing on the Upper Canada Academy had reached a record £5,000. Lord urged Ryerson to remain overseas until more money could be raised. He also wrote that in the meantime he had drawn another £500 against Ryerson's own credit to keep the Academy's doors open. Things were becoming desperate. Anson Green, who assumed the position of the Academy's treasurer later that summer, was far from persuaded that Ryerson's efforts in Britain would avail much. "To me," he wrote, "this was a day of great anxiety, requiring strong faith, untiring zeal, and much prayer. I had no books from the former Treasurer to guide me; and the workmen were clamouring for their pay! A debt of more than $16,000, and an empty treasury! Rooms without furniture, and students pressing for accommodation."[46]

When Canadian Methodists gathered in Belleville about a month after the General Conference in the United States was over, they were in a decidedly sullen mood. Not only had their claim against the Methodist Book Concern been dashed for the last time, but also the Upper Canada Academy was now teetering on the brink of financial ruin. There was much grumbling that Egerton Ryerson's talents would have been put to far better use lobbying for Canadian interests among the Americans in Cincinnati than they had been overseas begging donations from the Wesleyans. Lord bore the brunt of the blame – both for failing to find a way to get Ryerson home and for his own mishandling of Canadian affairs in the United States. It was now too late for anything but recriminations. In their frustration, the Canadians passed a resolution that was as futile as it was final. "We feel it due to ourselves to say that," it ran in part, "we still entertain the opinions which we have formerly expressed as to the equitableness of our claims on the Methodist Book Concern and we deeply regret that the General Conference has thought proper to refuse to us a participation in the Stock to which we have so largely contributed, and which we had been led to expect from the acts of former General Conferences." With that the affair came to what many believed was an unsatisfactory conclusion. That it would ultimately aid the Canadians in ridding themselves of William Lord and the rest of the British Wesleyans, at least for a time, had not yet become clear.[47]

A large part of the dissatisfaction Canadian Methodists felt with the settlement flowed from a mistaken conviction that they were being treated no differently than any other wholesaler. "The American Conference," John Carroll would later note with sarcasm, "in lieu of our claim, gave the Canada Book Room the privilege of purchasing books at their Concern at forty per cent., a discount which any publishing house will give to agents who have no vested claims! And this wonderful privilege was to end, if I mistake not, in 1870." But, of course, Carroll did mistake. The discount offered was in fact 7 per cent higher than any other wholesaler could obtain from the Concern, and the terms were to expire some eighteen years earlier than Carroll noted. That this appears to have been lost on the Canadians in the throes of their disappointment, however, only made it that much easier for them to treat the Concern's products as straightforward commodities that were no different from the offerings of any other publisher. If they were to buy these books, they would buy them entirely for their value as commercial wares suitable for whatever market – commercial or denominational – they chose to serve. Thus, while the Methodist Book Concern's books and periodicals continued to be set apart from the offerings of rival publishers in the United States as denominational status objects, in Upper Canada this key aspect of their cultural production became wholly obscured and irrelevant.[48]

It did not take long for Canadian Methodists to grasp that the voiding of the rhetorical connection between patronage and denominational identity in Canada, combined with a program of steep discounts, effectively opened the way to a new supply of inexpensive books that no longer compromised their religious identities as loyal Wesleyans. Indeed, even William Lord seemed to have intuited this new reality. His own report concluded with the hopeful view that the settlement as secured would, "open at once a friendly intercourse between the two Connexions, and ... afford considerable pecuniary benefit to the Canada Connexion." There was only one problem with Lord's diplomatic sentiment: apart from the fact that his chief motive for making it was self-exculpatory, he meant not a word of it. Supporting a "friendly intercourse" between American and Canadian Methodists was the last thing Wesleyan missionaries in Upper Canada wanted. And as long as British Wesleyan Matthew Lang retained control over the affairs of the Toronto Book Room, the likelihood that Canadians would derive any "pecuniary benefit" from the terms of their settlement with the Methodist Book Concern would remain vanishingly small.[49]

The following month, in accordance with the terms outlined in the settlement, Matthew Lang travelled to New York with John Ryerson and Ephraim Evans to settle all outstanding debts that the Canadians continued to owe to the Methodist Book Concern. The errand must have struck all three as gallingly ironic. Only two months earlier, Canadians had continued to hope that such a journey might be undertaken to collect money from, rather than pay money to the Methodist Book Concern. With their accounts now in order, the *Christian Advocate* sent all three preachers on their way with the extravagantly sunny claim, "The brethren parted, cherishing for each other much good will and brotherly affection." On the contrary, it is hard to imagine that Lang did not take at least a moment between these fond farewells to shake the dust from his sandals. Needless to say, Lang brought with him no books and left behind no outstanding orders with the Concern. And when he resumed his place at the Methodist Book Room in Toronto, he immediately set about running the storefront and supplying the province's preachers with books and periodicals as though the settlement with the Americans did not even exist.[50]

Although *The Village Blacksmith* was not selling well, plans were soon laid for the risky production of more local editions, including a hymnbook, as well as an "edition of the life of Rev. J. Smith, as also that of John Nelson." In the meantime, the months passed without a single order being placed with the Methodist Book Concern. John Ryerson, in whose home the Book Committee met at least occasionally in the following months, was becoming quietly but steadily more frustrated with Lang's unwavering refusal to take advantage of the Methodist Book Concern's discounts. Indeed, so annoyed had John Ryerson become with Lang and his policies in Toronto that on the one occasion he actually wanted something from the London Book Room, he wrote to his brother overseas to make the purchase on his behalf. It was shocking conduct considering his position as a member of the Book Committee – but it nevertheless allowed him to avoid paying the irritating surcharge Lang levied against Canadian preachers who obtained books through him. When Lang finally relented and placed a reluctant order with the Methodist Book Concern for some bibles and other miscellaneous titles that autumn, it was already too late. By that time, John Ryerson had made up his mind: Lang's days at the Toronto Book Room were numbered.[51]

Once that decision had been made, the Ryerson brothers worked together tirelessly to wrest control of the *Christian Guardian* and the Toronto Book Room – and with it Methodism's entire infrastructure for book distribution in Upper Canada – away from the Wesleyans. These events presaged not only an imminent dissolution of the union with the Wesleyans, but also created a space in which Canadian Methodists could establish new distribution agreements and structures, new publishing and bookselling practices, and a new understanding of American books as straightforward commodities perfectly divorced from the religious identities of their owners. That, in turn, meant the Toronto Book Room could reinvigorate its market by setting aside the Concern's denominationalism and appealing to Upper Canadians regardless of their religious convictions. In the process, the Methodist Book Concern's inexpensive wares became such an integral part of that strategy that subsequent changes in polity, including an eventual reunion with the Wesleyans in 1847, could little affect it. Indeed, so enduring did this market become in the shadow of these changes that, as Methodism continued to gain social respectability, the lingering animus that many Upper Canadians had continued to hold against the widespread use of American books in the colony after the War of 1812 entered a period of steady decline. Before any of that could happen, however, Matthew Lang had to go – and so did the rest of the Wesleyans.

Chapter Six

"Their Own Book Concern": A Methodist Book Market for All Upper Canadians

By the spring of 1836, the Ryerson brothers had had enough of the Wesleyans. Enough of their domineering ways. Enough of their conservative politics. Enough of their continual genuflecting to the Church of England. And above all, enough of their overpriced books. "The Union works *badly, very badly, for us,* and I am sick, in my very soul sick of it," William Ryerson complained bitterly to his brother Egerton that May. "I wish, most heartily wish," he concluded, "it had never taken place." John Ryerson added that as far as money was concerned, "We have received nothing from them & have lost much by them." This was nowhere more evident than in Wesleyan mismanagement of the Toronto Book Room. "The high price of books & the trifling discount which is made on them, the expence [*sic*] of gitting [*sic*] them here … make the circumstances of the Book concern perfectly horible [*sic*]," he continued. "Indeed, so far from the book agents or the English preachers who have been, or are, in this country trying to assist us in any way, their principle [*sic*] object appears to be, to flease [*sic*] us & git [*sic*] all out of us they can." With the market for books in disarray and attendance at Toronto's two Methodist churches down almost 25 per cent since the union with the British Wesleyans, John Ryerson and his brothers were determined to usher in change – beginning with electing "a Canadian preacher for book agent."[1]

Recent historians have tended to approach mid-nineteenth century religious history in Upper Canada from one of two dominant perspectives. Either they have looked for emergent forms of a nascent but distinct national character rooted in British North America's wider interdenominational landscape, or more recently, they have sought to foreground the enduring impact of transatlantic British cultural influences. Chief among the latter group, Todd Webb argues persuasively that Canadian Methodists went out of their way to emphasize their British character and outlook, especially after 1840 as they loudly professed themselves to be "as British as the British themselves, if not more so." When the Wesleyans and the Canadians finally agreed to set aside their differences 1847, the way became open, writes Goldwin French, "for an even greater infusion of Wesleyan influence than under the previous union." Other historians, looking beyond Methodism's internal workings to its interaction with other religious denominations in the province, have found common ground with William Westfall's powerful argument that as the century progressed, a "Protestant consensus" emerged that ultimately opened the way for the development of a geopolitically distinct religious character that contributed to the formation of an embryonic national identity. Methodism occupies a central place in this framework as the largest denomination and ultimately as an unofficial but "truly national church encompassing the full range of Canada's cultural identity." On one key point, however, all these scholars seem to agree: the cultural influence of American Methodism, however pronounced it may have been early in the nineteenth century, had by this time withered away entirely.[2]

Yet, there is ample evidence to suggest that this was not quite so. Upper Canadian Methodists, for example, consistently sent delegates to every General Conference of the Methodist Episcopal Church from 1836 until and well beyond the middle decades of the nineteenth century. Much to the horror of the Wesleyans, moreover, when the union between themselves and the Canadians was dissolved in 1840, the Canadians made a belated attempt to have "the entire question" subjected "to the arbitrament [*sic*] of the American Bishops." And just when things seemed darkest on the eve of the dissolution of that union, when it was not clear what his own fate might be, no less a figure than Egerton Ryerson mused openly about relocating to the United States and taking a pulpit in New York City. All this suggests something more than a defunct transnational attachment between Methodists in Upper Canada and their coreligionists in the United States. Nowhere were these attachments more evident than in the revival of the Methodist Book Concern's market in Upper Canada in the late 1830s. Egerton Ryerson had certainly made a serious effort to supplant that market with books and periodicals from the London Book Room, an effort that was continued by British Wesleyan Matthew Lang after he became Upper Canada's first official book steward in May 1835, but logistical complications and irremediably higher costs finally set this end beyond practicable reach.[3]

This chapter sets out to complicate existing historiography by unfolding the way in which the Methodist Book Concern's resurgent market in Upper Canada influenced cultural developments in the colony at a time when Canadian Methodists and British Wesleyans variously cooperated and competed with one another as they moved in and out of ecclesiastical union. Once the Americans had fully and finally rejected the Canadian claim against the Methodist Book Concern at their General Conference in 1836, the premise that purchasing a book published by the Concern somehow underscored a reader's loyalty to and membership in the Methodist Episcopal Church could no longer hold in Upper Canada. This change was reflected in the advertising strategies of the Methodist Book Room in Toronto as it urged Canadians of all stripes to purchase its wares not because they conferred material benefit on Methodist endeavours, but simply because they were the least expensive offerings on the market. This fundamental redefinition of the Toronto Book Room's market in purely commercial terms had several important – and surprisingly far-reaching – consequences.

First, by the time an arrangement to resume the union with the Wesleyans was sorted out, in 1847, Canadian Methodists had become so successful at selling the Methodist Book Concern's inexpensive products on a wholly commercial basis that only the most perfunctory effort was made to renew a relationship with the Wesleyan Book Room in London. Thus, because the Toronto Book Room was by then generating a reliable source of revenue for the denomination, the degree to which Wesleyan missionaries could reassert their influence by relying on their former strategy of being "Lords of the Treasury" was greatly diminished. Second, the Book Room's open and undisguised sale of American books also helped to soften anti-American sentiment among members of Upper Canada's broader reading public, particularly after Methodists found themselves in a position to exert through Egerton Ryerson a sustained influence over the development of the province's educational system and its public libraries. Third, and perhaps most importantly, the commercial reorientation of the Toronto Book Room, together with an unyielding determination on the part of its book stewards to appeal to readers beyond Methodism's denominational margins, was the first critical step in a long journey that would set the stage for the Toronto Book Room – and later the Methodist Book and Publishing House, as it was known after 1874 – to become one of the largest publishers in Canada as well as a major sponsor of Canadian writing.

I

By the time Canadian Methodists gathered in Toronto for their annual conference in June 1837, William Lord had already returned to England. William Harvard, Lord's replacement as president of the Conference of the Wesleyan Methodist Church in Canada and a man described as holding "highly conservative opinions," had been in the colony since the previous autumn. Ordained by British Wesleyans in 1810, Harvard was older, more experienced, and more formidable than his predecessor, having already served extensive terms in Britain, India, and Ceylon before accepting a post in Upper Canada. "On this side of the Atlantic," John Carroll notes, "he was found to be commanding in person, almost the *facsimile* of General Washington; dignified in his carriage; polite in his manners; pre-eminently Christian in his spirit; and unusually faithful as a minister."[4]

William Harvard's first order of business appears to have been to make sure that control over the Toronto Book Room and the *Christian Guardian* did not fall back into Canadian hands. And, if somehow that did happen, he was at least going to make sure that those Canadian hands would be bound by appropriate Wesleyan constraints. Perhaps Harvard, Matthew Lang, and Ephraim Evans, who together with John Ryerson made up the membership of the Book Committee, had already heard rumours of what the Ryersons were hoping to achieve at the upcoming conference. Perhaps they even knew that, in addition to John Ryerson's resolution to let his own name stand for book steward, that he had been actively lobbying his brother Egerton to seek the editorship of the *Christian Guardian* as well. However that may be, Harvard was taking no chances. Under his direction, members of the Book Committee met ahead of the conference to draft an extensive set of new rules intended not only to curtail the autonomy of the editor of the *Christian Guardian*, whoever that might turn out to be, but also to regulate the affairs of the Toronto Book Room in minute detail.

With the positions of Matthew Lang and perhaps even Ephraim Evans under immediate threat, and with them Wesleyan control over both the Toronto Book Room and the *Christian Guardian*, the Book Committee created a third locus of authority in the form of a much larger Book Committee with the power to override the decisions of the book steward in matters both cultural and financial. Nothing could be published without this new Book Committee's prior authorization. No money could be spent without its approval. Composed of the "President and Secretary of the Conference, the Superintendent of Missions, the Chairman of the Toronto District, the preachers resident in Toronto City, and the superintendents of the Yonge Street and Toronto Circuits," the new Book Committee was required to meet on a monthly basis in order to keep a close eye on the entire business. To facilitate such oversight, members of the committee were afforded free and open access to all the offices and warehouses of the Toronto Book Room. Should even a single member of the committee judge the editor of the newspaper or the book steward negligent or "unfaithful to the trust reposed in him," the Book Committee was authorized summarily to suspend either or both until the next conference at which a formal appeal could be entertained.[5]

By any measure these were extraordinary provisions. Once passed, the editor of the *Christian Guardian* and the book steward became the only officers in the Upper Canadian Methodist polity subject to summary suspension should members of a supervisory committee deem their performance objectionable. This new structure seems to have been enough to dissuade Egerton Ryerson from letting his name stand for editor – at least for the moment. John Ryerson, however, remained undaunted and coasted to an easy victory over Matthew Lang when delegates to the Canada Conference voted in Toronto later that same June. As things turned out, the composition of the new and larger Book Committee promised to make it quite amenable to Ryerson's agenda. Indeed, Ephraim Evans, who returned for one final year as editor of the *Christian Guardian*, was the only member of the committee on whom William Harvard could invariably rely to support his own views. As for the Canadian Methodist side, John Ryerson was joined by his brothers William, as a preacher "resident in Toronto City," and Egerton, who took over the role of conference secretary from William Case. John Ryerson also served simultaneously as the chairman of the Toronto District; the two remaining votes would be cast not only by fellow Canadian Methodists, but by Ryerson's own district subordinates, Hamilton Biggar and Rowley Heyland of the Toronto and Yonge Street circuits. With the Book Committee thus dominated by Canadian Methodists, British Wesleyans would find it all but impossible to interfere with the Toronto Book Room until the next annual conference. By then, it would be far too late. In the meantime, John Ryerson had a free hand to govern the affairs of the Toronto Book Room as he saw fit.

II

The resumption of Canadian Methodist control over the Toronto Book Room had enduring consequences for the continued development of Methodist religious identity in Upper Canada. Having "a Canadian preacher for book agent" reopened the market to the Methodist Book Concern's inexpensive books and periodicals in a way that no longer threatened to undermine the political advances that Methodists in the colony had achieved as a consequence of their union with British

Wesleyans; moreover, it destabilized the union itself by eliminating one of the key material benefits Canadian Methodists had originally hoped to enjoy as participants in the London Book Room's transatlantic market for books. With proof that British books would remain expensive and difficult to acquire even with a British Wesleyan conducting the Toronto Book Room's affairs, together with a purely commercial approach to the market that rendered the Concern's denominational rhetoric meaningless in Upper Canada, the stage was set for John Ryerson to displace the London Book Room's offerings with books that were more affordable and more readily available from New York. From this time forward, the vast majority of books found in Methodist hands in Upper Canada, whatever fluctuations might occur in Canadian Methodist polity, would be unashamedly American in manufacture.

Lang, Harvard, and Evans clearly played a role in crafting many of the new policies intended to place pre-emptive administrative strictures on the autonomy of the book steward. Nevertheless, one of the clearest indications that these men had met their match in the Ryerson brothers can be found in a blanket change to the standard discount Methodist preachers were entitled to receive from the Toronto Book Room on all resale orders. Under the arrangement Egerton Ryerson had made with the London Book Room back in 1833, the province's preachers, who were obliged to obtain all their inventory from the Toronto Book Room, were eligible for a paltry 10 per cent discount. Under the new terms instituted by John Ryerson in 1837, that discount was increased to 16 per cent "on all purchases ... as some compensation for their trouble and responsibility." This steeper discount was just a tiny fraction below the 17½ per cent discount the Toronto Book Room received on books it ordered from the Wesleyan Book Room in London for which the latter did not own the copyright – a discount that, moreover, was exclusive of the duties and premiums John Ryerson complained about so bitterly in his earlier letter to Egerton. What this meant in practice was that the Toronto Book Room could no longer afford to sell the bulk of the London Book Room's offerings to the province's preachers without incurring a loss on every sale it made. Thus, as long as this new discount remained in force, the book steward, whoever he might be, would have no choice but to stock his shelves in Toronto by relying on the 40 per cent discount that Lord and Case had secured for Canadians on the Methodist Book Concern's wares at the 1836 General Conference.[6]

John Ryerson, now firmly in control at the Toronto Book Room and unhampered by the Book Committee thanks to his brothers William and Egerton, set about dispensing with as much of Lang's left over business as he could. First on the agenda was finding a way to clear the shelves of Lang's remaining London Book Room stock together with unsold copies of that ill-advised Canadian edition of *The Village Blacksmith*. Nothing, of course, was ever again heard of Lang's plans to publish a Canadian "edition of the life of Rev. J. Smith, as also that of John Nelson." Not all the irons that Lang had left in the fire, however, could be dispensed with quite so easily.

Under Matthew Lang's direction, work on "a small Pocket Edition of the best tunes, suited to the various meters of our hymns, and familiar to the Methodists, particularly from Europe" was already well advanced by the time the Methodist delegates met in conference the previous June. As it happened, before John Ryerson could even assume his new role at the Toronto Book Room, Alex Davidson, who had been commissioned by Lang to prepare a "Book of Sacred Music," had completed his work on the project. Ryerson might well have been able to let Davidson's manuscript languish for a time without too much complaint from the Book Committee, but both he and his Canadian brethren almost certainly felt the need for a hymnbook of their own almost as keenly as the British Wesleyans did. Hymnbooks were special books for evangelicals, and ones that spoke powerfully to their collective religious identity. From a purely practical point of view, moreover, everyone in a singing congregation needed to have the same hymnbook so that worshippers could all turn to the correct hymn when a number was called out. Thus, the uneven use of an American hymnbook, even one unencumbered by the Methodist Book Concern's rhetoric, would be awkward and impractical.[7]

Canadians and Wesleyans were agreed on this much, then: a new hymnbook for Methodists in Upper Canada was very much to be desired. The only question that remained when Ryerson assumed control of the Toronto Book Room was not whether such a book would appear, but on whose press it would be printed. Type for musical notation was not yet available in Upper Canada, and because such notation was required, the hymnbook could not be printed in the colony. That left John Ryerson with just two options: he could either look across the border to the United States or across the Atlantic to England. There can be little doubt about where William Harvard would have wanted the business to be directed: "not so much" as William Ryerson had remarked a month earlier, "for *our good*, as for their own benefit and the advantage of the English Connexion." And although John Ryerson could rely on his Canadian Methodist majority on the Book Committee to support his decision, William Harvard and that Wesleyan cat's-paw Ephraim Evans still had it within their power to stir up trouble if they chose to dig in their heels. With that in mind, and with no practical way to exclude Evans as editor of the *Christian Guardian*, the Ryersons did what they could to make sure that Harvard's preferences would not be consulted on the matter of where the hymnbook was to be printed.[8]

III

The ink on the Conference minutes recording his election was hardly dry before John Ryerson rushed his first large order to the Methodist Book Concern. By midsummer, book agents in New York had already printed two notices in the *Christian Advocate* indicating that some four boxes of books were on their way to "J Ryerson, Toronto, U.C. via Rochester." Around the same time, Ryerson dispatched James Evans – who, unlike his brother Ephraim, had never repudiated American Methodism – to New York "to superintend the publication of several books made or translated into the Chippeway language." It was a remarkable move considering that only four years earlier, when Canadian Methodist anxieties about the dangers of the Concern's imprint had been approaching their apogee, Egerton Ryerson had used the *Guardian*'s own press to publish Evans's first Native translation in Toronto. Now, with the Methodist Book Concern's rhetorical bond between a book's material and cultural production entirely severed in British North America, John Ryerson appears to have let economy of time and money fully govern his choices. Since no special type or musical notation was required, and since Evans did not have his books stereotyped in New York, there can be no other explanation for why Ryerson chose not to publish Evans's translations in Toronto on his own press.[9]

It is a testament to the extent to which John Ryerson and his brothers were now convinced that the Methodist Book Concern's wares, emptied of their denominational status, could no longer compromise Methodism in Upper Canada that these changes unfolded in a time of serious political upheaval in the province. With the editorial support of Ephraim Evans at the *Christian Guardian* firmly behind the province's conservatives – a good example of just the kind of political interference the British Wesleyans were only too happy to encourage – they had finally regained control of the Legislative Assembly a month earlier. This led to further political polarization in Upper Canada as moderate reformers reorganized themselves in anticipation that a sympathetic new lieutenant governor, Sir Francis Bond Head, might be amenable to their perspectives. Tensions continued to rise, moreover, when Bond Head, after quickly losing patience with the political paralysis in the colony, prorogued the Assembly and inadvertently invited an open rebellion by setting himself against the province's reformers. Despite this political turmoil, and the fears it stoked among some that American-style republicanism might yet swamp the province and sever connections with the British metropole, John Ryerson persisted in his reliance on the Methodist Book Concern to fill his shelves in Toronto and, from there, the saddlebags of the province's itinerant preachers.[10]

Although their power to influence, much less control, the business transacted at the Toronto Book Room was now greatly reduced, the British Wesleyans appear to have done what they could to keep an eye on Ryerson and, where possible, impede his new policies. For example, although Ephraim Evans had planned to travel to New York almost immediately after the conclusion of that year's annual conference, he was prevented from doing so when Joseph Stinson, who held the denomination's purse strings, failed to provide the money he needed for the trip. "I have been very much disappointed," Evans complained in a letter to his wife written towards the end of July, "in not hearing from Brother Stinson, and the Banks all being closed, and money very scare, I have not been able to buy, borrow, or steal enough for my journey ... I have nothing to do, and have to watch and pray much to keep from murmuring every moment." At the time, Evans seemed not to have realized how important his role on the Book Committee of the Canada Conference had become to the British Wesleyans: since Matthew Lang's defeat, he had become the only member of the committee besides William Harvard who could be counted on to champion Wesleyan interests and, as needed, oppose whatever the Ryersons may have been doing behind the scenes. Stinson's consistent foot dragging ultimately prolonged Evans's delay from four weeks to something closer to four months. But as things finally turned out, the Wesleyans might just as well have let Evans travel. After all, he and Harvard remained a minority on the Book Committee and as such were quite as powerless to stop the Ryersons as those preachers had become determined to have their own way.[11]

While Evans quietly nursed his frustrations, John Ryerson hurriedly called a "special Meeting" of the new Book Committee before Egerton left town to ensure that the Toronto Book Room would be supplied with its own hymnbook cheaply, quickly, and in the way that the Ryerson brothers thought best. In addition to himself and his brothers Egerton and William, only Ephraim Evans, whose daily presence at the *Guardian* office would have made it all but impossible to exclude, attended. Despite the absence of almost half of the committee, including not coincidentally the new president of the Conference, William Harvard, important and expensive business was transacted. With almost unseemly dispatch, the Book Committee resolved that "an edition of 2,000 copies of the 'Sacred Harmony' be published forthwith" and that "Brother James Evans, who is about to proceed to New York, be respectfully requested to superintend its publication, and to get it printed part in plain, and part in patent notes, if practicable." If James's brother Ephraim Evans had any objections, they were brushed aside without comment. Harvard's anticipated displeasure when he found out that John Ryerson and his brothers had pushed through a decision to commission a new hymnbook in New York and not London seems to have been equally inconsequential in the minds of the committee's majority.[12]

An edition as large as this was a risky undertaking from almost any perspective. Although their meeting was not convened directly under those Toronto Book Room shelves that continued to groan under the weight of unsold copies of Lang's edition of *The Village Blacksmith*, the Ryersons were not inattentive to how much hung on the success of this undertaking. Everything would come down to price. A hymnbook was a practical tool that had to find its way into the hands of the overwhelming majority of those making up local congregations. With that in mind, and in order to save time and money, and retain control over the binding process, the Book Committee ordered James Evans to import the books in sheets. This was important since, although the Methodist Book Concern had been selected on grounds of economy and convenience alone, a hymnbook possessed a unique denominational character. Used in communal worship as well as for private devotion, it was the one book, besides the Bible, that could be found in the saddlebags of Methodist preachers everywhere. *Sacred Harmony* appeared in 1838, and it bore no indication that it had been printed using stereotype plates manufactured in New York. Instead, the title page simply declared that it has been "published" by John Ryerson at the Conference Office in Toronto, as indeed, it had been. For those who purchased it and sang from its pages, the circumstances of this hymnbook's material production were entirely irrelevant. What really mattered was the book's utility, affordability, and widespread availability. And that is exactly how the Ryersons wanted it.[13]

John Ryerson was far less coy when it came to the general stock of the Toronto Book Room. He did not wait for all the various denominational, cultural, and commercial complications attendant on the relatively protracted production of the hymnbook to be resolved before directing his energies towards reinvigorating that business. As soon as he had on hand a large shipment of books from New York, he ran his first Toronto Book Room catalogue, in the 6 September issue of the *Christian*

Guardian. In what must have struck some readers as oddly symmetrical to his brother's 1833 "BEAUTIFUL ENGLISH EDITIONS" catalogue, John Ryerson's catalogue consisted of thirty-five items under the heading "JUST RECEIVED *from* New York and for sale at the Wesleyan-Methodist Book-Room." Unlike Lang, and even his own brother before him, John Ryerson put a great deal of energy into issuing new and larger catalogues on an ongoing basis. The regular appearance of those catalogues also demonstrated that Ryerson's efforts were bearing real fruit: books were selling once again.[14]

The very next week Ryerson published a new catalogue listing hundreds of new titles – so many that it is highly unlikely he had them all on hand at the time of publication. This was the largest catalogue the Toronto Book Room had ever issued by a wide margin, and it was grounded in an appeal that was entirely economic in nature. Ryerson made no mention of how the profits from the sale of these books would be used to help starving widows and feckless orphans, rescue the souls of destitute settlers, or preach the Gospel to benighted Natives. These books were to be bought because they were cheap. "A *bonus* of ten *per cent.*," the advertisement proclaimed, "will be given in Books, on all orders for Sabbath schools, if accompanied by *cash*."[15]

Aggressive pricing of this kind had its desired effect: by the time John Ryerson completed his tenure as book steward, in June 1842, the holdings of Methodist Sunday school libraries across the province had grown fourfold, from 2,604 volumes to 11,372 volumes. Yet another catalogue appeared the following week in which Ryerson included, for the first time, brief book reviews of selected titles then in stock. By late October, the book steward was promising another large shipment from New York. "Our friends," the notice concluded, "especially in distant parts of the Province, will please send their orders immediately, that they may be executed before the close of navigation." In early November, James Evans left New York bringing with him "nine large boxes of books" from the Methodist Book Concern as well as seventeen boxes of stereotype plates for *Sacred Harmony* that the book agents had advised him would result in long-term economies when second and subsequent editions were eventually needed. To preachers and customers scattered all across the colony's preaching circuits, the changes John Ryerson had made – in less than half a year – in the price and availability of books must have seemed just short of revolutionary.[16]

The final step in Ryerson's reforms occurred on 29 November 1837, when on the eve of William Lyon Mackenzie's Rebellion, the Book Committee of the Canada Conference met to deal with the debt Canadian Methodists continued to owe the London Book Room. Attended by

William Harvard and Ephraim Evans, as well as John and William Ryerson, the committee authorized the book steward "to borrow the sum of £250 from the U.C. Academy, for the purchase of Bills of Exchange, to pay John Mason and T. Tegg & Co. of London." This was an astonishing move. Far from having an excess of funds to cover shortfalls at the Toronto Book Room, the Academy continued to teeter daily on the verge of bankruptcy as, in the words of John Ryerson, "the income of the institution [did] not more than pay half the expenses." Indeed, as even William Harvard probably knew, all of the £250 the Book Committee allotted to pay John Mason at the Wesleyan Book Room in London would have to come out of John Ryerson's own pocket. How had things become so terribly desperate? Moreover, why was there suddenly such urgency to settle things with London?[17]

Four days before the Book Committee passed this resolution, Egerton Ryerson had written a long letter to Robert Alder complaining that promises made by the government to extend financial support to the Upper Canada Academy had not been met – and, although they knew it not, would not be met until February 1838. John Ryerson, meanwhile, had been obliged to secure a personal loan from the province's receiver general for the enormous amount of £1,200. Nor was it even yet forgotten that all this trouble would have been saved had William Lord not recklessly insisted on representing the Canadian claim against the Methodist Book Concern in Ryerson's place. "It is also the full conviction from leading brethren," he observed angrily, "that had I attended the American General Conference, instead of being in England, such an arrangement would have been made as to have secured to our Connexion what was due us from the New York Book Concern, which amounts to more than I obtained in England." Instead, John Ryerson was now personally in debt to the banks and to the receiver general for £2,000, Egerton Ryerson for £3,400, and Ephraim Evans for £2,000. That John Ryerson, a man on whom debt did not weigh lightly, was willing to make such a payment to Mason under these conditions is a clear indication that either the British Wesleyans were exerting enormous pressure on the Canadians to clear their debt with the London Book Room, or that John Ryerson himself was almost morbidly anxious to be free of it. Whatever the cause, this left Upper Canadian Methodists less dependent on John Mason for books and periodicals than at any time since October 1833. Even more importantly, it seems to have helped raise new doubts in the minds of the Ryerson brothers about the continued value of the union between themselves and the British Wesleyans.[18]

Although the failure of the Upper Canada Rebellion was followed by a strong backlash of conservatism across the province, John Ryerson's policies at the Toronto Book Room remained largely unaltered. Ephraim Evans, meanwhile, used the *Christian Guardian* to show that the colonial administration had the support of the province's British Wesleyans in putting down the rebels. Perhaps in part because Canadian Methodists were now less dependent on the Wesleyans for the functioning of their denominational economy – such as it was – both John and Egerton Ryerson began to shift their sympathies towards an emergent reformism in the province that was more moderate in tone than William Lyon Mackenzie's. In March 1838, John Ryerson wrote to Egerton to complain about the *Christian Guardian*'s gratuitous anti-Americanism and its appeasement of a new wave of conservative sentiment so pronounced it even threatened to resurrect John Strachan's pretensions to religious establishment. The best way to put a stop to it, John argued for a second time, was for his brother Egerton to finally step forward "to take the Editorship of the *Guardian* again."[19]

Tensions between the Ryersons and the British Wesleyans reached a final breaking point when, on 12 April 1838, the colonial government publicly executed two of the rebels for treason. John and Egerton Ryerson judged the executions to be unforgivably and indefensibly draconian, while William Harvard and the *Christian Guardian* not only applauded the government's action, but also published a pastoral letter urging the province's Methodists "to institute an inquiry in all their Societies for any who had compromised their character of loyalty during the late events." This was too much to bear. The following month, Egerton Ryerson issued a very public and thoroughly embarrassing rebuke of the *Guardian* and the Wesleyans in the *Upper Canada Herald*. "The discipline of the church does not authorize us to become the judge of another man's political opinions," Ryerson insisted, much to the exasperation of both Harvard and Evans.[20]

Many were tempted to see in this distressingly public conflict the beginning of the end of the union of the British Wesleyans and the Canadian Methodists. As earlier developments in the affairs at the Toronto Book Room clearly show, however, that cleavage had begun to open long before this. Disagreement over the supply of books and periodicals to the colony's Methodists, and John Ryerson's retaking of the Toronto Book Room on behalf of Canadian Methodist interests, had helped to prepare the ground for this later more public break with Harvard and his British Wesleyan brethren. Had John and Egerton Ryerson not already worked so well together to reassert control of the Toronto Book Room despite the opposition of Harvard and Evans, and in the process vastly diminished their dependency on the London Book Room, it seems less certain Egerton Ryerson would have responded as quickly and as firmly as he did. It is somewhat ironic, then, that although John Ryerson provided his brother with both encouragement and a model for retaking control of the *Christian Guardian*, it would be John, and not Egerton, who would lose his nerve as the union began to splinter beyond repair.

IV

When the Conference of the Wesleyan Methodist Church in Canada convened in late June 1838 under the presidency of William Harvard, delegates elected Egerton Ryerson editor of the *Christian Guardian*, as planned. John Ryerson continued in his post as book steward at the Toronto Book Room. With these complementary positions now under Canadian control for the first time since before the union, it soon became painfully clear that the Ryersons had lost all interest in appeasing Wesleyan sensibilities. John Ryerson, of course, continued his earlier policy of publishing catalogues offering American books at the Book Room and through Methodist preachers across the province – always and loudly for the cheapest possible prices. Egerton, meanwhile, lost no time resurrecting his favourite political hobbyhorse in the form of a string of editorials demanding that the Clergy Reserves be secularized. And this was exactly the sort of thing the Wesleyans did not want to see in the *Christian Guardian*. Indeed, it was the very thing William Lord had been dispatched to Upper Canada years earlier to stop. When it became clear to Wesleyans overseas that Harvard was incapable of preventing Ryerson from "meddling in partisan politics," the London Missionary Committee dispatched the reliable Robert Alder to once again "put a *quietus* on the *Guardian* ... and to bring the Canadian body into a greater state of submission to the parent Conference." Upon arriving, however, Alder soon discovered that the circumstances on the ground were much altered since he had last visited the province.[21]

A year later, when the delegates to the Canaada Conference met again in Hamilton in June 1839, Robert Alder was among them – confident and eager to set in motion the same strategy that had helped him secure the upper hand at the time of the union some seven years earlier. "If we are to do anything with the Yankee," he had quipped in a letter to a leading Wesleyan overseas, back in the summer of 1832, "we must be Lords of the Treasury." Although Alder no longer had the dexterous aid of the Ryerson brothers at his disposal, he remained formidable even without their help and managed to push through several resolutions that increased Wesleyan control over the purse strings in Upper Canada. Alder was unable, however, to prevent the re-election of both John and Egerton Ryerson to their influential posts in Toronto. His interventions thus had little impact on the daily operations of either the *Christian Guardian* or the Toronto Book Room. Egerton Ryerson continued his editorial policies. John Ryerson continued to turn a profit by relying on the Methodist Book Concern to stock his shelves – although he no longer made a point of advertising that the books on offer were imported from the United States. Perhaps this was meant as a concession to Alder and the Wesleyans. If so, it was a very small one. Indeed, with the Book Room operating on strictly economic rather than denominational principles, John Ryerson might easily have argued that the supplier on whom he chose to rely was completely irrelevant as long as the books were cheap, of good quality, and readily available. Certainly, everyone knew that the Methodist Book Concern continued to offer Canadians the best terms they could find anywhere.[22]

By the spring of 1840, an impossible impasse had grown up between the Ryersons and the British Wesleyans. As far as the latter were concerned, Egerton Ryerson was to blame for most of the trouble. With the union now on the verge of collapse, Egerton and his brother John travelled to Baltimore to attend the General Conference of the Methodist Episcopal Church. American Methodists, and Nathan Bangs in particular, commiserated with the Ryersons and offered to secure Egerton a church in New York City if Canadian delegates to the Canada Conference failed to stand with him against the Wesleyans. Indeed, so worried was Ryerson about that possible reversal that he took the trouble to set things in order for a hasty return later that summer. "I have concluded and made arrangements," he wrote in late May, "to take a station in the city of New York for one, if not for two years." John Ryerson had similar plans to retreat to the safety of an American pulpit sometime the following year if things turned out as badly as they both feared.[23]

After returning north to attend the Canada Conference – possibly for the last time – Egerton Ryerson found himself unexpectedly cleared of all charges by a vote of fifty-nine to eight. More than that, he and his brother William were selected as representatives to attend the Conference of the Wesleyan Methodist Church in Britain later that summer to sort out the difficulties that had grown up between the two bodies. The choice was so inexpressibly injudicious that it amounted to a deliberate insult. Egerton and William Ryerson sailed for England on the first of July and did not return to Upper Canada for almost three months. John Ryerson, meanwhile, in the absence of his brothers, suddenly lost his nerve and scrambled to dispatch an order to the London Book Room. As soon as the shipment arrived, he rushed a new catalogue into the pages of the *Christian Guardian*. "JUST RECEIVED," it read, "at the Methodist Book Room, No. 9 Wellington Building, the following BOOKS from London." Although a striking departure from past practice – and one that demonstrated an extraordinary willingness on his part to incur financial losses at the Book Room if it meant easing tensions with the Wesleyans – in the end it was all for nothing. As many no doubt expected, Egerton and William Ryerson had not managed to smooth things over. On the contrary, the brothers' perceived obduracy – perhaps best exemplified by a marathon speech Egerton delivered to the British Wesleyans that tested the patience of conference delegates for an astonishing ten hours – had only inflamed things further. John Ryerson was able to run his new catalogue just twice more before his brothers returned to the province to announce that the union had been unilaterally dissolved by the Wesleyans. The news appears to have shaken John Ryerson badly. He did not run another catalogue in the *Christian Guardian* for almost an entire year.[24]

The ten months following Egerton and William Ryerson's return to Upper Canada were dark ones for the province's Methodists. Despite the passage of several blustering resolutions that roundly condemned British Wesleyan unilateralism, Canadian Methodists must have been astonished when, among the eleven preachers who abandoned them for the Wesleyans, they counted not only expected turncoats like Ephraim Evans, but also their respected elder in the faith, William Case. There was, moreover, a great deal of anxiety among Canadians more generally as the Act of Union to unite the upper and lower provinces came into effect in February 1841. Canadian Methodists, meanwhile, used the *Christian Guardian* to put on a brave face. George Playter, for example, published two influential letters arguing that the dissolution of the union was illegal and that, indeed, it was the Wesleyans who were behaving as schismatics. Joseph Stinson and Matthew Richey, for their part, tried to draw the Americans into the debate by writing to the editor of the *Western Christian Advocate* in an attempt to justify their continued presence in the colony. Not surprisingly, they were rebuffed. "We still think that the labors of the Wesleyan preachers in Upper Canada are not only uncalled for," the editors responded, "but that they are a hindrance to the promotion of religion among the Methodists, and others, in Upper Canada; and, with the light we now have, we would say we hope the English Wesleyans will go where they are more needed."[25]

In the meantime, John Ryerson toured the eastern parts of what was now called Canada West to bolster morale and began publishing extracts from his journal in the *Christian Guardian*. Despite the air of assurance these entries projected, however, John Ryerson found himself deeply divided. When not busy shoring up the flagging confidence of his fellow Methodists, the book steward quietly prostrated himself before Joseph Stinson and offered terms that amounted to little less than complete capitulation in an effort he believed would ultimately save institutional Methodism from ruin. According to Stinson, Ryerson promised that, in exchange for reunification, his brethren would place everything – church property, chapels, the Upper Canada Academy, and even the Toronto Book Room – "under the control of the British Conference," while his brother Egerton reluctantly played the role of sacrificial lamb. "I have observed by the discussion, especially by a pamphlet lately published by the [Wesleyan Methodist Missionary] Committee in London, & also in conversation with Mr Stinson, that the whole affair is made to appear as much as possible a matter of difference between the Committee & me personally, & epithets have been multiplied against me in proportion to the want of facts," a beleaguered Egerton Ryerson wrote with an equal measure of candour and bitterness to Nathan Bangs in New York that May: "It is also thought that if there should be failure of success, I could then honorably retire to the U.S. I am no theorist; but I hate despotism as I do Satan, & I love liberty as I do life." Terms this grovelling must have struck the British Wesleyans as almost implausible. In any event, they did not remain on the table long enough for the British Wesleyans to take advantage of them.[26]

By the end of June 1841, evidence that the tide had turned was beginning to mount. As membership statistics from the province's preaching circuits were enumerated it soon became clear which of the two parties was having the greater success. Despite whatever losses they suffered when the union with British Wesleyans was dissolved, Methodist membership rolls had grown by more than 660 to a total of more than 17,000 formal members across the province. Numbers like that encouraged the Ryersons, even John Ryerson, to harden their resolve against their Wesleyan brethren. William Ryerson, an early opponent of the union, was elected president of the Canada Conference, and John Ryerson was returned once again to the Toronto Book Room as book steward. Anson Green, an immigrant from the United States, was elected secretary of the Conference. This, however, was only the beginning. By late August, a petition to reconstitute the Upper Canada Academy as a degree-granting institution under the new name Victoria College passed through both the Legislative Assembly and the Legislative Council. Within days, Lord Sydenham, governor general of the newly united Canadas, gave the bill his royal assent. Egerton Ryerson, far from being forced out of the province, was appointed the first president of Victoria College by its Board of Governors in early September.[27]

With all these victories to buoy him up, for the first time in almost a year, John Ryerson published a new catalogue in the *Christian Guardian* advertising American books. What was far more striking than Ryerson's own renewed willingness to resupply his shelves with the Methodist Book Concern's discounted wares, however, was that the British Wesleyans who remained in the province to oppose the Canadians did not once point to John Ryerson's business practices in Toronto as evidence of a compromised religious identity or proof of American cultural hegemony. The absence of such accusations – especially when such accusations would have been so easy to make in the pages of their new denominational periodical, *The Wesleyan* – amounted to powerful evidence on all sides that Canadian Methodists had at last succeeded in fully reframing the Methodist Book Concern's books in the minds of most Upper Canadians as purely commercial goods that implied no disloyalty on the part of those who purchased and read them.[28]

With the "dark night of doubts and fears" now passed, John Ryerson, and later his successor at the Toronto Book Room, Alexander MacNab, carried on the affairs of the business largely in accordance with the policies put in place after the Canada Conference of 1837. Indeed, so much confidence did MacNab have in the future of the Toronto Book Room that he might have been guilty of overstocking the shelves. After receiving two large shipments of books from the Methodist Book Concern, in August and October 1843, he published a notice in the *Christian Guardian* to "direct attention to a Catalogue of Books handed us by the Book Steward on our last page to-day and to say, that it contains but a very limited selection, from the unusually large, diversified, and valuable stock now on hand, at our Establishment." Around the same time, John Ryerson and Anson Green were just returning from New York with stereotype plates for a supplement to their popular hymnbook, *Sacred Harmony*. A year later, however, when Anson Green agreed to take over responsibility for the Book Room from MacNab, he was astonished to find it "in a ruinous condition ... only reporting a gain of nine dollars, and that without making any allowance for shelf-worn books, bad debts, or for paying an appropriation to the Contingent Fund."[29]

Green, a far more hardheaded book steward than MacNab, concentrated his efforts to return the Toronto Book Room to profitability by forging ever closer ties with the Methodist Book Concern as well as by opening up relations with any other publisher – religious or secular – willing to offer him books and periodicals on advantageous terms. Green also used his catalogues to place an even greater emphasis on the value and affordability of his offerings. "A LARGE STOCK OF NEW BOOKS, AT REDUCED PRICES" one such catalogue printed in October

1844 declared. Eschewing all appeals to Methodists as distinct consumers, Green instead extended discounts of 10 per cent – equal to those offered to Methodist preachers under the terms of the 1833 agreement with the London Book Room – to "Ministers of other Denominations" while stressing for a third time that the prices given in the catalogue were "the cheapest we have ever published." In the end, the religious affiliations of those who purchased their books from the Toronto Book Room mattered as little to Green as those publishers supplying them. Thus, while the Methodist Book Concern's decidedly denominational market in the United States continued to grow because it was closed off from all competitors – and because it had an enormous number of decidedly denominational readers – Green's market in Canada was thoroughly commercial in its orientation and founded on a principle of complete openness. Appeals to denominational identity or religious outcomes mattered far less in such a context than guaranteeing potential customers the lowest possible prices.[30]

As Anson Green continued to expand his market in Canada West by offering the lowest possible prices and the steepest possible discounts to readers of all stripes, including those enrolled in the province's common schools, John Ryerson was once again quietly laying plans for an eventual reunion with the Wesleyans. A year later, he and Green made a trip to England to attend the international convention of the Evangelical Alliance. While there they were encouraged to learn that British Wesleyan support for the establishment principle had largely evaporated in the heat of the Disruption of the Church of Scotland, the Oxford Movement, and the refusal of the Church of England to repudiate Puseyism. In response to these changed circumstances, Green and Ryerson presented a proposal that would form the basis for reunion between the two bodies the following year. With both sides weary of competition, reunion was finally effected in June 1847.[31]

Recent historians generally agree that, with one or two minor exceptions, the terms of reunion were essentially the same as those in 1833. But while that may have been true in matters of ecclesiastical polity, there was nevertheless less evidence to support the view that a perfect facsimile of British Wesleyanism in Canada West was desirable. This was nowhere clearer than when it came to the Toronto Book Room. Unlike the agreement reached in 1833, the terms of reunion were unaccompanied by any agreement to resume importing books and periodicals from the London Book Room. It was now recognized on both sides that such an arrangement would be hopelessly impractical. Instead, the Toronto Book Room became increasingly intent on growing its market beyond its own denominational boundaries by taking advantage of the Methodist Book Concern's discounts to undercut its competitors in Canada. As this commercial approach to the market in Canada became both more entrenched and more successful, British Wesleyans simply gave up all interest in governing the affairs of the Toronto Book Room.[32]

V

As the Wesleyans accommodated themselves to the fact that the London Book Room's wares would never find much of a market in Canada as long as the book steward continued to place such enormous emphasis on the cost of goods and the commercial aspects of the business, something at least as remarkable was happening outside the denomination and in the province's nascent public education system. Although it has generally been understood that Methodism throughout the first half of the nineteenth century was obliged in all things to conform to the province's cultural mainstream by shedding its connections to American Methodists, for the first time in the colony's history, the current of influence showed clear signs of beginning to flow in the opposite direction. That is, Methodist determination to frame books from the United States as straightforward commercial goods to be judged on their material and economic merits rather than their significance as cultural status objects was beginning to take hold more broadly. And, as so often was the case, Egerton Ryerson was at the centre of these efforts.

Ever attentive to the importance of colonial politics and the balance of power between the province's conservatives and reformers, Egerton Ryerson made the surprising decision to side with Governor General Charles Metcalfe in the spring of 1844 when the latter undemocratically refused to make his Executive Council responsible to the elected Legislative Assembly. Ryerson published a series of nine tracts arguing in favour of Metcalfe's prerogative to act against the wishes of his counsellors. By that October, in large part thanks to Ryerson's intervention, the conflict reached a plateau when elections returned a majority of candidates in agreement with the governor general's position. That Metcalfe was grateful to Ryerson is beyond doubt. Indeed, it was widely believed, despite Ryerson's own strenuous denials, that his subsequent appointment as the province's chief superintendent of education – a monumental achievement for a Canadian Methodist under any circumstances but especially so considering that the Methodists and Wesleyans remained estranged from one another at that time – was a reward for his service in the controversy. Reward or not, the appointment had long-term consequences for both Methodists and Wesleyans, for the wider province, and especially for American publishers hoping to market their wares in Canada.[33]

At the time that Egerton Ryerson took up his new post, despite the revival of the Methodist Book Concern's market in Canada, and the refusal of the Wesleyans to point to that market as a sign of Methodist disloyalty, suspicion of American books in the province continued to linger in some quarters – particularly among those inclined to hold strongly conservative views. Unsurprisingly, much of that suspicion found new life after the Upper Canada Rebellion – led as it had been by that radical reformer, admirer of republicanism, and former mayor of Toronto, William Lyon Mackenzie. "Every Canadian school book," thundered the conservative *Patriot*, "ought to be *written* by a Briton, *printed* by a Briton, and *sold* by a Briton." Robert Baldwin Sullivan, Robert Baldwin's cousin and a political turncoat, reported as a member of Lieutenant Governor George Arthur's Executive Council that American history books in particular taught Canadian students to believe that "the British Government ... is a chimerical monster ... Ireland is a joyless land of bogs, pigs and catholics [*sic*], and Scotland an out of the way place in which the mountains and the men have a national and barbarous prejudice against decent covering." By the early 1840s, even some of the province's teachers had begun to grumble. One protested that the American books he was forced to rely on in the classroom were "decidedly anti-British," while another complained that an unnamed history of the United States depicted "British soldiers in the darkest colours."[34]

With the province's reformers so completely put out by Ryerson's advocacy on behalf of Metcalfe's unilateralism, and with his own position as chief superintendent of education far from secure, the former editor of the *Christian Guardian* had to at least appear to be on the side of the conservatives. Of course, he did not share any of their prejudices about American books – everything he and his brother John had accomplished at the Toronto Book Room attested to that fact. But while Egerton Ryerson was abroad on extensive educational tours of Europe and America, the political landscape of the province changed dramatically. Metcalfe was abruptly forced from office by illness, while Baldwin and his supporters continued to gain influence. Ryerson lost another supporter when, in the midst of a massive influx of potato famine victims in 1847, typhus broke out and claimed the life of Roman Catholic Bishop Michael Power, a man Ryerson understood to be a staunch ally in his struggle for public education. Under these circumstances, it is not difficult to imagine how doubtful the ground under Egerton Ryerson's feet must have felt when he returned to Canada. "It is quite certain," his brother John warned him in February 1847, just a few months before a reunion with the Wesleyans took effect, "that combined and powerful efforts are being made against you by certain parties, no doubt with a determination to destroy you as a public man, if they can. The feeling of the 'radical' party is most inveterate. They are determined, by hook or by crook, to turn you out of the office of Chief Superintendent of Education."[35]

In the summer of 1847 – at a time when Anson Green was in the middle of negotiating yet steeper discounts with the Methodist Book Concern while continuing to call attention to the "very moderate prices" of books at the Toronto Book Room – Egerton Ryerson submitted a *Special Report on the Operations of the Common School Act of 1846* to the Legislative Assembly. Its purpose was, in part, to defend Section XXX of the 1846 Act banning the use of "foreign Books" – a euphemism universally understood to mean American books – from all of the British colony's common schools. In keeping with the criticisms and views of political conservatives, Ryerson's report denounced such books "because they are, with very few exceptions, anti-British, in every sense of the word." Ryerson, however, went further than that – further than all but a small handful of the most outspoken ideological critics. "I believe it will be found, on inquiry," he speculated darkly, "that in precisely those parts of Upper Canada where the United States Books had been used most extensively, there the spirit of insurrection in 1837 and 1838, was most prevalent." What Ryerson's *Report* failed to foreground, of course, was that it was precisely in those parts of the colony where Methodists had been the most successful in establishing preaching circuits and Sunday school libraries that "the United States Books had been used most extensively."[36]

This was, of course, merely a pose. As subsequent events would demonstrate, Egerton Ryerson's opposition to American schoolbooks was adopted not to prevent these books from entering the province, but as a strategy to shore up his support among conservatives and thereby prevent a growing tide of reform resentment from sweeping him out of his post. Ryerson well knew that he could not maintain a legal ban on American books in the province's common schools for long without leaving himself, the Toronto Book Room, and Methodist preachers across the province, open to the charge of hypocrisy. Not surprisingly, Ryerson began to back away almost immediately from this unqualified condemnation of American books. Having successfully adopted the role of chief critic, he was uniquely placed to soften his resolve, and by extension the resolve of his conservative supporters, by stages. That is precisely what he did.[37]

By early 1848, Ryerson was striking a decidedly different tone. In his *Annual Report of Normal, Model, and Common Schools in Upper Canada*, Ryerson suggested that his earlier efforts to procure textbooks from the

National Board of Education in Dublin were not undertaken to displace American schoolbooks, but merely to encourage standardization across classrooms. At the same time, Ryerson provided a far more nuanced critique of American schoolbooks by quietly narrowing the focus of his censure to geography schoolbooks, and American Jesse Olney's popular geographies in particular, describing them as "almost exclusively American [and] particularly hostile against everything British." In the next breath, however, Ryerson recommended American Jedidiah Morse's "new Geography" as the "most impartial, the best constructed, the cheapest and best adapted geography for Canada with which I have yet met." Ryerson extolled the quality of its many maps and woodcuts, as well as the text itself. Indeed, so outstanding was Morse's book that Ryerson had gone so far as to contact the publishers directly – Methodist publishers Harper and Brothers in New York – to arrange for a Canadian edition of the work. "The enterprising publishers have intimated," Ryerson enthused, "that if I would prepare an additional quarto page or two on the statistics, commerce, &c., of Canada, they would insert it and publish an edition of their geography expressly for Canada." Morse's geographies were just the beginning. In the months and years ahead, Egerton Ryerson continued to soften his stance against American schoolbooks in a subtle, but remarkably consistent fashion.[38]

As founding editor of the *Christian Guardian*, Ryerson knew how effective a periodical could be in shifting public opinion. No doubt with his broader cultural agenda at least partly in mind, in January 1848 Ryerson established the *Journal of Education for Upper Canada*. Later that year, he reprinted a review of his 1846 *Report on a System of Public Elementary Instruction for Upper Canada* and his subsequent *Special Report on the Operation of the Common School Act of 1846* that had originally appeared in the *Official Monthly District School Journal for the State of New York*. The American reviewer, while praising Ryerson's initiatives more generally, took strong exception to the prohibition on schoolbooks produced in the United States. "On this subject," the reviewer complained, "there will be increasing public sentiment in favour of using the *best books*, and employing the *best Teachers*, whether of British or American origin. We hope, ere long, to see this restrictive feeling give place to a more generous and liberal policy."[39] There is nothing particularly surprising about these sentiments. After all, one would expect an American writer to object to a ban on American schoolbooks. What is striking is that Ryerson chose to use his new *Journal* to disseminate these sentiments to readers in Canada.

His reasons for publishing it were soon clear. Ryerson wanted to bring his policy into contention, and by publishing a piece that opposed it, he afforded himself a strategic opportunity to reflect publicly on the ban and even to speculate on how that ban might evolve in the future. Ryerson knew, of course, that it was incumbent on him to offer at least a perfunctory justification of the prohibition. Indeed, Ryerson's justification was so cursory and so brief that it amounted to little more than a prelude to his subsequent announcement that major changes were in the offing. "When we advance a step further in our School System," he wrote, "by providing for the establishment of Common School Libraries in Upper Canada, we doubt not but our Board of Education will readily adopt and recommend perhaps nineteenth-twentieths of the admirable and cheap publications which constitute the Common School Libraries of the States of Massachusetts and New-York." Here was a truly remarkable shift in rhetoric. A straightforward juxtaposition of the soaring anti-Americanism found in Ryerson's 1847 *Special Report* with the conciliatory sentiments expressed in this later piece would make it difficult to credit that they were even the product of the same pen. Yet, here readers learned that, not only was the ban on American schoolbooks undertaken as a strictly temporary measure, but also that as Upper Canadian libraries began to take shape, the province would effectively become an open market to American publishers. This was, not coincidentally, precisely the same policy that Anson Green was following at the Toronto Book Room to such effect as he supplied the rapidly expanding Sunday school libraries across the province.[40]

As Ryerson well knew, Methodists by that time had been at work for twenty years or more building such libraries. With that in mind, he measured his own success in supplying common school libraries against the already considerable holdings of the province's Sunday school libraries. Beginning with his *Annual Report* for 1848, Ryerson included statistics for the number of volumes in the province's Sunday school and common school libraries. That year, he reported 46,926 volumes in Sunday school libraries, but only 1,579 volumes in common school libraries. Two years later, the figures stood at 73,662 volumes in Sunday school libraries and just 4,752 volumes in common school libraries. The problem, Ryerson knew, was one of policy. Sunday school libraries were funded largely by private donation, and were not subject to the provisions or restrictions outlined in the Common School Act. Thus, denominational actors, and most especially his fellow Methodists, were and would remain free to continue filling the shelves of their burgeoning libraries with the cheapest and most readily available books from the United States. Ryerson's experience at the Toronto Book Room had taught him that, even with government monies at his disposal, the only practicable way to close the gap between Sunday school and common school libraries would be to liberalize his own policies governing the importation of American books.[41]

In 1853, Ryerson claimed to open a "new epoch in the intellectual and social history of Upper Canada" when he issued for the first time a general catalogue of books for common school libraries. Here Ryerson set aside without reservation his earlier policies against the use of American schoolbooks. "It will be seen," he wrote, "that the books selected, embrace nearly the whole field of human knowledge – at least so far as it is embraced in the works of popular reading – including the best works of the kind that issue from both the English and American press." Ryerson distributed his catalogues to school trustees with instructions to select titles that would be underwritten by the legislative grant provided in the Common School Act of 1850. The only books to be excluded were those "hostile to the christian [*sic*] religion" and "controversial works on theology." Such catalogues were also used to begin stocking the shelves of free public libraries. Thus, Ryerson moved from being one of Canada's sternest, if thoroughly disingenguous, critics of American books to the chief enabler of a policy that opened the way for a unified North American market for schoolbooks of all kinds. Egerton Ryerson's work as an itinerant preacher, editor of the *Christian Guardian*, and bookseller at the Toronto Book Room all played a key part in this evolution since these experiences had taught him, as well as his fellow Methodists, that books could be treated as straightforward commercial goods in a public market regardless of their geopolitical origins.[42]

VI

Back at the Toronto Book Room, Anson Green remained as intent as ever on filling his shelves and the shelves of the province's burgeoning Sunday school libraries with the best books obtained on the best terms. Although he would not have scrupled to pursue that end with British imprints, high costs continued to rule out the London Book Room and, indeed, virtually all British publishers with the exception of the British and Foreign Bible Society. British books, in the main, were simply too expensive. Green would instead rely on those publishers offering him the best prices. The Methodist Book Concern was most often – but not always – Green's preferred supplier. "In addition to our usual supply of Sabbath School Books," began one advertisement appearing in early July 1847, "we now offer to the public those of the American Sunday School Union, at the Society's prices in Rochester, with the addition merely of the duties and cost of importation."[43]

Exceptions of this kind only served to prove the rule that no other publisher could reliably undercut the Methodist Book Concern for long.

In September 1847, yet another large shipment of Methodist books left New York for the Toronto Book Room. Treating them as nothing more than inexpensive commercial goods with a potentially universal appeal, Green urged Canadians – Methodist as well as non-Methodists alike – to buy them for no other reason than their incomparable affordability. "We have no hesitation," an advertisement appearing about that time ran, "in saying that purchases can be made at the Wesleyan Book Room at as low a figure as any reasonable person could expect – or as any unreasonable person could make them in any establishment in the Province. If there be the least doubt on this subject, we suggest that whoever is skeptical should procure the catalogue of any Canadian house and then compare the prices with the prices attached to similar works in the catalogue issued by our esteemed colleague, the Book Steward." The distance between these straightforward economic appeals and the denominational rhetoric the Methodist Book Concern had pioneered to build and sustain its sprawling market in North America could hardly have been more pronounced.[44]

Green knew he had a good thing going with the Methodist Book Concern. Yet, he wondered if it might not be made even better. As the Canadian representative at the General Conference of the Methodist Episcopal Church held in 1848 – just a year after the Canadians and the British Wesleyans restored their union – Green set about securing a new agreement with the Americans that would result in even steeper discounts. Arguing that the Canadian claim against the Concern had never been properly recognized, Green reported, "I was able to convince the committee that, in reality, they gave us nothing for our stock in their Book Concern." The end result was an agreement so favourable that anything better would have seen the Americans actually paying Green to take their books: The Toronto Book Room would now receive all books and periodicals "at cost price." So advantageous were these terms that the Americans, to protect their own interests in the United States, further stipulated that "the books purchased by the Book Concern in Canada shall not be disposed of in such places as will bring them into competition with the Book Concern in the United States." Remarkably, this extraordinary agreement remained in place for more than fifteen years – until the outbreak of the American Civil War.[45]

With an agreement as advantageous as this now secured, there was little reason for Anson Green to waste time cultivating business relationships with other publishers. Whatever interest he may have had in the London Book Room before the General Conference, by this time had atrophied to almost nothing. Apart from a single resolution passed in 1850 by the Book Committee directing Green to "write to John Mason,

London, requiring of him if he could not furnish the periodicals published by the English Conference at 50 per cent. discount for circulation in Canada," there is little evidence to suggest that the London Book Room's relatively expensive wares occupied much space at all on Methodist shelves in Toronto. By that time, moreover, the Toronto Book Room was on a very firm financial footing. "The Book-room is prospering fine," Green cooed, "We are paying off our debts, have enlarged our building, prepared a vault for the safety of our public documents, and increased our annual grants to Church funds to $800."[46]

A relationship as close as this one between the Toronto Book Room and the Methodist Book Concern would have been enough on its own to ensure the continuance of cordial, even friendly, relations between American and Canadian Methodists. Yet, it seems unlikely that affections did not run deeper than the niceties a strictly economic relationship would necessitate. The rhetorical context in which the Concern's market in Canada had operated for decades would have made it difficult for Canadian Methodists to view its products in quite the same fundamentally uncomplicated fashion that Green's unyielding emphasis on the singular importance of "very moderate prices" might otherwise imply. For many Methodists, particularly those whose membership extended back more than a dozen years, the imprint of the Methodist Book Concern no doubt remained a subtle, but telling reminder of their ongoing membership, not in a single denominational body governed by a common polity, but in an imagined community of transnational readers whose integrity had proven to be far more durable than any of Canadian Methodism's various ecclesiastical arrangements in the previous half-century.[47]

VII

When Canadian Methodists gathered in Brockville for their annual conference in the summer of 1850, they welcomed into their midst a veteran preacher from the United States whose labours in Upper Canada's backwoods almost half a century earlier had earned him a permanent place in their memories. A record of Nathan Bangs's last visit to British North America is preserved in a series of articles he penned for the *Christian Advocate* in which he marvelled at the many hopeful changes that had taken place since he first preached to the colony's "thoughtless and wicked" settlers of old. In the intervening years, Bangs had visited the province on at least one other occasion, in the summer of 1826, to promote the sale and distribution of what was then his new denominational newspaper, the *Christian Advocate*. At that time, Canadian Methodists still operated under the direct supervision of the General

Conference in the United States; British Wesleyan missionaries in Canada remained largely isolated on the eastern side of the Ottawa River; John Strachan's conservative coterie was at the height of its powers under the patronage of Lieutenant Governor Peregrine Maitland; and Egerton Ryerson, whose rebuttal of Strachan had only just appeared in the *Colonial Advocate*, remained an obscure and anonymous figure shielded from public scrutiny by William Lyon Mackenzie's press.[48]

By 1850, it was abundantly clear that Methodist fortunes had changed dramatically. Bangs delighted to boast, not only that Canadian Methodists had achieved "their full share of religious influence" in the province, but also that Egerton Ryerson was "an officer of the government, holding an office of high trust and responsibility, having a general oversight of all the schools in the province." Given his own work as sometime senior book agent of the Methodist Book Concern and founder of the *Christian Advocate*, Bangs was particularly effusive about the fact that Canadian Methodists also had "their own Book Concern established here, in which they keep a suitable variety of books on religious and scientific subjects on sale, and likewise publish the 'Christian Guardian,' a weekly paper which is exerting a hallowed influence on the community throughout the province."[49]

When he had an opportunity to visit Anson Green at the Toronto Book Room and run his eyes over the books filling its shelves, Nathan Bangs must have wondered at how much things had changed – as well as, oddly, how they had stayed the same. In some ways, Green's mid-century offerings were quite different from the books that he had bought from the saddlebags of Methodist preachers while still a young man living in Niagara. The Toronto Book Room's books were printed on machine-made paper. They were bound in cloth rather than plain wrappers, and some of them had been produced from stereotyped plates rather than set type. Yet, they were exactly the same books – written by the same authors, issued in the same editions, printed on the same presses, and constructed of the same materials – as the books Bangs would have so often perused himself at the offices of the Methodist Book Concern near his home in New York City. Green's stock, after all, came almost exclusively from the Methodist Book Concern. Yet, from a cultural point of view, and in this different geopolitical context, they were not at all the same.

Anson Green, unlike his counterparts in the United States, did not promote the sale of the Methodist Book Concern's books in denominational terms at the Toronto Book Room. His advertisements and catalogues instead framed the books he offered to the whole of Canada's reading public as straightforward commodities. They were to be preferred to the offerings of other booksellers not because they indicated something about the purchaser's religious identity, but simply because they were the least expensive on the market. Ironically, the Concern's explicitly denominational strategies in the United States had become so effective at insulating its market there, and its economies of scale so large as that market grew as part of Methodism's wider expansion, that the generous discounts the Concern provided to the Toronto Book Room meant that Green no longer needed to imitate those strategies himself. It was much easier for him to simply undercut the prices of rival booksellers in the province. The result was that, although Methodists in the United States and Upper Canada sold the very same books printed on the very same presses, the nature of these two markets – one emphatically denominational and the other strictly commercial – could hardly have been more different.

The Toronto Book Room's insistence on a wholly commercial approach to its provincial market had surprisingly enduring consequences. Indeed, the Methodist Book Room's thoroughly commercialist reorientation set it apart from the Methodist publishing houses in both Britain and North America. Unlike the London Book Room and the New York Methodist Book Concern, the Methodist Book Room in Toronto no longer defined its market in denominational or even religious terms. As Green's advertisements made clear, the market he intended to reach was composed of all members of the Canadian reading public. This remarkable and highly unusual strategy led to large profits and enormous long-term cultural influence in the nation as a whole.

The Methodist Book and Publishing House, as the Toronto Book Room later came to be known, leveraged the steep discounts afforded to it by Methodists in the United States to set the business on the firmest of financial footings by allowing the book stewards to consistently undercut religious and secular competitors across the entire province. As the business grew to become not only one of the nation's largest, but in the words of Lorne Pierce, the "Mother of Publishers in Canada," it boasted a catalogue of offerings that included "many of the most important books and outstanding authors of the Dominion." The emergence of a publishing agenda that was not merely non-denominational but deliberately inclusive of all Canadian readers anticipated, and perhaps even played a part in bringing about, a later desire on the part of Methodists to become not merely a church in the nation, but a church for the nation. The first steps on that journey – although remarkably easy to miss – came when John Ryerson and Anson Green finally and fully rejected the Methodist Book Concern's denominational rhetoric and insisted that the books they sold under the Methodist banner should and would appeal to all Canadians no matter their religious belief or affiliation.[50]

Conclusion

"Making Our Methodist Book Room a Cultural Mecca for Canada"

In the autumn of 1970, Canadian novelist Graeme Gibson clambered up a weathered bronze statue of Egerton Ryerson – a statue that had loomed at the corner of Church and Gould streets in Toronto since 1889 – to drape around its hoary shoulders a brightly coloured American flag. When Gibson resumed his place on the sidewalk, he led a small crowd of college students in an irreverent rendition of "I'm a Yankee Doodle Dandy" around the statue's base. Gibson and his students were not protesting Ryerson's liberal policies towards the widespread use of American books in the province's schools and libraries in the nineteenth century. Nor were they objecting that the statue commemorating Ontario's first chief superintendent of education, and that served as the locus of their protest, had been manufactured in New York. The true object of their ire was what they held to be the shameful and precipitous sale of the Ryerson Press – since 1919 the name of the trade arm of the Methodist Book and Publishing House – to American publisher McGraw-Hill for more than two million dollars. Even those who worked at the Press seem to have understood that its loss was somehow a betrayal of the man it had been named to commemorate: on the day of the official announcement, an unnamed employee slipped out to the Press's main lobby and quietly covered Ryerson's portrait with black cloth.[1]

Gibson was not alone in his dismay. Many in the Canadian literary community shared his sense of distress at the sale – and with good reason. The Methodist Book and Publishing House had evolved from its earliest days as a supplier of denominational books and periodicals into a soaring pillar of Canadian culture. In 1874, when the British Wesleyans decided that the game in Canada was no longer worth the candle, Methodists from across most of the country united to form the Methodist Church of Canada. Five years later, the Methodist Book and Publishing House came under the direction of famed book steward William Briggs and redoubled its long-standing commercial practice of securing "the best rates and discounts" for all Canadians by remaining in "constant communication with all the prominent publishing houses of England, Scotland and the United States." Briggs's ongoing cultivation of these commercial relationships was so successful that he, like John Ryerson and Anson Green before him, aimed to be all things to all readers: "We can supply you with any book you want," he boasted in one advertisement, "no matter what the subject or where published." Indeed, in the years following Confederation, Briggs and his successors did far more than merely supply Canadian readers with books printed on foreign presses: they also took decisive steps to support, publish, and promote a growing body of original works – including secular works – written by Canadians expressly for the Canadian market.[2]

When Samuel Fallis took over as book steward in 1919, he and his newly hired editor Lorne Pierce worked to deepen and extend this work by transforming the Methodist Book and Publishing House and the newly minted Ryerson Press into, as Pierce termed it, the "the cultural Mecca of Canada." In 1925, after the Methodists united with the Presbyterians and the Congregationalists to form the United Church, Pierce continued to promote Canadian writers in the context of a church that had for some decades already been acknowledged as the dominant Protestant force in Canada. Building on the United Church's nationalist vision for itself, Pierce oversaw the publication of a flood of Canadian books in all genres – poetry, novels, art books, textbooks, and non-fiction – authored by writers from every corner of the country, including to name just a few, Lucy Maud Montgomery, Earl Birney, P.K. Page, Marjorie Pickthall, Dorothy Livesay, Evelyn Richardson, A.M. Kline, Alice Munro, and many others. Between 1937 and 1964, the Ryerson Press boasted no fewer than twenty separate works that had gone on to win Governor General's Awards. When Lorne Pierce finally retired, he did so with every confidence that as Canada and the United Church continued to grow together, so too would the Press that he had laboured so long to advance.[3]

Pierce's faith soon proved to be sadly misplaced. Although the Ryerson Press was still Canada's largest publishing house at the time of his retirement in 1960, a host of grim problems emerged almost immediately. Within just a single decade, it had become painfully clear that the Ryerson Press was no longer sustainable and had to be sold to the highest bidder before its value fell even further. The public announcement of its sale to McGraw-Hill provoked a lengthy bout of national hand-wringing. Newspapers everywhere issued panicked editorials. The United Church was swamped with letters of protest – including letters from Lorne Pierce's own children. The New Democratic Party erected pickets to protest the Americanization of Canada and the use of American textbooks in Canadian schools – something Egerton Ryerson certainly knew a thing or two about. Finally, the provincial government established a Royal Commission on Book Publishing to sort out what exactly had gone wrong. But by then it was too late. The Ryerson Press had been sold, the stock liquidated, and the hallowed Ryerson imprint turned over for all time to McGraw-Hill.[4]

Historians have puzzled at length over what caused the Ryerson Press to fail so dramatically. Some argue that its editorial vision faltered after the retirement of Lorne Pierce. Others that the Press rashly overextended itself when it purchased expensive new colour printing equipment. Still others contend that enormous demographic shifts in Canada led to a decline in both the United Church and the Ryerson Press from which neither organization was ever able to recover. This unyielding focus on the end of the Ryerson Press, however, has obscured a critical question about its beginning. Why did the Methodist Book and Publishing House, as the Methodist or Wesleyan Book Room in Toronto became known after 1874, evolve to become such an important trade publisher with clear commercial, cultural, and nation-building interests in the first place? Remarkably, most of the scholarship on Methodist publishing in Canada has taken this evolution largely for granted. Although it has often been remarked that there was an undoubted tension between the religious and commercial agendas of the Methodist Book and Publishing House, and that this tension discomfited at least some Methodists, the more fundamental question is not why that tension existed, but rather why the unusual impulse to adopt a commercialist approach at the House was so strong and so enduring.[5]

This question is worth asking partly because neither John Wesley's London Book Room nor the Methodist Book Concern in the United States evolved in a similar fashion. Apart from producing a smattering of non-denominational children's literature in the nineteenth century, the Wesleyan Book Room in London, as well as its trade arm Epworth Press, remained focused entirely on producing and selling books of a religious and Methodist character. Admittedly, Wesleyanism never grew to dominate the religious landscape in Britain as Methodism did in Canada, and as a result, the idea of publishing books for the nation as a whole might not have readily occurred to the London Book Room's book stewards. But Methodism was at least as dominant in the United States as it was in Canada. Indeed, by the end of the nineteenth century, about 75 per cent of the world's Methodists lived in the United States, making America the undisputed "powerhouse of world Methodism." The Methodist Book Concern in New York, meanwhile, grew to become the largest American publisher of any stripe, whether religious or commercial, by the middle of the nineteenth century. Yet, Methodists in the United States remained unwavering in their commitment to supplying primarily their own denominational market. On those very few occasions that the Concern did stray beyond those confines, the books and periodicals it offered were strictly religious in character.[6]

What was different in Canada? Why did Methodist publishing evolve in such a singular way north of the US border? For an answer, one must look back to the cultural and religious concerns of Canadian Methodists in the 1830s and 1840s – a time when they found themselves torn between their investment in and loyalty to American Methodism, on the one hand, and the political advantages closer relations with the British Wesleyans promised, on the other. Of course, Methodism in Canada, unlike Methodism in the United States, had to contend for its place in a society where the shadow of church establishment complicated its existence. This has led some historians to speculate that, because the *Christian Guardian* had been founded, in part, to agitate for equal religious rights in the colony, Methodist publishing in Canada had always been focused on achieving wide political outcomes. Yet, this ignores the fact that the New York *Christian Advocate* was itself hardly an apolitical publication – although it has at times been so mischaracterized by both British Wesleyans and later scholars. Just as the *Christian Guardian* under Egerton Ryerson repeatedly agitated for the secularization of the Clergy Reserves in Upper Canada, so too did the *Christian Advocate* take firm editorial positions on a wide range of controversial political and legislative matters, including slavery, taxation, temperance, and suffrage. Indeed, Egerton Ryerson himself argued that the *Christian Advocate* was the very model from which the *Christian Guardian* drew its editorial inspiration: "The N.Y. Ch. Advocate has always been most watchful and zealous in detecting and exposing any measures that had the least tendency towards a union of Church and State," wrote Ryerson in 1832, "and our polemic's argument from that example is like a sword."[7]

A more satisfying explanation seems to lie in the direction that the Methodist Book Room in Toronto adopted in the 1830s and 1840s in response to the final refusal by the General Conference of the Methodist Episcopal Church in the United States to compensate Canadian Methodists for their financial interest in the Methodist Book Concern. As far as John Ryerson and Anson Green were concerned, the Canadian claim against the Concern was never fully resolved. American delegates to the General Conference, however, believed that those claims had been fairly settled when they extended to Canadians an offer of steep discounts on their books and periodicals in 1836. John Ryerson and his successors were certainly determined to take advantage of those discounts, but they did so only after repudiating the Methodist Book Concern's denominational rhetoric and reframing the books and periodicals they imported to Upper Canada from the United States as nothing more than straightforward commercial goods. As a result, the stewards of the Toronto Book Room began to target potential customers from across the colony as a whole, not on the basis of any shared religious identity, but rather on the grounds that the Toronto Book Room's wares were the least expensive on the market.

The scale of the Methodist Book Concern's operation in New York guaranteed that the Toronto Book Room could reliably undercut its local competitors – particularly after 1848 when the Concern's agents agreed to supply Anson Green with books and periodicals "at cost price." Under these extremely favourable terms, Green wasted no time whatsoever on denominational appeals, arguing instead that "purchases can be made at the Wesleyan Book Room at as low a figure as any reasonable person could expect – or as any unreasonable person could make them in any establishment in the Province." As the Book Room's commercialist approach paid dividends, a new space was opened for the Methodist Book and Publishing House, and later the Ryerson Press, to begin making different sorts of claims on the identities of customers that were equally expansive – claims with the power to tell them who they were, not in the Church, but in the nation. Indeed, it is perhaps no coincidence that the undiscriminating commercialism of the Methodist Book Room in Toronto, first pioneered by John Ryerson and Anson Green, anticipated – and almost certainly helped galvanize – emergent nationalist ambitions in the wider Methodist and later United Church.[8]

By the early 1960s, however, that grand vision of the United Church's nationalist destiny was fading fast. As church attendance declined and the country's demographic composition grew steadily more diverse, it became increasingly difficult to imagine that the Church's boundaries and interests could ever be coterminous with those of the nation. Thus, the relationship between a faltering Church and its publisher would soon become for some not only awkward, but even unseemly. James Taylor, a managing editor with the Ryerson Press, confirmed as much when he argued, in 1970, "A church should not be operating a commercial business in a competitive market. For if the business makes money, the church is tainted with the practices of big business: if the business is run at cost, the church is undercutting businesses that must show profit; and if the business loses money, the church has to subsidize it from the funds donated by members for other purposes – a practice which, if continued for any extended time, might be considered fraud." How utterly discordant Taylor's argument would have sounded to the ears of John Ryerson, Anson Green, and William Briggs – all of whom, like John Dickins and his successors at the Methodist Book Concern in New York, urged their customers in various formulations and at every opportunity to "purchase no Books which we publish of any other person." Yet, by the time Taylor put pen to paper, it was clear that the Ryerson Press had not only lost its editorial vision: it had lost all vision of any rightful place in the nation's wider cultural life.[9]

Thus, John Ryerson's and Anson Green's commercialization of the Toronto Book Room seems to have been both its making and its undoing. The market for Methodist books in Upper Canada began as an extension of the Methodist Book Concern's market in the United States. Both denominational and transnational in character, that market was insulated from the offerings of rival presses by a pervasive rhetoric that tied the purchase of its books to the interests of the wider Methodist Episcopal Church in North America. When Ryerson and Green finally and fully rejected the Concern's rhetoric, but continued to rely on the Concern's discounted wares to commercially undercut their competitors in Canada, the ground was laid for both church and publisher, not necessarily in that order, to set sights on the nation as a whole. But when the United Church's own nationalist vision began to falter, just as the Concern's denominational vision had been deliberately set aside in Canada more than a century earlier, there was nothing left to take its place. Suddenly, it seemed not only incongruous but also wrong for the United Church to continue owning the Ryerson Press – regardless of the profits or losses incurred. That the balance sheet had been showing more losses than profits since Lorne Pierce's retirement may have have had less to do with the loss of that man's remarkable talents and outlook than it did with the fact that when books fail to make any sort of claim whatsoever on the identities of their purchasers, they become not only less potent as cultural status objects, but also, ultimately, less viable even as mere commercial goods.

Notes

Introduction: "Reading the Most Useful Books"

1 John Wesley, *The Works of John Wesley*, vol. 10, *The Minutes of Conference* (Nashville: Abingdon Press, 2011), 82, 340, 360, ed. Henry Rack; hereafter Wesley *Minutes of Conference* (Rack). Isabel Rivers, "John Wesley as Editor and Publisher," in *The Cambridge Companion to John Wesley*, eds. Randy L. Maddox and Jason E. Vickers (Cambridge: Cambridge University Press, 2010), 150–1; Frank Cumbers, *The Book Room: The Story of the Methodist Publishing House and Epworth Press* (London: Epworth Press, 1956), 1–10; Scott McLaren, "Brandishing Their Grey Goose Quills: The Struggle to Publish an Official Life of John Wesley, 1791–1805" *Book History* 17 (2014): 191–2.

2 Valentine Cunningham, "Daniel Defoe," in *The Blackwell Companion to the Bible in English Literature*, eds. Rebecca Lemon, Emma Mason, Jonathan Roberts, and Christopher Roland (Chichester: Blackwell, 2012), 346; Exodus 31:18; Henri-Jean Martin, *The History and Power of Writing* (Chicago: University of Chicago Press, 1994), 8, 11–12, 32–3, 74–5, 107ff; Harold Innis, *Empire and Communications* (Toronto: Dundurn Press, 2007), 33, 46; Florian Ebeling, *The Secret History of Hermes Trismegistus: Hermeticism from Ancient to Modern Times* (Ithaca: Cornell University Press, 2007), 4–7. See also Scott McLaren, "The End of Religion and the Death of the Book," *Mémoires du livre* 6, no. 2 (2015), http://id.erudit.org/iderudit/1032705ar (accessed 15 Apr. 2018).

3 Harold Bloom, *How to Read and Why* (New York: Scribner, 2000), 21; John Wesley, *A Concise Ecclesiastical History, from the Birth of Christ to the Beginning of the Present Century, in Four Volumes* (London: J. Paramore, 1781), 4:169ff. See also William Bowman, *The Imposture of Methodism Display'd* (London: Joseph Lord, 1740); George Lavington, *The Enthusiasm of Methodists and Papists Compared* (London: J. and P. Knapton, 1754); John

Free, *A Display of the Bad Principles of the Methodists* (London: Printed for the author and sold by Mr Sanby [*sic*], Mr J. Scott, and Mr Cook, 1759); Richard Challoner, *A Caveat against the Methodists* (London: M. Cooper, 1760).

4 Vicki Tolar Burton, *Spiritual Literacy in John Wesley's Methodism: Reading, Writing, and Speaking to Believe* (Waco, TX: Baylor University Press, 2008), 13; Richard Heitzenrater, *Wesley and the People Called Methodists*, 2nd ed. (Nashville, TN: Abingdon Press, 2013), 41, 46–8, 58–73; Geordan Hammond, *John Wesley in America: Restoring Primitive Christianity* (Oxford: Oxford University Press, 2014), 104; Mark A. Noll, *The Rise of Evangelicalism: The Age of Edwards, Whitefield, and the Wesleys* (Downers Grove, IL: InterVarsity Press, 2010), 96–8.

5 Bloom, *How to Read and Why*, 21; John Wesley, *The Letters of John Wesley*, ed. John Telford (London: Epworth Press, 1960), 8:247, hereafter Wesley, *Letters* (Telford); Wesley, *Minutes of Conference* (Rack), 82, 340, 360.

6 John Wesley, *The Complete English Dictionary, Explaining those Hard Words, Which Are Found in the Best English Writers* (London: W. Strahan, 1753); John Strachan, *Documents and Opinions: A Selection*, ed. John L.H. Henderson (Toronto: McClelland and Stewart, 1969), 92; hereafter Strachan, *Documents and Opinions* (Henderson). Nathan O. Hatch, *The Democratization of American Christianity* (New Haven, CT: Yale University Press, 1989), 204.

7 S. Olin, "Letter to the Editor," *Christian Advocate*, 25 Mar. 1836, 123.

8 James Green, "The Rise of Book Publishing," in *An Extensive Republic: Print, Culture, and Society in the New Nation, 1790–1840*, eds. Robert Gross and Mary Kelley (Chapel Hill, NC: University of North Carolina Press, 2010), 94–7.

9 Hatch, *Democratization*, 127, 142; David Paul Nord, *Faith in Reading: Religious Publishing and the Birth of the Mass Media in America* (Oxford: Oxford University Press, 2004), 6–7.

10 Leslie Howsam, "The Nineteenth-Century Bible Society and 'The Evil of Gratuitous Distribution,'" in *Free Print and Non-Commercial Publishing since 1700*, ed. James Raved (London: Ashgate, 2000), 119–34.

11 Scott McLaren, "'May I Print Any of Your Books?' John Wesley and the Rise of Methodist Publishing in America," *Papers of the Canadian Society of Church History* (2016): 136–9.

12 Neil Semple, *The Lord's Dominion: The History of Canadian Methodism* (Montreal: McGill-Queen's University Press, 1996), 42; John Webster Grant, *A Profusion of Spires: Religion in Nineteenth-Century Ontario* (Toronto: University of Toronto Press, 1988), 63–4; George Sheppard, *Plunder, Profit, and Paroles: A Social History of the War of 1812 in Upper Canada* (Montreal: McGill-Queen's University Press, 1994), 25; William Westfall, *Two Worlds: The Protestant Culture of Nineteenth-Century Ontario*

(Montreal: McGill-Queen's University Press, 1990), 21–8; David Mills, *The Idea of Loyalty in Upper Canada, 1784–1850* (Montreal: McGill-Queen's University Press, 1988), 52.

13 Semple, *Lord's Dominion*, 50–1, 70–1.

14 Elizabeth Cooper, "Religion, Politics, and Money: The Methodist Union of 1832–1833," *Ontario History* 81 (1989): 94, 102; Todd Webb, "How the Canadian Methodists Became British: Unity, Schism, and Transatlantic Identity, 1827–54," in *Transatlantic Subjects: Ideas, Institutions, and Social Experience in Post-Revolutionary British North America*, ed. Nancy Christie (Montreal: McGill-Queen's University Press, 2008), 165–6; Egerton Ryerson, *Canadian Methodism: Its Epochs and Characteristics* (Toronto: W. Briggs, 1882), 304.

15 Goldwin S. French, *Parsons & Politics: The Rôle of Wesleyan Methodists in Upper Canada and the Maritimes from 1780 to 1855* (Toronto: Ryerson Press, 1962), 254.

1 "What a Boon Were These Publications": Buying and Selling Methodist Books in Early Upper Canada

1 Abel Stevens, *The Life and Times of Nathan Bangs* (New York: Carlton & Porter, 1863), 17, 21–2.

2 Ibid., 29.

3 Ibid., 37, 39. See also Seth Crowell, *The Journal of Seth Crowell: Containing an Account of His Travels as a Methodist Preacher for Twelve Years* (New York: Printed by J.C. Totten, 1813), 25–8.

4 Stevens, *Bangs*, 40–3.

5 Ibid., 44; Nathan Bangs, *Christian Advocate*, 4 May 1854, 72.

6 Methodist Episcopal Church, *Journals of the General Conference of the Methodist Episcopal Church* (New York: Carleton & Phillips, 1855), 1:45; hereafter *Journals* (MEC). Richard Landon, "Robert Addison's Library," in *History of the Book in Canada*, vol. 1, *Beginnings to 1840*, eds. Patricia Lockhart Fleming, Gilles Gallichan, and Yvan Lamonde (Toronto: University of Toronto Press, 2004), 1:211–12; hereafter *History of the Book in Canada* (Fleming). Stevens, *Bangs*, 37.

7 Methodist Episcopal Church, *Doctrines and Disciplines of the Methodist Episcopal Church in America* (Philadelphia: Printed by Jenry Tuckniss and sold by John Dickins, 1798); Methodist Episcopal Church, *Minutes of the Methodist Conferences, Annually Held in America: From 1773 to 1794, Inclusive* (Philadelphia: Printed by Henry Tuckniss and sold by John Dickins, 1795); John Fletcher, *The Works of the Rev. John Fletcher* (Philadelphia: Printed by Joseph Crukshank and sold by John Dickins, 1791); Thomas Coke and Henry Moore, *The Life of the Rev. John Wesley: A.M. Including an Account of*

the Great Revival of Religion, in Europe and America, of Which He Was the First and Chief Instrument (London: G. Paramore, 1792); John Wesley, *Sermons on Several Occasions: In Four Volumes* (Philadelphia: Printed by J. Crukshank and sold by John Dickins, 1801); John Wesley, *An Extract of the Rev. Mr John Wesley's Journals* (Philadelphia: Printed by Henry Tuckniss and sold by John Dickins, 1795).

8 Joseph Alleine and Richard Baxter, *The Solemn Warning of the Dead: Or, an Admonition to Unconverted Sinners and a Call to the Unconverted* (New York: Printed by John C. Totten for the Methodist Episcopal Church, 1804), 81; Jeffrey Meyers, *Samuel Johnson: The Struggle* (New York: Basic Books, 2008), 43.

9 Stevens, *Bangs*, 51–65. See also Mark Noll, *America's God: From Jonathan Edwards to Abraham Lincoln* (Oxford: Oxford University Press, 2002), 349; George Rawlyk, *The Canada Fire: Radical Evangelicalism in British North America, 1775–1812* (Montreal: McGill-Queen's University Press, 1994), 106.

10 Stevens, *Bangs*, 13, 131–52, 236–43, 263–4, 325.

11 Nancy Christie, "'In These Times of Democratic Rage and Delusion': Popular Religion and the Challenge to the Established Order, 1760–1815," in *The Canadian Protestant Experience, 1760–1990*, ed. George Rawlyk (Montreal: McGill-Queen's University Press, 1993), 28–9; George Rawlyk, *The Canada Fire: Radical Evangelicalism in British North America, 1775–1812* (Montreal: McGill-Queen's University Press, 1994), 117–18; George Parker, *The Beginnings of the Book Trade in Canada* (Toronto: University of Toronto Press, 1985), 19–20; Janet Friskney, "Christian Faith in Print," in *History of the Book in Canada* (Fleming), 1:139.

12 Burton, *Spiritual Literacy*, 13, 77–81, 247–61; Henry Rack, *Reasonable Enthusiast: John Wesley and the Rise of Methodism*, 3rd ed. (London: Epworth Press, 2002), 123, 346–59; John Wesley to George Holder, 8 Nov. 1790, in Wesley, *Letters* (Telford), 8:247.

13 Scott E. Casper and Joan Shelley Rubin, "The History of the Book in America," in *The Oxford Companion to the Book*, eds. Michael Suarez and H.R. Woudhuysen (Oxford: Oxford University Press, 2010), 1:425–6.

14 James Green, "English Books and Printing in the Age of Franklin," in *The Colonial Book in the Atlantic World*, eds. Hugh Amory and David D. Hall (Chapel Hill, NC: University of North Carolina Press, 2007), 270–83.

15 Wesley, *Minutes of Conference* (Rack), 374. John Wesley, *The Works of John Wesley*, vols. 18–22, *Journals and Diaries*, eds. W. Reginald Ward and Richard P. Heitzenrater (Nashville, TN: Abingdon Press, 1993), 5:47, 2:322n85; hereafter *Journals and Diaries* (Ward and Heitzenrater). Dee Andrews, *The Methodists and Revolutionary America, 1760–1800: The*

Shaping of an Evangelical Culture (Princeton, NJ: Princeton University Press, 2000), 40.

16 Jesse Lee, *A Short History of the Methodists, in the United States of America; Beginning in 1766, and Continued Till 1809: To Which Is Prefixed, a Brief Account of Their Rise in England, in the Year 1729, &c.* (Baltimore, MD: Magill and Clime, 1810), 27.

17 Wesley, *Minutes of Conference* (Rack), 190, 207, 235, 291. See also Thomas B. Shepherd, *Methodism and the Literature of the Eighteenth Century* (New York: Haskell House, 1966), 71, 253.

18 Francis Asbury, *The Journal and Letters of Francis Asbury*, 3 vols., eds. Elmer T. Clark, J. Manning Potts, and Jacob S. Payton (London: Epworth Press, 1958), 1:28; Joseph Pilmore, Frank Bateman Stanger, Frederick E. Maser, and Howard Maag, *The Journal of Joseph Pilmore, Methodist Itinerant, for the Years August 1, 1769, to January 2, 1774* (Philadelphia: Printed by Message Pub. Co. for the Historical Society of the Philadelphia Annual Conference of the United Methodist Church, 1969); John H. Wigger, *Taking Heaven by Storm: Methodism and the Rise of Popular Christianity in America* (Chicago, IL: University of Illinois Press, 1998), 78.

19 Asbury, *Journal and Letters*, 1:46, 1:164; Andrews, *Revolutionary America*, 44; John H. Wigger, *American Saint: Francis Asbury and the Methodists* (Oxford: Oxford University Press, 2009), 56, 85.

20 Asbury, *Journal and Letters*, 1:85; Lee, *Short History*, 46–7.

21 David Hempton, *Methodism: Empire of the Spirit* (New Haven, CT: Yale University Press, 2005), 58. See also Rack, *Reasonable Enthusiast*, 247; Andrews, *Revolutionary America*, 22, 25, 28, 230; Wigger, *Taking Heaven by Storm*, 179–80; Wigger, *American Saint*, 271–5, 402; Wesley, *Minutes of Conference* (Rack), 190, 207, 235, 291. See also Shepherd, *Methodism*, 71, 253.

22 Lee, *Short History*, 49.

23 James Penn Pilkington, *The Methodist Publishing House: A History* (Nashville, TN: Abingdon Press, 1968), 1:37, 1:41; Andrews, *Revolutionary America*, 48–50; David Hempton, *Methodism and Politics in British Society 1750–1850* (London: Hutchinson, 1984), 45.

24 Asbury, *Journal and Letters*, 1:326, 1:413; Wigger, *American Saint*, 114–20; Wigger, *Taking Heaven by Storm*, 23–4; Pilkington, *Methodist Publishing*, 1:49–50, 1:51–5.

25 Lee, *Short History*, 49; Methodist Episcopal Church, *Minutes of the Annual Conference of the Methodist Episcopal Church for the Years 1775–1828* (New York: T. Mason and G. Lane, 1840), 16; hereafter MEC, *Minutes … 1775–1828*. Pilkington, *Methodist Publishing*, 1:55.

26 Nathan Bangs, *A History of the Methodist Episcopal Church: Revised and Corrected*, 4 vols. (New York: Carlton & Porter, 1860), 2:67–9; Pilkington,

Methodist Publishing, 1:43; Andrews, *Revolutionary America*, 40–4, 68ff; Wigger, *American Saint*, 118, 159ff.

27 Andrews, *Revolutionary America*, 197; Wigger, *Taking Heaven by Storm*, 19; Hatch, *Democratization*, 90–1.

28 Lee, *Short History*, 129; Pilkington, *Methodist Publishing*, 1:71, 1:77; Andrews, *Revolutionary America*, 198; Robert Emory, *History of the Discipline of the Methodist Episcopal Church* (New York: Lane & Scott, 1851), 81–2.

29 Pilkington, *Methodist Publishing*, 1:95.

30 Melville Horn, ed., *Posthumous Pieces of the Reverend John William de la Fletchere* (Philadelphia, PA: Parry Hall, 1793), n.p.; original emphasis. See also Pilkington, *Methodist Publishing*, 1:102.

31 For additional examples of this rhetoric aimed directly at readers, see Lucas Endicott, "Settling the 'Printing Business': John Dickins and the Methodist Episcopal Book Concern 1789–1798," *Methodist History* 48, no. 2 (2010): 88–9.

32 *Journals* (MEC), 1:45–6; Bangs, *History*, 4:427.

33 Richard Preston, *Kingston before the War of 1812: A Collection of Documents* (Toronto: Champlain Society, 1959), 292.

34 William Warburton and Richard Hurd, *The Works of the Right Reverend William Warburton: To Which Is Prefixed a Discourse by Way of General Preface, Containing Some Account of the Life, Writings, and Character of the Author by Richard Hurd*, new ed. 12 vols. (London: Printed by Luke Hansard & Sons ... for T. Cadell and W. Davies, 1811), 7:92.

35 Semple, *Lord's Dominion*, 42; Grant, *Profusion of Spires*, 38–45; Curtis Fahey, *In His Name: The Anglican Experience in Upper Canada, 1791–1854* (Ottawa: Carleton University Press, 1991); Christopher Adamson, "God's Continent Divided: Politics and Religion in Upper Canada and the Northern and Western United States," *Comparative Studies in Society and History* 36, no. 3 (1994): 432.

36 Michael Smith, *A Geographical View of the Province of Upper Canada and Promiscuous Remarks on the Government: In Two Parts, with an Appendix: Containing a Complete Description of the Niagara Falls, and Remarks Relative to the Situation of the Inhabitants Respecting the War* (Hartford, CT: Printed for the Author by Hale & Hosmer, 1813), 63–4.

37 John Carroll, *Case and His Cotemporaries: Or, the Canadian Itinerants' Memorial: Constituting a Biographical History of Methodism in Canada, from Its Introduction into the Province, Till the Death of the Rev. Wm. Case in 1855*. 5 vols. (Toronto: S. Rose, 1867–77), 1:7–12.

38 Rawlyk, *Canada Fire*, 102; Wigger, *Taking Heaven by Storm*, 17; Smith, *Geographical View*, 61.

39 Smith, *Geographical View*, 60.

40 Nathan Bangs, *Journals and Notebook of Nathan Bangs, 1805–1806, 1817*, ed. Scott McLaren, http://www.yorku.ca/scottm/journals/1805sep27.htm
41 Bangs, *Journals*, http://www.yorku.ca/scottm/journals/1805sep29.htm
42 Fahey, *In His Name*, 94–5; Todd Webb, *Transatlantic Methodists: British Wesleyanism and the Formation of an Evangelical Culture in Nineteenth-Century Ontario and Quebec* (Montreal: McGill-Queen's University Press, 2013), 139; Anna Jameson, *Winter Studies and Summer Rambles in Canada*, 3 vols. (London: Saunders and Otley, 1838), 2:218; George Lavington, *The Enthusiasm of Methodists and Papists Compared, in Three Parts* (London: J. and P. Knapton, 1754), 23.
43 Stevens, *Bangs*, 120.
44 Carroll, *Case*, 1:25, 1:39–40, 1:95–6; Bangs, *History*, 1:74. Original emphases.
45 Patricia Lockhart Fleming, "First Printers and the Spread of the Press," in *History of the Book in Canada* (Fleming), 1:63–4.
46 Jameson, *Winter Studies*, 1:34; E. Jennifer Monaghan, *Learning to Read and Write in Colonial America* (Amherst, MA: University of Massachusetts Press, 2007), 284–5, passim.
47 Fiona Black, "Importation and Book Availability," in *History of the Book in Canada* (Fleming), 1:115.
48 Egerton Ryerson, *The Loyalists of America and Their Times: From 1620 to 1816*, 2 vols. (Toronto: W. Briggs, 1880), 2:249; Stevens, *Bangs*, 37; Carroll, *Case*, 1:28, 1:133; Bertrum MacDonald, "Print in the Backwoods," in *History of the Book in Canada* (Fleming) 1:185. Bangs makes no mention of the province's first subscription library opened in Newark in 1800. See Parker, *Book Trade*, 21.
49 Parker, *Book Trade*, 19–20; Friskney, "Christian Faith in Print," 1:139.
50 *Journals* (MEC) 1:46.
51 Stevens, *Bangs*, 64, 80, 86. James Lackington, *Memoirs: Of the First Forty-Five Years of the Life of James Lackington, the Present Bookseller in Chiswell-Street, Moorfields, London: Written by Himself: In a Series of Letters to a Friend* (London: Printed for and sold by the Author; W. Bulgin, Bristol; and All Other Booksellers, 1791).
52 Lackington, *Memoirs*, 87, 48.
53 Ibid., 176.
54 Stevens, *Bangs*, 88–91; H.F. Mathews, *Methodism and the Education of the People, 1791–1851* (London: Epworth Press, 1949), 75.
55 Methodist Episcopal Church (MEC), *Pocket Hymn-Book, Designed as a Constant Companion for the Pious* (Philadelphia, PA: Printed by Henry Tuckniss ... for Ezekiel Cooper ... Near the Methodist Church, 1802), ii; Pilkington, *Methodist Publishing*, 1:78–9.
56 Carroll, *Case*, 1:257.
57 Ibid., 1:182.

58 Ibid., 1:97–8, 89, 113, 182; Stevens, *Bangs*, 105–6. See also Nathan Bangs, *The Life of the Rev. Freeborn Garrettson*: (New York: Published by J. Emory and B. Waugh, at the Conference Office, 1829), 160.
59 Stevens, *Bangs*, 143.

2 "Rekindling the Canada Fire": Books, Periodicals, and the Revival of Methodism after the War of 1812

1 Sheppard, *Plunder*, 40ff; Jeremy Black, *The War of 1812 in the Age of Napoleon* (Norman, OK: University of Oklahoma Press, 2009), passim.
2 Carroll, *Case*, 1:24; Playter, *History*, 84, 98–100, 105, 109.
3 Brock to Liverpool, 3 Dec. 1811, 146, quoted in Sheppard, *Plunder*, 25.
4 Bangs, *History*, 2:348; Playter, *History*, 108–9; William Charles Henry Wood, ed., *Select British Documents of the Canadian War of 1812* (Toronto: Champlain Society, 1920), 1:350.
5 William Case, "Account of the Late Revivals in the Province of Upper Canada," *Methodist Magazine* 2, no. 1 (1819), 33; Carroll, *Case*, 1:261, 1:288–9; Playter, *History*, 143; George Henry Cornish, ed., *Cyclopaedia of Methodism in Canada: Containing Historical, Educational, and Statistical Information, Dating from the Beginning of the Work in the Several Provinces of the Dominion of Canada, and Extending to the Annual Conferences of 1880* (Toronto: Methodist Book and Publishing House, 1881), 31.
6 Carroll, *Case*, 1:286.
7 *Journals* (MEC), 1:172; Bangs, *History*, 1:249–50, 2:95.
8 Pilkington, *Methodist Publishing*, 149–50.
9 More direct evidence of book depositories in Upper Canada exists after the War of 1812. William Case, for example, made just these kinds of arrangements to store "the publications of the Book-Concern, in New York" in people's homes when he was presiding elder of the province. See Carroll, *Case*, 2:304.
10 N. Bethune, *Memoir of the Right Reverend John Strachan, D.D., L.L.D., First Bishop of Toronto* (Toronto: Henry Rowsell, 1870), 40–50.
11 Grant, *Profusion of Spires*, 68. See also Webb, *Transatlantic Methodists*, 52; Rawlyk, *Canada Fire*, 123; Christie, "Democratic Rage," 41–2; Semple, *Lord's Dominion*, 46; French, *Parsons & Politics*, 68; Sheppard, *Plunder*, 8–9, 189–91, 229–30; Elizabeth Jane Errington, *The Lion, the Eagle, and Upper Canada: A Developing Colonial Ideology* (Montreal: McGill-Queen's University Press, 1987), 89ff.
12 Quoted in Parker, *Beginnings*, 24. See also Michael Peterman, "Literary Cultures and Popular Reading in Upper Canada," in *History of the Book in Canada* (Fleming), 1:396.

13 Fahey, *In His Name*, passim; J. Donald Wilson, "The Pre-Ryerson Years," in *Egerton Ryerson and His Times*, eds. Neil McDonald and Alf Chaiton (Toronto: Macmillan, 1978), 29.

14 Archives of Ontario, Strachan Papers, vol. 1, 1792–1822, John Strachan to James Brow, 27 Oct. 1803; Strachan, *Documents and Opinions* (Henderson), 25; Mills, *The Idea of Loyalty*, 52; Westfall, *Two Worlds*, 21–8; John Strachan to Hargreave, 7 Mar. 1831, quoted in French, *Parsons & Politics*, 126; Sheppard, *Plunder*, 22–4, 189–90; Errington, *Lion*, 167–9.

15 Fahey, *In His Name*, 39, 89, 220; Cornish, *Cyclopaedia*, 31–2.

16 Playter, *History*, 143.

17 Semple, *Lord's Dominion*, 46; French, *Parsons & Politics*, 71.

18 *Journals* (MEC), 1:151–2; Playter, *History*, 164–7; Webb, *Transatlantic Methodists*, 50–5; quoted in French, *Parsons & Politics*, 72.

19 *Journals* (MEC), 1:215.

20 George G. Findlay and William West Holdsworth, *The History of the Wesleyan Methodist Missionary Society*, 5 vols. (London: Epworth Press, 1921), 1:387. United Church of Canada Archives (hereafter UCCA), Methodist Episcopal Church (hereafter MEC), box 1, file 1, no. 4, Enoch George to the London Methodist Missionary Society, 28 May 1821; George Peck, *Early Methodism within the Bounds of the Old Genesee Conference from 1788 to 1828, or, the First Forty Years of Wesleyan Evangelism in Northern Pennsylvania, Central and Western New York, and Canada* (New York: Carlton & Porter, 1860), 503–4.

21 C. Stuart, *The Emigrant's Guide to Upper Canada* (London: Longman, Hurst, Rees, Orme, and Brown, 1820), 227–8; William Case, "State of Religion in Upper Canada," *Methodist Magazine* 3, no. 10 (Oct. 1820), 94–6; Carroll, *Case*, 2:294–5; Playter, *History*, 193.

22 Candy Gunther Brown, *The Word in the World: Evangelical Writing, Publishing, and Reading in America, 1789–1880* (Chapel Hill, NC: University of North Carolina Press, 2004), 144–5. See also Hatch, *Democratization of American Christianity*, 125–6.

23 William Case, "Utility of the Magazine," *Methodist Magazine* 8, no. 3 (Mar. 1825), 109; Jeffery McNairn, *The Capacity to Judge: Public Opinion and Deliberative Democracy in Upper Canada, 1791–1854* (Toronto: University of Toronto Press, 2000), 28, 132, 149; John Hare and Jean-Pierre Wallot, "The Business of Printing and Publishing," in *History of the Book in Canada* (Fleming) 1:72; Scott McLaren, "Before the Christian Guardian: American Methodist Periodicals in the Upper Canadian Backwoods, 1818–1829," *Papers of the Bibliographical Society of Canada* 49, no. 2 (2011): 143–65.

24 Carroll, *Case*, 1:257.

25 *Journals* (MEC), 1:171–2.

26 Carroll, *Case*, 1:196, 2:131.

27 William Case, "Account of the Late Revivals of Religion in the Province of Upper Canada," *Methodist Magazine* (Jan. 1819), 33–8.

28 William Case, "Canada Conference," *Methodist Magazine* 7, no. 10 (Oct. 1824), 398–9.

29 Alvin Torry, *Autobiography of Rev. Alvin Torry: First Missionary to the Six Nations and the Northwestern Tribes of British North America* (Auburn: W.J. Moses, 1861), 46, 67; Stevens, *Bangs*, 110; Playter, *History*, 74; Semple, *Lord's Dominion*, 150–3; Playter, *History*, 74, 295.

30 Alvin Torry: "Grand-River Mission," *Methodist Magazine* 7, no. 10 (Jan. 1824), 33–5; "Religious and Missionary Intelligence: Grand River (U.C.) Mission," *Methodist Magazine* 8, no. 12 (Dec. 1825), 479; and "Religious and Missionary Intelligence: Grand River (U.C.) Mission," *Methodist Magazine* 8, no. 5 (May 1825), 199–201.

31 Peter Jones, *Life and Journals of Kah-Ke-Wa-Quo-N -by (Rev. Peter Jones,) Wesleyan Missionary* (Toronto: Anson Green, at the Wesleyan Printing Establishment, 1860), 38–9, 106.

32 Fitch Reed, "State of Religion in Upper Canada," *Methodist Magazine* 4, no. 9 (Sept. 1821), 351–3.

33 William Case, "Upper Canada District," *Methodist Magazine* 5, no. 5 (May 1822), 198; Fitch Reed, "Upper Canada Mission," *Methodist Magazine* 5, no. 5 (May 1822), 195.

34 Preston, *Kingston before the War of 1812*, 292; Egerton Ryerson, *Claims of the Churchmen and Dissenters of Upper Canada Brought to the Test* (Kingston: Herald Office, 1828), 43; Stevens, *Bangs*, 22; Nathan Bangs, "The Importance of Study to a Minister of the Gospel," *Methodist Magazine* (Sept. 1822), 345–7.

35 See *Methodist Magazine*: Oct. 1822, 377–82; Nov. 1822, 417–21; Dec. 1822, 454–7; Jan. 1823, 30–5; Feb. 1823, 63–7; Mar. 1823, 102–7; Apr. 1823, 141–5; May 1823, 189–96; June 1823, 216–20; July 1823, 264–7; and Aug. 1823, 302–6.

36 Wesleyan-Methodist Church in Canada (WMCC), *The Minutes of the Annual Conferences of the Wesleyan-Methodist Church in Canada, from 1824 to 1845 Inclusive: With Many Official Documents and Resolutions Not before Published: To Which Is Added the Marriage Act*, ed. Anson Green (Toronto: Published by Anson Green, 1846), 8–9; hereafter *Minutes* (WMCC). UCCA, MEC, box 1, file 1, Canada Conference Minutes (hereafter CCM), 1824–1828.

37 Nathan Bangs, *Letters to Young Ministers of the Gospel, on the Importance and Method of Study* (New York: Published by N. Bangs and J. Emory, for the Methodist Episcopal Church, at the Conference Office, 1826), iv, 197–8.; UCCA, MEC, box 1, file 1, CCM, 1824–28. Interestingly, these resolutions were excised from Anson Green's 1846 published *Minutes of the Annual Conferences*.

38 Anson Green and S.S. Nelles, *The Life and Times of the Rev. Anson Green, D.D.* (Toronto: Methodist Book Room, 1877), 25; Egerton Ryerson, *"The Story of My Life": Being Reminiscences of Sixty Years' Public Service in Canada*, eds. J. George Hodgins, S.S. Nelles, John Potts, and Henry Wright Smith (Toronto: W. Briggs, 1883), 38; Carroll, *Case*, 3:67–8; C.B. Sissons, ed., *Egerton Ryerson: His Life and Letters*, 2 vols. (Toronto: Clarke, Irwin, 1937–47), 1:575.

39 *Journals* (MEC) 1:224, 1:302; Playter, *History*, 234–6, 244; Green, *Life and Times*, 38–9; Semple, *Lord's Dominion*, 71–4; French, *Parsons & Politics*, 75–8.

40 Playter, *History*, 288; *Minutes* (WMCC), 13; Thomas Webster, *History of the Methodist Episcopal Church in Canada* (Hamilton: Printed at the Canada Christian Advocate Office, 1870); Thomas Webster, *Life of Rev. James Richardson* (Toronto: J.B. Magurn, 1876), 112; Bangs, *History*, 3:322–3; Stevens, *Bangs*, 243–4.

41 Green, *Life and Times*, 90–1; Playter, *History*, 259, 289; "Terms," *Christian Advocate* 9 Sept. 1826, 1.

42 "Revivals of Religion," *Christian Advocate*, 23 Dec. 1826, 62; "Canada Conference," *Christian Advocate*, 26 Sept. 1826, 10.

43 *Christian Advocate*, 13 June 1827, 178. See also Methodist Episcopal Church and Sunday School Union, *Hints to Aid in Forming and Conducting Sunday Schools* (New York: B. Waugh and T. Mason), 1833.

44 Grant, *Profusion of Spires*, 52, 111–12; Carroll, *Case*, 2:123–4; John Carroll, *My Boy Life: Presented in a Succession of True Stories* (Toronto: W. Briggs, 1882), 135; Playter, *History*, 195; Fitch Reed, "State of Religion in Upper Canada" *Methodist Magazine* 4, no. 9 (Sept. 1821), 351.

45 Semple, *Lord's Dominion*, 368–70; J.I. Little, *Borderland Religion: The Emergence of an English-Canadian Identity* (Toronto: University of Toronto Press, 2004), 268–9; S.D. Clark, *Church and Sect in Canada* (Toronto: University of Toronto Press, 1948), 99–100; Allan Greer, "The Sunday Schools of Upper Canada," *Ontario History* 67 (1975): 172–5.

46 Carroll, *My Boy Life*, 135; UCCA, Thomas Webster Papers, box 1, file 1, Memoirs "A Story of Early Pioneer Life in Canada West."

47 Playter, *History*, 215; British and Foreign Bible Society, *Twenty-Second Report of the British and Foreign Bible Society* (London: British and Foreign Bible Society, 1826), 56; Reed, "State of Religion in Upper Canada," 351; Case, "Upper Canada District," 198; Carroll, *My Boy Life*, 135.

48 Pilkington, *Methodist Publishing*, 158; Brown, *Word in the World*, 62; James E. Kirby, Russell E. Richey, and Kenneth E. Rowe, *The Methodists* (Westport, CT: Greenwood Press, 1996), 170–2.

49 *Journals* (MEC), 1:287; 1:295, Grant, *Profusion of Spires*, 97–8; Greer, "Sunday Schools," 175; Fahey, *In His Name*, 65; Kirby, Richey, and Rowe, *Methodists*, 181.

50 Carroll, *My Boy Life*, 158, 211, 237–8, 248, 276; Edith Firth, *The Town of York: A Collection of Documents of Early Toronto*, 2 vols. (Toronto: Champlain Society for the Government of Ontario; University of Toronto Press, 1962), 1:210n47.

51 Semple, *Lord's Dominion*, 369. "Sabbath School Books," *Christian Advocate*, 7 Apr. 1827, 123; "Sunday School in Canada," *Christian Advocate*, 13 July 1827, 178.

52 "List of Sunday School Depositories," *Christian Advocate*, 3 Aug. 1827, 190.

53 French, *Parsons & Politics*, 75–7; Semple, *Lord's Dominion*, 71ff; Ryerson, *Claims*, 19–20; Ryerson, *Canadian Methodism*, 258–60.

54 John Howison, *Sketches of Upper Canada, Domestic, Local, and Characteristic: To Which Are Added, Practical Details for the Information of Emigrants of Every Class; and Some Recollections of the United States of America* (London: G. & W.B. Whittaker, 1821), 275; Jameson, *Winter Studies*, 1:100.

55 The names of the following Upper Canadian preachers appear in Bangs's column of Book Concern correspondents between these two dates: Avah Adams (14, 21, and 28 Sept. 1827; 18 Jan. 1828), George Bissell (31 Aug. 1827), David Breakenridge (14 Sept. 1827), William Brown (7 Sept., 23 Nov., and 7 Dec. 1827), William Case (24 Aug., 5 Oct., 2, 9, and 23 Nov., and 28 Dec. 1827; 4 and 18 Jan. 1828), Sylvanus Keeler (28 Sept. 1827), Thomas Madden (4 Jan. 1828), Francis Metcalf (9 Nov. and 14 Dec. 1827; 11 Jan. 1828), George Poole (21 Dec. 1827), John Ryerson (26 Oct. 1827), James Wilson (24 Aug., 19 Oct. and 28 Dec. 1827), David Wright (2 and 30 Nov. 1827), and possibly Matthew Whiting (31 Aug. 1827).

3 "Rancorous Calumnies and Abuse": Contending for Methodism in Print

1 "Review of a Sermon, Preached by the Honourable and Reverend John Strachan," *Colonial Advocate*, 11 May 1826; Carroll, *Case*, 3:86–8; Green, *Life and Times*, 83.

2 Quoted in French, *Parsons & Politics*, 72.

3 Green, *Life and Times*, 184.

4 Christie, "Democratic Rage," 40; Fahey, *In His Name*, 25, 89ff.

5 Ryerson, *Canadian Methodism*, 141; Westfall, *Two Worlds*, 19ff; French, *Parsons & Politics*, 111; Fahey, *In His Name*, 76–6, 97; McNairn, *Capacity to Judge*, 181; Carol Wilton, *Popular Politics and Political Culture in Upper Canada, 1800–1850* (Montreal: McGill-Queen's University Press, 2000), 45.

6 Strachan, *Documents and Opinions* (Henderson), 92–3.

7 Ryerson, *Canadian Methodism*, 145, 154; Ryerson, *My Life*, 24; Sissons, *Ryerson*, 1:3.
8 Ryerson, *My Life*, 27, 32; Sissons, *Ryerson*, 1:7.
9 Carroll, *Case*, 3:110, 3:192; Ryerson, *My Life*, 27, 32.
10 Charles Lindsey, *The Life and Times of Wm. Lyon Mackenzie: With an Account of the Canadian Rebellion of 1837, and the Subsequent Frontier Disturbances, Chiefly from Unpublished Documents* (Toronto: Samuel Pike, 1863), 1:40–1.
11 Wilton, *Popular Politics*, 39; McNairn, *Capacity to Judge*, 128, 132, 149.
12 Ryerson, *Canadian Methodism*, 143.
13 Carroll, *Case*, 1:192; Joseph Sanderson, *The First Century of Methodism in Canada*, vol. 2 (Toronto: W. Briggs, 1908), 177; Bethune, *Memoir*, 49; William Lyon Mackenzie, *Sketches of Canada and the United States* (London: E. Wilson, 1833), 343.
14 Wilton, *Popular Politics*, 37–8, 152; William Kilbourn and Rosemary Kilbourn, *The Firebrand: William Lyon Mackenzie and the Rebellion in Upper Canada* (Toronto: Dundurn Press, 2008), 69.
15 McNairn, *Capacity to Judge*, 143; Wilton, *Popular Politics*, 152; Green, *Life and Times*, 113. John Strachan, *The John Strachan Letter Book: 1812–1834* ed. George Spragge (Toronto: Ontario Historical Society, 1946), 164; hereafter *Strachan Letter Book* (Spragge).
16 Ryerson, *Claims*, 26, 32, 35, 39, 40, 49.
17 Ryerson, *My Life*, 25, 27; Nathaniel Burwash and Alfred Henry Reynar, *Egerton Ryerson* (Toronto: Morang, 1909), 6.
18 Ryerson, *Claims*, 30; Strachan, *Documents and Opinions* (Henderson), 92–3.
19 Ryerson, *Claims*, 43–5.
20 Ibid., 54, 55, 83.
21 Ibid., 68–9; original emphasis.
22 Sissons, *Ryerson*, 1:69; Ryerson, *My Life*, 116; Carroll, *Case*, 3:192.
23 Bethune, *Memoir*, 125–6.
24 Ryerson, *Canadian Methodism*, 143.
25 Semple, *Lord's Dominion*, 150–3; Stevens, *Bangs*, 110; Playter, *History*, 74; Torry, *Autobiography*, 46.
26 William Case, "Religious and Missionary Intelligence," *Methodist Magazine* 5, no. 11 (Nov. 1822), 428–9, and "Upper Canada Mission," *Methodist Magazine* 6, no. 6 (June 1823), 233; Torry, *Autobiography*, 67; Carroll, *Case*, 2:403.
27 Torry, *Autobiography*, 59; Joyce Banks, "'And Not Hearers Only': Books in Native Languages," in *History of the Book in Canada* (Fleming), 1:284.
28 William Case, "Grand-River Mission, Upper-Canada," *Methodist Magazine* (Oct. 1824), 398; Semple, *Lord's Dominion*, 153; Donald B. Smith, *Sacred Feathers: The Reverend Peter Jones (Kahkewaquonaby) & the Mississauga Indians* (Toronto: University of Toronto Press, 1987), 61.

29 Torry, *Autobiography*, 158–9, 182; Smith, *Sacred Feathers*, 46.
30 Semple, *Lord's Dominion*, 155; Smith, *Sacred Feathers*, 13–6, 41–7, 64; William Case, "Methodist Indian Missions," *Christian Advocate*, 25 Nov. 1826, 46; Kyle Wyatt, "Rejoicing in This Unpronounceable Name: Peter Jones's Authorial Identity," *Papers of the Bibliographical Society of Canada* 47, no. 2 (2009): 159.
31 Webster, *History*, 202.
32 Jones, *Life and Journals*, 38–9, 106.
33 Ibid., 45–6.
34 Alvin Torry, "Grand River Mission, Upper Canada," *Methodist Magazine* (Dec. 1825), 477–80; Jones, *Life and Journals*, 46; Patricia Fleming, *Upper Canadian Imprints, 1801–1841: A Bibliography* (Toronto: University of Toronto Press, 1988), no. 254.
35 Fleming, *Imprints*, nos. 287, 297, 384.
36 Ryerson, *My Life*, 58; Playter, *History*, 292–3; Jones, *Life and Journals*, 84; Smith, *Sacred Feathers*, 99; *Christian Advocate*, 14 Apr. 1827, 127.
37 Bethune, *Memoir*, 108–10, 113; *Strachan Letter Book* (Spragge), 265; Strachan, *Documents and Opinions* (Henderson), 95–9; Errington, *Lion*, 247; Sissons, *Ryerson*, 1:81–2.
38 John Strachan, *Observations on the Provision Made for the Maintenance of a Protestant Clergy, in the Provinces of Upper and Lower Canada, under the 31st Geo. III.* (London, 1827), passim; Ryerson, *My Life*, 81; Sissons, *Ryerson*, 1:82–3, 1:219; Bethune, *Memoir*, 126; Fleming, *Imprints*, no. 402.
39 French, *Parsons & Politics*, 114, Wilton, *Popular Politics*, 45, Fahey, *In His Name*, 75–6; Sissons, *Ryerson*, 1:76; Fleming, *Imprints*, no. 396.
40 Jones, *Life and Journals*, 106, 148, 155; Fleming, *Imprints*, no. 401; *Christian Advocate*, 29 Aug. 1828, 201.
41 Playter, *History*, 234, original emphasis; Ryerson, *Canadian Methodism*, 259; Green, *Life and Times*, 148. Unfortunately, Ryan's pamphlets are no longer extant.
42 Semple, *Lord's Dominion*, 73ff.; Sissons, *Ryerson*, 1:93.
43 Green, *Life and Times*, 123, 129; Sissons, *Ryerson*, 1:85.
44 Jones, *Life and Journals*, 206; *Christian Advocate*, 27 Mar. 1829, 2.
45 Sissons, *Ryerson*, 1:105–6.
46 Jones, *Life and Journals*, 217; *Christian Advocate*, 3 July 1829, 173.
47 Jones, *Life and Journals*, 221, 225–7; Fleming, *Imprints*, no. 435.
48 McNairn, *Capacity to Judge*, 181.
49 Elizabeth Hulse, "Working in a Newspaper Office: The *Upper Canada Herald* 1829–1833," in *History of the Book in Canada* (Fleming), 1:86–8; Sissons, *Ryerson*, 1:91–2, 1:95, 1:109; Fleming, *Imprints*, no. 445.

50 Wilton, *Popular Politics*, 40; UCCA, Egerton Ryerson Papers (ERP), box 1, file 6, William Case to Egerton Ryerson, 7 Apr. 1829.
51 Green, *Life and Times*, 112.

4 "Schemes and Evils of Divisions": Denominational Identities and the Public Market for Print

1 Green, *Life and Times*, 134; original emphasis. *Christian Guardian*, 11 Sept. 1830.
2 Leslie Howsam, *Cheap Bibles: Nineteenth-Century Publishing and the British and Foreign Bible Society* (Cambridge: Cambridge University Press, 1991), 33; *Christian Advocate*, 8 Oct. 1830, 23, and 22 Oct. 1830, 31.
3 *Christian Guardian*, 17 Apr. 1830, 170–1; Patricia Fleming, "Paper Evidence in Toronto Imprints, 1798 to 1841," *Papers of the Bibliographical Society of Canada* 19, no. 1 (1980): 33.
4 *Journals* (MEC) 1:302; Playter, *History*, 236; Webster, *History*, 188–9; UCCA, MECC, CCM, 1829–32.
5 Fahey, *In His Name*, 75–6; Playter, *History*, 337–8; Smith, *Sacred Feathers*, 101; Wilton, *Popular Politics*, 45; Ryerson, *My Life*, 385; Semple, *Lord's Dominion*, 71–6.
6 *Journals* (MEC) 1:311; R. Sutton, H.B. Bascom, and George Lane, *The Methodist Church Property Case: Report of the Suit of H.B. Bascom ... [Et Al.] vs. George Lane, and Others ... in the Circuit Court, United States, for the Southern District of New York, May 17–29, 1851* (New York: Lane & Scott, 1851), 35.
7 *Journals* (MEC) 1:322, 1:338; Bangs, *History*, 3:390–1; Pilkington, *Methodist Publishing*, 211, 223.
8 Bangs, *History*, 3:391; Robert Emory, *The Life of the Rev. John Emory* (New York: George Lane, 1841), 107–8; *Journals* (MEC) 1:337–9.
9 Sutton, Bascom, and Lane, *Church Property*, 36; *Journals* (MEC) 1:407; UCCA, MEC, box 1, file 1, CCM, 1824–1828.
10 Semple, *Lord's Dominion*, 78.
11 Webster, *History*, 229.
12 UCCA, ERP, box 1, file 6, William Case to Egerton Ryerson, 7 Apr. 1829.
13 Jones, *Life and Journals*, 206, 295; Sissons, *Ryerson*, 1:102–5; Carroll, *Case*, 3:227; Green, *Life and Times*, 135; Janet Beverly Friskney, "Towards a Canadian 'Cultural Mecca': The Methodist Book and Publishing House's Pursuit of Book Publishing and Commitment to Canadian Writing, 1829–1926" (MA thesis, Trent University, Peterborough, ON, 1994), 36.
14 *Christian Guardian*, passim.
15 Sissons, *Ryerson*, 1:126–8.

16 *Christian Guardian*, 12 Dec. 1830, and 16 May 1832, 106; Fleming, *Imprints*, no. 441.
17 UCCA, MECC, box 1, file 1, Annual Conference Minutes, 1829–1832.
18 Ibid.
19 Webster, *History*, 257; French, *Parsons & Politics*, 136, 139–40.
20 Webb, *Transatlantic Methodists*, 76; French, *Parsons & Politics*, 134–5; Semple, *Lord's Dominion*, 79–80; British House of Commons, *Report from the Select Committee on the Civil Government of Canada* (London: King's Printer, 1828), 297.
21 Ryerson, *Canadian Methodism*, 299–300, 307–8; Webb, *Transatlantic Methodists*, 72–7.
22 *Journals* (MEC) 1:373, 1:369, 1:381, 1:407; Carroll, *Case*, 3:215; Bangs, *History*, 3:390–1, Emory, *Life*, 107–8.
23 Emory, *Life*, 333–4.
24 *Minutes* (WMCC), 18, 47.
25 *Journals* (MEC) 1:399.
26 Ibid., 1:400; Sutton, Bascom, and Lane, *Church Property*, 38; Bangs, *History*, 4:99.
27 John Carroll mistakenly notes the amount of the claim to have been $2,700. Carroll, *Case*, 4:5; *Journals* (MEC): 1:405; Green, *Life and Times*, 177, 315; Sutton, Bascom, and Lane, *Church Property*, 39.
28 Ryerson, *Canadian Methodism*, 309; French, *Parsons & Politics*, 137; Webb, *Transatlantic Methodists*, 165–6.
29 Ryerson, *Canadian Methodism*, 304; *Christian Guardian*, 20 June 1832, 126; UCCA, WMCC, MECC Conference Minutes, 1829–1832.
30 *Christian Guardian*, 16 May 1832, 106.
31 French, *Parsons & Politics*, 135–6; Ryerson, *Canadian Methodism*, 309; Sissons, *Ryerson*, 1:154. Original emphasis.
32 Sutton, Bascom, and Lane, *Church Property*, 39; Carroll, *Case*, 3:351–2.
33 UCCA, MEC, Journals of the New York Conference, 1800–39.
34 Carroll, *Case*, 3:352.
35 *Christian Guardian*, 27 June 1832; Webb, *Transatlantic Methodists*, 61–3, 78–9.
36 Semple, *Lord's Dominion*, 86–7.
37 Emory, *Life*, 85–110.
38 Carroll, *Case*, 3:353; French, *Parsons & Politics*, 138; Cooper, "Religion, Politics, and Money," 100–2.
39 Cooper, "Religion, Politics, and Money," 102–3; Semple, *Lord's Dominion*, 82.
40 French, *Parsons & Politics*, 165; original emphasis.
41 *Minutes* (WMCC), 50–2; Sissons, *Ryerson*, 1:154–5.
42 Green, *Life and Times*, 161; French, *Parsons & Politics*, 139.

43 Carroll, *Case*, 3:362; UCCA, WMCC, MECC Conference Minutes, 1829–32.
44 *Christian Guardian*, 29 Aug. 1832, n.p. It would have taken as long as two weeks for the *Guardian* to reach New York assuming Ryerson dispatched it immediately. In addition, type for the *Advocate* had to be set well in advance to allow enough time for printing.
45 *Christian Advocate*, 21 Sept. 1832, 15; Sutton, Bascom, and Lane, *Church Property*, 39; Green, *Life and Times*, 178.
46 Webster, *History*, 267–70, 285.
47 Sissons, *Ryerson*, 1:169–70; Carroll, *Case*, 3:367–70.
48 UCCA, ERP, box 1, file 10, Justus Williams to William Case and Egerton Ryerson.
49 French, *Parsons & Politics*, 140.
50 Sissons, *Ryerson*, 1:171, 1:175–6; Ryerson, *My Life*, 115; Carroll, *Case*, 3:362; *Christian Advocate*, 29 Mar. 1833, 124.
51 Sutton, Bascom, and Lane, *Church Property*, 39; *Minutes* (WMCC), 58–60, 63–6; French, *Parsons & Politics*, 140.
52 *Christian Advocate*, 13 Sept. 1833, 10.
53 French, *Parsons & Politics*, 138, 152; Webb, *Transatlantic Methodists*, 79; Semple, *Lord's Dominion*, 83; Cooper, "Religion, Politics, and Money," 103; Green, *Life and Times*.
54 "General Alphabetical Catalogue of Books," *Christian Advocate*, 18 Apr. 1835, 111; "A New Edition of Baxter's *Saints' Everlasting Rest*," *Christian Advocate*, 31 Mar. 1837, 127; Wesleyan Methodist Church, *Valuable Books Published by J. Mason, 14 City-Road; and Sold at 66 Paternoster Row* (London: John Mason, 1838).
55 UCCA, WMCC, Minutes of Annual Conferences, Appendix to the Conference Minutes, "The report of his mission to England." For more on the generally dim view Wesleyans and others took of the manufactured quality of American books, see Frederick Jobson, *America and American Methodism* (London: Virtue, Emmins, 1857), 31.
56 *Journals* (MEC) 1:118–19, 287, 349; Bangs, *History*, 3:265; *Minutes* (WMCC), 58.
57 Egerton Ryerson, "Impressions Made by Our Late Visit to England," *Christian Guardian*, 30 Oct. 1833; French, *Parsons & Politics*, 142–3; Semple, *Lord's Dominion*, 89–90; Wilton, *Popular Politics*, 155.
58 *Colonial Advocate*, 30 Oct. 1833; "English Affairs," *Christian Advocate*, 29 Nov. 1833, 53; Sissons, *Ryerson*, 1:193–205; French, *Parsons & Politics*, 142–4; Wilton, *Popular Politics*, 155; Webb, *Transatlantic Methodists*, 79.
59 Sissons, *Ryerson*, 1:206–12, 1:214–15, 1:217–18.
60 French, *Parsons & Politics*, 149; *Minutes* (WMCC), 75–85; Semple, *Lord's Dominion*, 86–90; Webster, *History*, 314.

5 "We Saw That All Was Gone": A Failed Claim and a Failing Union

1 Stevens, *Bangs*, 301–2.
2 Wilton, *Popular Politics*, 189–93; Mills, *Idea of Loyalty*, 107–8; Ryerson, *Canadian Methodism*, 274–80; Semple, *Lord's Dominion*, 90; French, *Parsons & Politics*, 161–2, 171.
3 *Christian Advocate*, 31 May 1833, 159; 7 June 1833, 163; and 14 June 1833, 167. *Minutes* (WMCC), 47–8.
4 *Christian Guardian*, 5 Mar. 1834, 67; original emphases.
5 French, *Parsons & Politics*, 147–9; *Minutes* (WMCC), 75; Webster, *History*, 314–23; Semple, *Lord's Dominion*, 90–2.
6 Wilton, *Popular Politics*, 144; Sissons, *Ryerson*, 1:243–4. Original emphasis.
7 *Christian Advocate*, 24 Oct. 1834, 35.
8 Carroll, *Case*, 3:475; French, *Parsons & Politics*, 151.
9 *Christian Guardian*, 19 Nov. and 17 Dec. 1834.
10 Ryerson, *My Life*, 146; Ryerson, *Canadian Methodism*, 322; French, *Parsons & Politics*, 152.
11 Sissons, *Ryerson*, 1:248; Webster, *Life*, 154–7, 179–80.
12 *Minutes* (WMCC), 109–11.
13 Carroll, *Case*, 4:2–3; French, *Parsons & Politics*, 153; Cornish, *Cyclopaedia of Methodism in Canada*, 113.
14 *Minutes* (WMCC), 110.
15 Ibid., 95; original emphases.
16 UCCA, WMCC, Minutes of Annual Conference, Appendix to Conference Minutes, "Report of the Sunday school Committee to Conference of 1834"; original emphasis. UCCA, WMCC, Minutes of Annual Conference, Appendix to Conference Minutes, "Sabbath School Report 1835."
17 John Tyson, "The Methodist National Anthem," in *Sing Them Over Again to Me: Hymns and Hymnbooks in America*, eds. Mark A. Noll and Edith Waldvogel Blumhofer (Tuscaloosa, AL: University of Alabama Press, 2006), 20–42.
18 *Minutes* (WMCC), 92; *Christian Advocate*, 10 July 1835, 42.
19 Carroll, *Case*, 4:6.
20 UCCA, ERP, box 1, file 13, S.S. Junkin to Egerton Ryerson, 20 July 1835.
21 Ibid., S.S. Junkin to Egerton Ryerson, 9 Sept. 1835, and box 1, file 14, S.S. Junkin to Egerton Ryerson, 21 Nov. 1835. Original emphasis.
22 *Christian Guardian*, 15 June 1835; Sissons, *Ryerson*, 1:254–5; French, *Parsons & Politics*, 152, 168; Semple, *Lord's Dominion*, 91–2.
23 Junkin to Ryerson, 21 Nov. 1835; Green, *Life and Times*, 192.
24 Fleming, *Imprints*, nos. 524, 645, and 832; Friskney, "Towards a Canadian Cultural Mecca,'" 82; Elizabeth Barnes, *States of Sympathy: Seduction and Democracy in the American Novel* (New York: Columbia University Press, 1997), 443.

25 It seems highly probable that the Methodist Book Concern would have published its own edition much earlier had not its New York premises been completely destroyed by fire in February 1836.
26 Carroll, *Case*, 4:68; Sissons, *Ryerson*, 1:279–81. Original emphasis.
27 Sissons, *Ryerson*, 1:286, 1:332; original emphasis.
28 Ibid., 1:333–4; Ryerson, *My Life*, 161.
29 Stevens, *Bangs*, 301–2; Bangs, *History*, 4:442ff; Richard Carwardine, "Trauma in Methodism: Property, Church Schism, and Sectional Polarization in Antebellum America," in *God and Mammon: Protestants, Money, and the Market, 1790–1860*, ed. Mark Noll, (Oxford: Oxford University Press, 2001), 195–216.
30 Pilkington, *Methodist Publishing*, 224, 237–8; "Methodist Book Concern," *Christian Advocate*, 19 Feb. 1836, 103; "Destruction of the Methodist Book Room by Fire!!," *Christian Advocate*, 29 Feb. 1836, 102.
31 "Methodist Book Concern," *Christian Advocate*, 19 Feb. 1836, 103; original emphasis.
32 *Christian Advocate*, 25 Mar. 1836, 123.
33 *Christian Advocate*, "Every Cent Will Tell," 8 Apr. 1836, 130, and 20 May 1836, 155; "Subscriptions and Donations to the Book Concern," 29 Apr. 1836, 142, and 25 Mar. 1836, 123.
34 *Christian Guardian*, 9 Mar. 1836, 71; UCCA, ERP, box 1, file 21, S.S. Junkin to Egerton Ryerson, 1 May 1836.
35 *Christian Guardian*, 6 Apr. 1836, 86.
36 Bangs, *History*, 4:227–8; Stevens, *Bangs*, 299; "Death of Bishop Emory!!," *Christian Advocate*, 25 Dec. 1835, 70; Matthew Simpson, *Cyclopaedia of Methodism: Embracing Sketches of Its Rise, Progress, and Present Condition, with Biographical Notices and Numerous Illustrations* (Philadelphia: Louis H. Everts, 1878), 577–8.
37 "General Book Concern" *Christian Advocate*, 29 Apr. 1835, 143; Webster, *History*, 324–6; *Journals* (MEC) 1:440, 1:442.
38 William Lord, "Address of the Rev. Wm. Lord to the General Conference," *Christian Advocate*, 24 June 1836, 173; UCCA, WMCC, Minutes of Annual Conference, Appendix to Conference Minutes, "Statement of the Questions on the Canada Claim."
39 See Meredith McGill, *American Literature and the Culture of Reprinting, 1834–1853* (Philadelphia, PA: University of Pennsylvania Press, 2003), 45–75, and "Copyright," in *An Extensive Republic: Print, Culture, and Society in the New Nation, 1790–1840*, eds. Robert Gross and Mary Kelley (Chapel Hill, NC: University of North Carolina Press, 2010), 198–211.
40 UCCA, WMCC, Minutes of Annual Conference, Appendix to Conference Minutes, "Report on the Book Claims"; Webster, *History*, 324.

41 *Journals* (MEC) 1:452; UCCA, WMCC, Minutes of Annual Conference, Appendix to Conference Minutes, "Report on the Book Claims."
42 Ryerson, *My Life*, 278; Stevens, *Bangs*, 259–61; UCCA, WMCC, Minutes of Annual Conference, Appendix to Conference Minutes, "Report on the Book Claims"; *Journals* (MEC) 1:416, 1:449, 1:478.
43 *Journals* (MEC) 1:461–3; Bangs, *History*, 4:236–9.
44 Ibid.
45 UCCA, WMCC, Minutes of Annual Conference, Appendix to Conference Minutes, "The Report of his [Ryerson's] Mission to England"; Brown, *Word in the World*, 240–1; *Journals* (MEC) 1:463; Bangs, *History*, 4:239.
46 UCCA, ERP, box 1, file 22, William Lord to Egerton Ryerson, 31 May 1836; Green, *Life and Times*, 207.
47 UCCA, ERP, box 1, file 26, William Lord to Egerton Ryerson, 20 Oct. 1836; UCCA, WMCC, Minutes of Annual Conference, 1833–74.
48 Carroll, *Case*, 4:5–6.
49 UCCA, WMCC, Minutes of Annual Conference, Appendix to Conference Minutes, "Report on the Book Claims."
50 "Final Adjustment of Canada Affairs," *Christian Advocate*, 29 July 1836, 195.
51 UCCA, UCC Board of Publications, box 1, file 1, Book Committee Journal of Proceedings, 15 Aug. and 17 Oct. 1836; Sissons, *Ryerson*, 1:362; *Christian Advocate*, 4 Nov. 1836; *Christian Guardian*, 23 Nov. 1836.

6 "Their Own Book Concern": A Methodist Book Market for All Upper Canadians

1 Sissons, *Ryerson*, 1:367–8; 1:376; original emphasis.
2 Webb, "How the Canadian Methodists Became British," 171; Webb, *Transatlantic Methodists*, 89–91; French, *Parsons & Politics*, 254; Westfall, *Two Worlds*, 11, 49, 52, 110; Semple, *Lord's Dominion*, 211; Grant, *Profusion of Spires*, passim.
3 *Journals* (MEC) 1:427, 2:25, 3:10–11; Green, *Life and Times*, 250–1; Ryerson, *My Life*, 269–70; Sissons, *Ryerson*, 1:543–4.
4 UCCA, UCC Board of Publications, box 1, file 1, Book Committee Journal of Proceedings, 12 June 1837. Carroll, *Case*, 4:130–1; original emphasis.
5 *Minutes* (WMCC), 153–4, 159.
6 Ibid., 157–8.
7 UCCA, UCC Board of Publications, box 1, file 1, Book Committee Journal of Proceedings, 15 Aug. and 17 Oct., 1836; UCCA, WMCC, Minutes of Annual Conference, Appendix to Conference Minutes, "Committee on the Improvement of Singing 1835"; UCCA, WMCC, Minutes of Annual Conference, 1833–74.

8 Sissons, *Ryerson*, 1.377; original emphasis.
9 *Christian Advocate*, 14 July 1837, 187, and 11 Aug. 1837, 203. Carroll, *Case*, 4:170; Banks, "Books in Native Languages," 286; Fleming, *Imprints*, no. 693.
10 French, *Parsons & Politics*, 154.
11 Carroll, *Case*, 4:172.
12 UCCA, UCC Board of Publications, box 1, file 1, Book Committee Journal of Proceedings, 15 July 1837.
13 UCCA, UCC Board of Publications, box 1, file 1, Book Committee Journal of Proceedings, Sept. 1837; *Christian Guardian*, 25 July 1838; Fleming, *Imprints*, no. 1197a.
14 *Christian Guardian*, 6 Sept. 1837, 176; original emphasis.
15 Ibid., 13 Sept. 1837, 179; original emphases.
16 UCCA, WMCC, Minutes of Annual Conference, Appendix to Conference Minutes, "Report of the Sabbath School Committee to Conference in 1842"; "Book Concern," *Christian Guardian*, 27 Sept. 1837, 187; "Book Concern New Supply of Books," *Christian Guardian*, 25 Oct. 1837, 203; Carroll, *Case*, 4:174.
17 UCCA, UCC Board of Publications, box 1, file 1, Book Committee Journal of Proceedings, 29 Nov. 1837; Sissons, *Ryerson*, 1:366.
18 Ryerson, *My Life*, 181; Sissons, *Ryerson*, 1:389–90, 1:392.
19 Sissons, *Ryerson*, 1:434; French, *Parsons & Politics*, 172.
20 French, *Parsons & Politics*, 161; Carroll, *Case*, 4:178–9.
21 Carroll, *Case*, 4:237; original emphasis.
22 UCCA, WMCC, Minutes of Annual Conference, 1833–1874; Sissons, *Ryerson*, 1:376; Semple, *Lord's Dominion*, 82, 93; French, *Parsons & Politics*, 180–1; *Christian Guardian*: 17 July 1839, 150; 24 July 1839, 154–5; and 31 July 1839, 158.
23 *Journals* (MEC) 2:25; Ryerson, *My Life*, 269–70; Sissons, *Ryerson*, 1:543–4.
24 Semple, *Lord's Dominion*, 95; Webb, *Transatlantic Methodists*, 81–3; French, *Parsons & Politics*, 187–8; Sissons, *Ryerson*, 1:549–51; *Minutes* (WMCC), 225; Ryerson, *My Life*, 272–3; *Christian Guardian*, 26 Aug. 1840, 175; Benjamin Gregory, *Side Lights on the Conflicts of Methodism during the Second Quarter of the Nineteenth Century, 1827–1852: Taken Chiefly from the Notes of the Late Rev. Joseph Fowler of the Debates in the Wesleyan Conference: A Centenary Contribution to the Constitutional History of Methodism* (London: Cassell, 1898), 291ff.
25 *Minutes* (WMCC), 245; French, *Parsons & Politics*, 31; Webb, "How the Canadian Methodists Became British," 177; "The Canadian and Wesleyan Methodists," *Western Christian Advocate*, 12 Mar. 1841, 186.
26 Ryerson, *Canadian Methodism*, 314, 430; *Christian Guardian*, 24 and 31 Mar., 7 and 14 Apr., and 12 May 1841; Sissons, *Ryerson*, 1:576–7; Ryerson, *My Life*, 230; French, *Parsons & Politics*, 222.

27 *Minutes* (WMCC), 263, 266; French, *Parsons & Politics*, 223; Ryerson, *My Life*, 301; Green, *Life and Times*, 247; Sissons, *Ryerson*, 1:580.
28 *Christian Guardian*, 25 Aug. 1841, 175.
29 *Christian Advocate*, 3 Aug. 1843, 11; 4 Oct. 1843, 31; 1 Nov. 1843, 6; and 21 May 1844, 163. Green, *Life and Times*, 267, 278.
30 *Christian Guardian*, 29 Oct. 1844, 7.
31 Ryerson, *Canadian Methodism*, 436; Webb, "How the Canadian Methodists Became British," 181–2; Semple, *Lord's Dominion*, 97.
32 Semple, *Lord's Dominion*, 98; Webb, "How the Canadian Methodists Became British," 183.
33 Egerton Ryerson, *Sir Charles Metcalfe: Defended against the Attacks of His Late Counsellors* (Toronto: Printed at the British Colonist Office, 1844); Anthony Di Mascio, *The Idea of Popular Schooling in Upper Canada: Print Culture, Public Discourse, and the Demand for Education* (Montreal: McGill-Queen's University Press, 2012), 142ff.
34 Quoted in James Love, "Cultural Survival and Social Control: The Development of a Curriculum for Upper Canada's Common Schools in 1846," *Social History* 15 (Nov. 1982): 360; George Arthur and Charles Rupert Sanderson, *The Arthur Papers: Being the Canadian Papers Mainly Confidential, Private, and Demi-Official of Sir George Arthur, in the Manuscript Collection of the Toronto Public Libraries*, 3 vols. (Toronto: Toronto Public Libraries and University of Toronto Press, 1957), 1:151–2; J. George Hodgins, ed., *Documentary History of Education in Upper Canada from the Passing of the Constitutional Act of 1791 to the Close of Rev. Dr Ryerson's Administration of the Education Department in 1876*, 28 vols. (Toronto: Warwick Bros. & Rutter, 1894–1910), 5:276–7, 6:309. Original emphases.
35 Mark McGowan, *Michael Power: The Struggle to Build the Catholic Church on the Canadian Frontier* (Montreal: McGill-Queen's University Press, 2005), 213–16; Ryerson, *My Life*, 413.
36 *Christian Guardian*, 23 June 1847, 143; Legislative Assembly, "An Act for the Better Establishment and Maintenance of Common Schools in Upper Canada," in Hodgins, *Documentary History*, 6:67. See also Susan E. Houston and Alison L. Prentice, *Schooling and Scholars in Nineteenth-Century Ontario* (Toronto: University of Toronto Press, 1991), 237; Egerton Ryerson, *Special Report on the Operations of the Common School Act of 1846*, in Hodgins, *Documentary History*, 7:110.
37 In spite of the obviously political context in which Ryerson made these controversial statements, many scholars have taken his criticism of American schoolbooks at face value. See, for example, Viola Elizabeth Parvin, *Authorization of Textbooks for the Schools of Ontario, 1846–1950* (Toronto: University of Toronto Press, 1965), 29; Paul Axelrod, *The Promise*

of Schooling: Education in Canada, 1800–1914 (Toronto: University of Toronto Press, 1997), 39; and Alison Prentice, *The School Promoters: Education and Social Class in Mid-Nineteenth Century Upper Canada* (Don Mills: Oxford University Press, 1999), 523. See also Scott McLaren, "Anti-British in Every Sense of the Word? Methodist Preachers, School Libraries, and the Problem of American Books in Upper Canada, 1820–1860," *Historical Papers of the Canadian Society of Church History* (2013): 55–76, and Sarah Brouillette, "Books of Instruction in Upper Canada and the Atlantic Colonies," in *History of the Book in Canada* (Fleming) 1:259–62.

38 *Upper Canada, Department of Public Instruction, and* Egerton Ryerson, *Annual Report of Normal, Model, and Common Schools in Upper Canada, for the Year 1848: With an Appendix* (Toronto: Rollo Campbell, 1849), 7–11; Olney's *A Practical System of Modern Geography* was first published in 1828. It and related volumes went through almost one hundred editions in the following decades. See Caryn Hannan, ed., *Connecticut Biographical Dictionary* (Hamburg, MI: State History Publications, 2008), 423; Ryerson, *Annual Report 1847*, 14.

39 *Journal of Education for Upper Canada* 6 (June 1848): 175; original emphases.

40 Ibid., 190.

41 Upper Canada, Department of Public Instruction, and Egerton Ryerson, *Annual Report of the Normal, Model and Common Schools in Upper Canada for the Year 1848: With an Appendix* (Toronto: Rollo Campbell, 1849), 30; Upper Canada, Department of Public Instruction, and Egerton Ryerson, *Annual Report of the Normal, Model and Common Schools in Upper Canada for the Year 1850: With an Appendix* (Toronto: Lovell and Gibson, 1851), 152; Hodgins, *Documentary History*, 9:35, 9:48.

42 Upper Canada, Department of Public Instruction, and Egerton Ryerson, *Annual Report of the Normal, Model and Common Schools in Upper Canada for the Year 1853: With an Appendix* (Toronto: King's Printer, 1854), 133, 145, and 189.

43 *Christian Guardian*, 7 July 1847, 152.

44 Ibid., 7 Oct. 1847, 202.

45 *Journals* (MEC) 3:50; Green, *Life and Times*, 361; Carroll, *Case*, 4:6.

46 UCCA, UCC Board of Publications, box 1, file 1, Book Committee Journal of Proceedings, 3 July 1850; Green, *Life and Times*, 334.

47 Benedict Anderson, *Imagined Communities: Reflections on the Origins and Spread of Nationalism* (London: Verso, 2006), passim.

48 Nathan Bangs, "A Visit to the Wesleyan Canada Conference," *Christian Advocate*, 4 July 1850, 107.

49 Stevens, *Bangs*, 354–62; Carroll, *Case*, 5:66–7. *Christian Advocate*, 11 July 1850, 111; 18 July 1850, 115; 1 Aug. 1850, 123; 8 Aug. 1850, 127; 22 Aug. 1850, 135.

50 Lorne Pierce, ed., *The Chronicle of a Century, 1829–1929: The Record of One Hundred Years of Progress in the Publishing Concerns of the Methodist, Presbyterian and Congregational Churches in Canada* (Toronto: United Church Publishing House, 1929), xv.

Conclusion: "Making Our Methodist Book Room a Cultural Mecca for Canada"

1 Ruth Bradley-St-Cyr, "The Downfall of the Ryerson Press" (Ph.D. dissertation, University of Ottawa, Ottawa, ON, 2014), 10–11, 199–200, 204; "A Great Teacher: The Ryerson Statue Unveiled," *Globe*, 25 May 1889, 16.
2 Friskney, "Towards a Canadian Cultural Mecca,'" 130, 137, 202.
3 Pierce, *Chronicle of a Century*, xv; Sandra Campbell, *Both Hands: A Life of Lorne Pierce of Ryerson Press* (Montreal: McGill-Queen's University Press, 2013), 179; Phyllis D. Airhart, *A Church with the Soul of a Nation: Making and Remaking the United Church of Canada* (Montreal: McGill-Queen's University Press, 2014), 4, 28; Semple, *Lord's Dominion*, 439; Webb, *Transatlantic Methodists*, 16; Friskney, "Towards a Canadian 'Cultural Mecca,'" 326.
4 Bradley-St-Cyr, "Downfall of Ryerson Press," 202–3; Ruth Panofsky, *The Literary Legacy of the Macmillan Company of Canada: Making Books and Mapping Culture* (Toronto: University of Toronto Press, 2012), 203, 214ff.
5 Campbell, *Both Hands*, 495ff; Airhart, *Soul of a Nation*, 127; John Webster Grant, "The Ryerson Press," in *The Oxford Companion to Canadian Literature*, ed. William Toye (Toronto: Oxford University Press, 1983), 722; Bradley-St-Cyr, "Downfall of Ryerson Press," 97ff.
6 Hempton, *Empire of the Spirit*, 4, 188; Hatch, *Democratization*, 204; Cumbers, *The Book Room*, 43ff; Pilkington, *Methodist Publishing*, passim.
7 Janet Beverly Friskney, "From Methodist Literary Culture to Canadian Literary Culture: The United Church Publishing House: The Ryerson Press, 1829–1970," in *Literary Cultures and the Material Book*, eds. Simon Eliot, Andrew Nash, and I.R. Willison (London: British Library, 2007), 379–80; French, *Parsons & Politics*, 140; Playter, *History*, 165–6; Egerton Ryerson, *Christian Guardian*, 6 June 1832, 118.
8 *Christian Guardian*, 6 Oct. 1847, 202; Green, *Life and Times*, 316.
9 James Taylor, letter to the editor, *Globe and Mail*, 17 Nov. 1970, 7; Bradley-St-Cyr, "Downfall of the Ryerson Press," 19; Pilkington, *Methodist Publishing*, 1:102.

Bibliography

Archives

Archives of Ontario
Strachan Papers, vol. 1, 1792–1822

United Church of Canada Archives (UCCA)
Egerton Ryerson Papers (ERP), 1824–1883
Methodist Episcopal Church (MEC) Fonds, 1800–1839
Methodist Episcopal Church in Canada (MECC) Fonds, 1828–1833, and 1835–1884
Thomas Webster Papers, 1834–1899
United Church of Canada (UCC) Board of Publications Fonds, Methodist Book Committee (MBC) Minutes and Reports, 1836–1855
Wesleyan Methodist Church (WMC) Collection, 1791–1893
Wesleyan Methodist Church in Canada (WMCC) Fonds, 1824–1874
William Case Papers, 1808–1809

United Methodist Archives, Drew University, Madison, New Jersey
Nathan Bangs Papers, 1802–1859

Newspapers and Magazines

Christian Advocate, New York, 1826–1828
Christian Advocate and Journal, New York, 1833–1865
Christian Advocate and Journal and Zion's Herald, New York, 1828–1833
Christian Guardian, York (Toronto), 1829+
Colonial Advocate, York (Toronto), 1824–1834
Journal of Education for Upper Canada, Toronto, 1848–1867
Kingston Chronicle, Kingston, 1819–1833

Methodist Magazine, New York, 1818+
Sunday School Guardian, Toronto, 1846+
Upper Canada Herald, Kingston, 1819+
Western Christian Advocate, Cincinnati, 1834+
Zion's Herald, Boston, 1823–1828

Books, Minutes, and Pamphlets

Alleine, Joseph and Richard Baxter. *The Solemn Warnings of the Dead: Or, An Admonition to Unconverted Sinners*. New-York: Printed by John C. Totten, for the Methodist Episcopal Church, and sold by Ezekiel Cooper and John Wilson, at the Book-Room, 1805.

Arthur, George, and Charles Rupert Sanderson. *The Arthur Papers: Being the Canadian Papers Mainly Confidential, Private, and Demi-Official of Sir George Arthur, in the Manuscript Collection of the Toronto Public Libraries*. 3 vols. Toronto: Toronto Public Libraries and University of Toronto Press, 1957.

Asbury, Francis. *The Journal and Letters of Francis Asbury*. 3 vols. Edited by Elmer T. Clark, J. Manning Potts, and Jacob S. Payton. London: Epworth Press, 1958.

Bangs, Nathan. *Journals and Notebook of Nathan Bangs, 1805–1806, 1817*. Edited by Scott McLaren. Accessed 15 April 2018. https://www.yorku.ca/scottm/journals/

– *Letters to Young Ministers of the Gospel, on the Importance and Method of Study*. New York: Published by N. Bangs and J. Emory, for the Methodist Episcopal Church, at the Conference Office, 1826.

– *A History of the Methodist Episcopal Church: Revised and Corrected*. 4 vols. New York: Carlton & Porter, 1860.

Bethune, N. *Memoir of the Right Reverend John Strachan, D.D., L.L.D., First Bishop of Toronto*. Toronto: H. Rowsell, 1870.

Bowman, William. *The Imposture of Methodism Display'd*. London: Joseph Lord, 1740.

British House of Commons. *Art. X. Report from the Select Committee of the House of Commons, on the Civil Government of Canada, 1828*. London: Westminster Review, 1829.

Carroll, John. *Case and His Cotemporaries: Or, the Canadian Itinerants' Memorial: Constituting a Biographical History of Methodism in Canada, from Its Introduction into the Province, Till the Death of the Rev. Wm. Case in 1855*. 5 vols. Toronto: S. Rose, 1867–1877.

– *My Boy Life: Presented in a Succession of True Stories*. Toronto: W. Briggs, 1882.

Challoner, Richard. *A Caveat against the Methodists*. London: M. Cooper, 1760.

Coke, Thomas, and Henry Moore. *The Life of the Rev. John Wesley: A.M. Including an Account of the Great Revival of Religion, in Europe and America, of Which He Was the First and Chief Instrument*. London: G. Paramore, 1792.

Cornish, George Henry, ed. *Cyclopaedia of Methodism in Canada: Containing Historical, Educational, and Statistical Information, Dating from the Beginning of the Work in the Several Provinces of the Dominion of Canada, and Extending to the Annual Conferences of 1880*. Toronto: Methodist Book and Publishing House, 1881.

Crowell, Seth. *The Journal of Seth Crowell: Containing an Account of His Travels as a Methodist Preacher for Twelve Years*. New York: Printed by J.C. Totten, 1813.

Emory, Robert. *The Life of the Rev. John Emory*. New York: George Lane, 1841.

– *History of the Discipline of the Methodist Episcopal Church*. New York: Lane & Scott, 1851.

Everett, James. *The Village Blacksmith, or, Piety and Usefulness Exemplified in a Memoir of the Life of Samuel Hick, Late of Micklefield, Yorkshire*. Toronto: Published by M. Lang for the Wesleyan Methodist Church in Canada, 1835.

Firth, Edith G., ed. *The Town of York: A Collection of Documents of Early Toronto*. 2 vols. Ontario Series 5, 8. Toronto: Champlain Society for the Government of Ontario; University of Toronto Press, 1962.

Fletcher, John. *The Works of the Rev. John Fletcher*. Philadelphia: Printed by Joseph Crukshank and sold by John Dickins, 1791.

– *Posthumous Pieces of the Reverend John William de la Fletchere*. Philadelphia: Printed by Parry Hall, and sold by John Dickins, 1793.

Free, John. *A Display of the Bad Principles of the Methodists*. London, 1759.

Garrettson, Freeborn, and Nathan Bangs. *The Life of the Rev. Freeborn Garrettson*. New-York: Published by J. Emory and B. Waugh, at the Conference Office, 1829.

Green, Anson, and S.S. Nelles. *The Life and Times of the Rev. Anson Green, D.D.* Toronto: Methodist Book Room, 1877.

Gregory, Benjamin. *Side Lights on the Conflicts of Methodism during the Second Quarter of the Nineteenth Century, 1827–1852: Taken Chiefly from the Notes of the Late Rev. Joseph Fowler of the Debates in the Wesleyan Conference: A Centenary Contribution to the Constitutional History of Methodism*. London: Cassell, 1898.

Hodgins, J. George, ed. *Documentary History of Education in Upper Canada from the Passing of the Constitutional Act of 1791 to the Close of Rev. Dr Ryerson's Administration of the Education Department in 1876*. 28 vols. Toronto: Warwick Bros. & Rutter, 1894.

Howison, John. *Sketches of Upper Canada, Domestic, Local, and Characteristic: To Which Are Added, Practical Details for the Information of Emigrants of Every Class, and Some Recollections of the United States of America*. London: G. & W.B. Whittaker, 1821.

Jameson, Anna. *Winter Studies and Summer Rambles in Canada*. 3 vols. London: Saunders and Otley, 1838.

Jobson, Frederick J. *America and American Methodism*. New York: Virtue, Emmins, 1857.

Jones, Peter. *Tracts in the Chippeway and English Comprising Seven Hymns, the Decalogue, the Lord's Prayer, the Apostle's Creed*. New York: Printed at the Conference Office, 1828.

– *Life and Journals of Kah-Ke-Wa-Quo-N -by (Rev. Peter Jones), Wesleyan Missionary*. Toronto: Anson Green, at the Wesleyan Printing Establishment, 1860.

Lackington, James. *Memoirs: Of the First Forty-Five Years of the Life of James Lackington, the Present Bookseller in Chiswell-Street, Moorfields, London: Written by Himself: In a Series of Letters to a Friend*. London: Printed for and Sold by the Author; W. Bulgin, Bristol; and All Other Booksellers, 1791.

– *The Confessions of J. Lackington: Late Bookseller, at the Temple of the Muses, in a Series of Letters to a Friend: To Which Are Added, Two Letters on the Bad Consequences of Having Daughters Educated at Boarding-Schools*, 2nd ed. London: Printed and Sold by Richard Edwards ... for the Author, 1804.

Lavington, George. *The Enthusiasm of Methodists and Papists Compared. In Three Parts*. London: J. and P. Knapton, 1754.

Law, William. *An Extract from Mr Law's Serious Call to a Holy Life*. New-York: Ezekiel Cooper & John Wilson, for the Methodist Connection, 1805.

Lee, Jesse. *A Short History of the Methodists, in the United States of America; Beginning in 1766, and Continued Till 1809: To Which Is Prefixed, a Brief Account of Their Rise in England, in the Year 1729, &c*. Baltimore, MD: Magill and Clime, 1810.

Lindsey, Charles. *The Life and Times of Wm. Lyon Mackenzie: With an Account of the Canadian Rebellion of 1837, and the Subsequent Frontier Disturbances, Chiefly from Unpublished Documents*. Toronto: Samuel Pike, 1863.

Methodist Episcopal Church. *Doctrines and Disciplines of the Methodist Episcopal Church in America*. Philadelphia: Printed by Jenry Tuckniss, Sold by John Dickins, 1798. – *Pocket Hymn-Book, Designed as a Constant Companion for the Pious*. Philadelphia: Printed by Henry Tuckniss ... for Ezekiel Cooper ... near the Methodist Church, 1802.

– *Journals of the General Conference of the Methodist Episcopal Church*. New York: Carlton & Porter, 1855.

Methodist Episcopal Church, and Sunday School Union. *Hints to Aid in Forming and Conducting Sunday Schools*. New York: B. Waugh and T. Mason, 1833.

Peck, George. *Early Methodism within the Bounds of the Old Genesee Conference from 1788 to 1828, or, the First Forty Years of Wesleyan Evangelism in Northern Pennsylvania, Central and Western New York, and Canada: Containing Sketches of Interesting Localities, Exciting Scenes, and Prominent Actors*. New York: Carlton & Porter, 1860.

Pilmore, Joseph, Frank Bateman Stanger, Frederick E. Maser, and Howard Maag. *The Journal of Joseph Pilmore, Methodist Itinerant, for the Years August*

1, 1769, to January 2, 1774. Philadelphia: Printed by Message Pub. Co. for the Historical Society of the Philadelphia Annual Conference of the United Methodist Church, 1969.

Playter, George F. *The History of Methodism in Canada: With an Account of the Rise and Progress of the Work of God among the Canadian Indian Tribes, and Occasional Notices of the Civil Affairs of the Province*. Toronto: Anson Green, 1862.

Preston, Richard A., ed. *Kingston before the War of 1812: A Collection of Documents*. Publications of the Champlain Society. Ontario Series, III. Toronto: Champlain Society, 1959.

Rowe, Elizabeth Singer. *Devout Exercises of the Heart, in Meditation et Soliloquy, Prayer and Praise*. New York: Ezekiel Cooper and John Wilson, for the Methodist Connection in the U. States, 1808.

Ryerson, Egerton. *Sir Charles Metcalfe: Defended against the Attacks of His Late Counsellors*. Toronto: Printed at the British Colonist Office, 1844.

– *The Loyalists of America and Their Times: From 1620 to 1816*. 2 vols. Toronto W. Briggs, 1880.

– *Canadian Methodism: Its Epochs and Characteristics*. Toronto: W. Briggs, 1882.

– *"The Story of My Life": Being Reminiscences of Sixty Years' Public Service in Canada*. Edited by J. George Hodgins, S.S. Nelles, John Potts, and Henry Wright Smith. Toronto: W. Briggs, 1883.

Sanderson, J.E. *The First Century of Methodism in Canada*, vol. 2. Toronto: W. Briggs, 1908.

Simpson, Matthew. *Cyclopaedia of Methodism: Embracing Sketches of Its Rise, Progress, and Present Condition, with Biographical Notices and Numerous Illustrations*. Philadelphia: Louis H. Everts, 1878.

Sissons, C.B., ed. *Egerton Ryerson: His Life and Letters*. 2 vols. Toronto: Clarke, Irwin, 1937–1947.

Smith, George. *History of Wesleyan Methodism*. 3 vols. London: Longman, Brown, Green, Longmans, and Roberts, 1857.

Smith, Michael. *A Geographical View of the Province of Upper Canada and Promiscuous Remarks on the Government: In Two Parts, with an Appendix: Containing a Complete Description of the Niagara Falls, and Remarks Relative to the Situation of the Inhabitants Respecting the War*. Hartford, CT: Printed for the Author by Hale & Hosmer, 1813.

Stevens, Abel. *The Life and Times of Nathan Bangs, D.D.* New York: Carlton & Porter, 1863.

Strachan, John. *Observations on the Provision Made for the Maintenance of a Protestant Clergy, in the Provinces of Upper and Lower Canada, under the 31st Geo. III. Cap. 31*. London, 1827.

– *The John Strachan Letter Book: 1812–1834*. Edited by George Warburton Spragge. Toronto: Ontario Historical Society, 1946.

– *Documents and Opinions: A Selection*. Edited by John H.L. Henderson. Carleton Library, No. 44. Toronto: McClelland and Stewart, 1969.

Stuart, C. *The Emigrant's Guide to Upper Canada*. London: Longman, Hurst, Rees, Orme, and Brown, 1820.

Sutton, R., H.B. Bascom, and George Lane. *The Methodist Church Property Case: Report of the Suit of H.B. Bascom ... [Et Al.] vs. George Lane, and Others ... in the Circuit Court, United States, for the Southern District of New York, May 17–29, 1851*. New York: Lane & Scott, 1851.

Torry, Alvin, and W. H. C. Hosmer. *Autobiography of Rev. Alvin Torry: First Missionary to the Six Nations and the Northwestern Tribes of British North America*. Auburn: W.J. Moses, 1861.

Upper Canada, Department of Public Instruction, and Egerton Ryerson. *Annual Report of the Normal, Model, and Common Schools, in Upper Canada, for the Year 1848: With an Appendix*. Toronto: Rollo Campbell, 1849.

– *Annual Report of the Normal, Model, and Common Schools, in Upper Canada, for the Year 1850: With an Appendix*. Toronto: Lovell and Gibson, 1851.

– *Annual Report of the Normal, Model, and Common Schools, in Upper Canada, for the Year 1853: With an Appendix*. Toronto: King's Printer, 1854.

Warburton, William, and Richard Hurd. *The Works of the Right Reverend William Warburton: To Which Is Prefixed a Discourse by Way of General Preface, Containing Some Account of the Life, Writings, and Character of the Author by Richard Hurd*. New ed. 12 vols. London: Printed by Luke Hansard & Sons ... for T. Cadell and W. Davies, 1811.

Webster, Thomas. *History of the Methodist Episcopal Church in Canada*. Hamilton: Printed at the Canada Christian Advocate Office, 1870.

– *Life of Rev. James Richardson: A Bishop of the Methodist Episcopal Church in Canada*. Toronto: J.B. Magurn, 1876.

Wesley, John. *The Complete English Dictionary, Explaining those Hard Words, Which Are Found in the Best English Writers*. London: W. Strahan, 1753.

– *A Calm Address to Our American Colonies By the Rev. Mr John Wesley*. London, 1775.

– *A Concise Ecclesiastical History, from the Birth of Christ to the Beginning of the Present Century, in Four Volumes*. London: J. Paramore, 1781.

– *Explanatory Notes upon the New Testament*. Philadelphia: Printed by Joseph Crukshank and sold by John Dickins, 1791.

– *An Extract of the Rev. Mr John Wesley's Journals*. Philadelphia: Printed by Henry Tuckniss and sold by John Dickins, 1795.

– *Sermons on Several Occasions: In Four Volumes*. Philadelphia: Printed by J. Crukshank and sold by John Dickins, 1801.

– *Letters of John Wesley*. 8 vols. Edited by John Telford. Standard ed. London: Epworth Press, 1960.

– *The Works of John Wesley*, vols. 18–24, *Journals and Diaries*. Edited by Richard P. Heitzenrater and W. Reginald Ward. 7 vols. Nashville: Abingdon Press, 1988–2003.

– *The Works of John Wesley*, vol. 10, *The Minutes of Conference*. Edited by Henry D. Rack. Nashville: Abingdon Press, 2011.

Wesleyan Methodist Church in Canada. *The Minutes of the Annual Conferences of the Wesleyan-Methodist Church in Canada, from 1824 to 1845 Inclusive: With Many Official Documents and Resolutions Not before Published: To Which Is Added the Marriage Act*. Edited by Anson Green. Toronto: Published by Anson Green, 1846.

Wesleyan Methodist Church, John Wesley, and Richard Green, eds. *Minutes of Several Conversations between the Rev. Mr Wesley, and Others: From the Year 1744, to the Year 1789*. London: Printed for the Author, and Sold at the New Chapel, City-Road, and at the Rev. Mr Wesley's Preaching-Houses in Town and Country, 1789.

– *Minutes of Several Conversations: Between the Preachers Late in Connection with the Rev. Mr Wesley*. London: Printed by G. Paramore, North-Green, Worship-Street, and sold by G. Whitfield, at the Chapel, City-Road and at All the Methodist Preaching-Houses in Town and Country, 1791.

The Whole Booke of Psalmes. New York: Stephen Daye, 1640.

Wood, William, ed. *Select British Documents of the Canadian War of 1812*. 3 vols. Publications of the Champlain Society 13–15, 17. Toronto: Champlain Society, 1920–1928.

Secondary Sources

Adamson, Christopher. "God's Continent Divided: Politics and Religion in Upper Canada and the Northern and Western United States, 1774 to 1841." *Comparative Studies in Society and History* 36, no. 3 (1994): 417–46.

Airhart, Phyllis D. *A Church with the Soul of a Nation: Making and Remaking the United Church of Canada*. McGill-Queen's Studies in the History of Religion. Series Two 67. Montreal: McGill-Queen's University Press, 2014.

Altick, Richard D. *The English Common Reader: A Social History of the Mass Reading Public, 1800–1900*. Chicago, IL: University of Chicago Press, 1957.

Anderson, Benedict R. O'G. *Imagined Communities: Reflections on the Origin and Spread of Nationalism*. Rev. ed. London: Verso, 2006.

Andrews, Dee. *The Methodists and Revolutionary America, 1760–1800: The Shaping of an Evangelical Culture*. Princeton, NJ: Princeton University Press, 2000.

Axelrod, Paul. *The Promise of Schooling: Education in Canada, 1800–1914*. Themes in Canadian Social History. Toronto: University of Toronto Press, 1997.

Banks, Joyce. "'And Not Hearers Only': Books in Native Languages." In *History of the Book in Canada*, vol. 1, *Beginnings to 1840*, edited by Patricia

Lockhart Fleming, Gilles Gallichan, and Yvan Lamonde, 278–88. Toronto: University of Toronto Press, 2004.

Barnes, Elizabeth. *States of Sympathy: Seduction and Democracy in the American Novel.* New York: Columbia University Press, 1997.

Black, Fiona A. "Importation and Book Availability." In *History of the Book in Canada*, vol. 1, *Beginnings to 1840*, edited by Patricia Lockhart Fleming, Gilles Gallichan, and Yvan Lamonde, 115–24. Toronto: University of Toronto Press, 2004.

Black, Jeremy. *The War of 1812 in the Age of Napoleon*. Campaigns and Commanders. Vol. 21. Norman, OK: University of Oklahoma Press, 2009.

Bloom, Harold. *How to Read and Why.* New York: Scribner, 2000.

Bradley-St-Cyr, Ruth. "The Downfall of the Ryerson Press." Ph.D. diss., University of Ottawa, Ottawa, ON, 2014.

Brouillette, Sarah. "Books of Instruction in Upper Canada and the Atlantic Colonies." In *History of the Book in Canada*, vol. 1, *Beginnings to 1840*, edited by Patricia Lockhart Fleming, Gilles Gallichan, and Yvan Lamonde, 259–62. Toronto: University of Toronto Press, 2004.

Brown, Candy Gunther. *The Word in the World: Evangelical Writing, Publishing, and Reading in America, 1789–1880*. Chapel Hill, NC: University of North Carolina Press, 2004.

Campbell, Sandra. *Both Hands: A Life of Lorne Pierce of Ryerson Press*. Montreal: McGill-Queen's University Press, 2013.

Carwardine, Richard. "Trauma in Methodism: Property, Church Schism, and Sectional Polarization in Antebellum America." In *God and Mammon: Protestants, Money, and the Market, 1790–1860*, edited by Mark Noll, 195–216. Oxford: Oxford University Press, 2001.

Casper, Scott, and Joan Shelley Rubin. "The History of the Book in America." In *The Oxford Companion to the Book*, edited by Michael F. Suarez and H.R. Woudhuysen, 1: 425–42. Oxford: Oxford University Press, 2010.

Christie, Nancy. "'In These Times of Democratic Rage and Delusion': Popular Religion and the Challenge to the Established Order, 1760–1815." In *The Canadian Protestant Experience*, edited by George Rawlyk, 9–47. Montreal: McGill-Queen's University Press, 1990.

Clark, Penney. "The Publishing of School Books in English." In *History of the Book in Canada*, vol. 2, *1840–1918*, edited by Yvan Lamonde. Patricia Lockhart Fleming, Fiona A. Black, 335–42. Toronto: University of Toronto Press, 2005.

Clark, S.D. *Church and Sect in Canada*. Toronto: University of Toronto Press, 1965.

Cooper, Elizabeth. "Religion, Politics, and Money: The Methodist Union of 1832–1833." *Ontario History* 81 (1989): 89–108.

Cumbers, Frank Henry. *The Book Room: The Story of the Methodist Publishing House and Epworth Press*. London: Epworth Press, 1956.

Cunningham, Valentine. "Daniel Defoe." In *The Blackwell Companion to the Bible in English Literature*, edited by Rebecca Lemon, Emma Mason, Jonathan Roberts, and Christopher Roland, 345–58. Chichester: Blackwell, 2012.

Di Mascio, Anthony. *The Idea of Popular Schooling in Upper Canada: Print Culture, Public Discourse, and the Demand for Education*. Montreal: McGill-Queen's University Press, 2012.

Ebeling, Florian. *The Secret History of Hermes Trismegistus: Hermeticism from Ancient to Modern Times*. Ithaca: Cornell University Press, 2007.

Endicott, Lucas. "Settling the 'Printing Business': John Dickins and the Methodist Episcopal Book Concern 1789–1798." *Methodist History* 48, no. 2 (2010): 81–91.

Errington, Elizabeth Jane. *The Lion, the Eagle, and Upper Canada: A Developing Colonial Ideology*. Montreal: McGill-Queen's University Press, 1987.

Fahey, Curtis. *In His Name: The Anglican Experience in Upper Canada, 1791–1854*. Carleton Library Series 163. Ottawa: Carleton University Press, 1991.

Findlay, George G., and William West Holdsworth. *The History of the Wesleyan Methodist Missionary Society*. 5 vols. London: Epworth Press, 1921–1924.

Fleming, Patricia. "Paper Evidence in Toronto Imprints, 1798 to 1841." *Papers of the Bibliographical Society of Canada* 19, no. 1 (1980): 22–37.

– *Upper Canadian Imprints, 1801–1841: A Bibliography*. Toronto, Ottawa: University of Toronto Press, Bibliothèque nationale du Canada, 1988.

– "First Printers and the Spread of the Press." In *History of the Book in Canada*, vol. 1, *Beginnings to 1840*, edited by Patricia Lockhart Fleming, Gilles Gallichan, and Yvan Lamonde, 61–9. Toronto: University of Toronto Press, 2004.

French, Goldwin S. *Parsons & Politics: The Rôle of the Wesleyan Methodists in Upper Canada and the Maritimes from 1780 to 1858*. Toronto: Ryerson Press, 1962.

Friskney, Janet Beverly. "Towards a Canadian 'Cultural Mecca': The Methodist Book and Publishing House's Pursuit of Book Publishing and Commitment to Canadian Writing, 1829–1926." MA Thesis, Trent University, Peterborough, ON, 1994.

– "Christian Faith in Print." In *History of the Book in Canada*, vol. 1, *Beginnings to 1840*, edited by Patricia Lockhart Fleming, Gilles Gallichan, and Yvan Lamonde, 138–44. Toronto: University of Toronto Press, 2004.

– "From Methodist Literary Culture to Canadian Literary Culture: The United Church Publishing House: The Ryerson Press, 1829–1970." In *Literary Cultures and the Material Book*, edited by Simon Eliot, Andrew Nash, and I. R. Willison, 379–85. British Library Studies in the History of the Book. London: British Library, 2007.

Grant, John Webster. *A Profusion of Spires: Religion in Nineteenth-Century Ontario*. Ontario Historical Studies Series. Toronto: University of Toronto Press, 1988.

Green, James. "English Books and Printing in the Age of Franklin." In *The Colonial Book in the Atlantic World*, edited by Hugh Amory and David D. Hall, 248–98. Chapel Hill, NC: University of North Carolina Press, 2007.

– "The Rise of Book Publishing." In *An Extensive Republic: Print, Culture, and Society in the New Nation, 1790–1840*, edited by Robert Gross and Mary Kelley, 75–127. Chapel Hill, NC: University of North Carolina Press, 2010.

Greer, Allan. "The Sunday Schools of Upper Canada." *Ontairo History* 67 (1975): 169–84.

Hammond, Geordan. *John Wesley in America: Restoring Primitive Christianity*. Oxford: Oxford University Press, 2014.

Hare, John, and Jean-Pierre Wallot. "The Business of Printing and Publishing." In *History of the Book in Canada*, vol. 1, *Beginnings to 1840*, edited by Patricia Lockhart Fleming, Gilles Gallichan, and Yvan Lamonde1, 71–8. Toronto: University of Toronto Press, 2004.

Hatch, Nathan O. *The Democratization of American Christianity*. New Haven, CT: Yale University Press, 1989.

Heitzenrater, Richard P. *Wesley and the People Called Methodists*. 2nd ed. Nashville, TN: Abingdon Press, 2013.

Hempton, David. *Methodism and Politics in British Society 1750–1850*. London: Hutchinson, 1984.

– *Methodism: Empire of the Spirit*. New Haven, CT: Yale University Press, 2005.

Houston, Susan E., and Alison L. Prentice. *Schooling and Scholars in Nineteenth-Century Ontario: A Project of the Ontario Historical Studies Series for the Government of Ontario*. Ontario Historical Studies Series. Toronto: University of Toronto Press, 1988.

Howsam, Leslie. *Cheap Bibles: Nineteenth-Century Publishing and the British and Foreign Bible Society*. Cambridge Studies in Publishing and Printing History. Cambridge: Cambridge University Press, 1991.

– "The Nineteenth-Century Bible Society and 'The Evil of Gratuitous Distribution.'" In *Free Print and Non-Commercial Publishing since 1700*, ed. James Raven, 119–34. London: Ashgate, 2000.

Hulse, Elizabeth. "Working in a Newspaper Office: The *Upper Canada Herald* 1829–1833." In *History of the Book in Canada*, vol. 1, *Beginnings to 1840*, edited by Patricia Lockhart Fleming, Gilles Gallichan, and Yvan Lamonde, 86–8. Toronto: University of Toronto Press, 2004.

Innis, Harold. *Empire and Communications*. Toronto: Dundurn Press, 2007.

Kilbourn, William, and Rosemary Kilbourn. *The Firebrand: William Lyon Mackenzie and the Rebellion in Upper Canada*. Toronto: Dundurn Press, 2008.

Kirby, James E., Russell E. Richey, and Kenneth E. Rowe. *The Methodists*. Denominations in America, no. 8. Westport, CT: Greenwood Press, 1996.

Landon, Richard. "Robert Addison's Library." In *History of the Book in Canada*, vol. 1, *Beginnings to 1840*, edited by Patricia Lockhart Fleming, Yvan Lamonde, and Gilles Gallichan, 211–12. Toronto: University of Toronto Press, 2004.

Little, J.I. *Borderland Religion: The Emergence of an English-Canadian Identity, 1792–1852*. Toronto: University of Toronto Press, 2004.

Love, James. "Cultural Survival and Social Control: The Development of a Curriculum for Upper Canada's Common Schools in 1846." *Social History* 15, no. 30 (1982): 357–82.

MacDonald, Bertrum. "Print in the Backwoods." In *History of the Book in Canada*, vol. 1, *Beginnings to 1840*, edited by Patricia Lockhart Fleming, Gilles Gallichan, and Yvan Lamonde, 184–7. Toronto: University of Toronto Press, 2004.

Martin, Henri Jean. *The History and Power of Writing*. Chicago: University of Chicago Press, 1994.

Mathews, H.F. *Methodism and the Education of the People, 1791–1851*. London: Epworth Press, 1949.

McGill, Meredith L. *American Literature and the Culture of Reprinting, 1834–1853*. Material Texts. Philadelphia, PA: University of Pennsylvania Press, 2003.

– "Copyright." In *An Extensive Republic: Print, Culture, and Society in the New Nation, 1790–1840*, edited by Robert Gross and Mary Kelley, 198–211. Chapel Hill, NC: University of North Carolina Press, 2010.

McGowan, Mark. *Michael Power: The Struggle to Build the Catholic Church on the Canadian Frontier*. Montreal: McGill-Queen's University Press, 2014.

McLaren, Scott. "Before the Christian Guardian: American Methodist Periodicals in the Upper Canadian Backwoods, 1818–1829." *Papers of the Bibliographical Society of Canada* 49, no. 2 (2011): 143–65.

– "Anti-British in Every Sense of the Word? Methodist Preachers, School Libraries, and the Problem of American Books in Upper Canada, 1820–1860." *Historical Papers of the Canadian Society of Church History* (2013): 55–76.

– "Brandishing Their Grey Goose Quills: The Struggle to Publish an Official Life of John Wesley, 1791–1805." *Book History* 17 (2014): 191–220.

– "The End of Religion and the Death of the Book," *Mémoires du livre* 6, no. 2 (2015). Accessed 15 April 2018. http://id.erudit.org/iderudit/1032705ar

– "'May I Print Any of Your Books?' John Wesley and the Rise of Methodist Publishing in America." *Papers of the Canadian Society of Church History* (2016): 127–44.

McNairn, Jeffrey L. *The Capacity to Judge: Public Opinion and Deliberative Democracy in Upper Canada, 1791–1854*. Toronto: University of Toronto Press, 2000.

Meyers, Jeffrey. *Samuel Johnson: The Struggle*. New York: Basic Books, 2008.

Mills, David. *The Idea of Loyalty in Upper Canada, 1784–1850*. Montreal: McGill-Queen's University Press, 1988.

Monaghan, E. Jennifer. *Learning to Read and Write in Colonial America*. Studies in Print Culture and the History of the Book. Amherst, MA; Worcester, MA: University of Massachusetts Press; American Antiquarian Society, 2005.

Noll, Mark A. *America's God: From Jonathan Edwards to Abraham Lincoln*. Oxford: Oxford University Press, 2002.

– *The Rise of Evangelicalism: The Age of Edwards, Whitefield, and the Wesleys*. History of Evangelicalism. Downers Grove, IL: InterVarsity Press, 2010.

Nord, David. *Faith in Reading: Religious Publishing and the Birth of Mass Media in America*. Religion in America Series. Oxford: Oxford University Press, 2004.

Panofsky, Ruth. *The Literary Legacy of the Macmillan Company of Canada: Making Books and Mapping Culture*. Toronto: University of Toronto Press, 2012.

Parker, George L. *The Beginnings of the Book Trade in Canada*. Toronto: University of Toronto Press, 1985.

Parvin, Viola Elizabeth. *Authorization of Textbooks for the Schools of Ontario, 1846–1950*. Toronto: Published in association with the Canadian Textbook Publishers' Institute at the University of Toronto Press, 1965.

Peterman, Michael. "Literary Cultures and Popular Reading in Upper Canada." In *History of the Book in Canada*, vol. 1, *Beginnings to 1840*, edited by Patricia Lockhart Fleming, Gilles Gallichan, and Yvan Lamonde, 395–408. Toronto: University of Toronto Press, 2004.

Pierce, Lorne, ed. *The Chronicle of a Century, 1829–1929: The Record of One Hundred Years of Progress in the Publishing Concerns of the Methodist, Presbyterian and Congregational Churches in Canada*. Toronto: United Church Publishing House, 1929.

Pilkington, James Penn. *The Methodist Publishing House: A History*. Nashville, TN: Abingdon Press, 1968.

Prentice, Alison L. *The School Promoters: Education and Social Class in Mid-Nineteenth Century Upper Canada*. Canadian Social History Series. Toronto: University of Toronto Press, 2004.

Rack, Henry D. *Reasonable Enthusiast: John Wesley and the Rise of Methodism*. 3rd ed. London: Epworth Press, 2002.

Rawlyk, George. *The Canada Fire: Radical Evangelicalism in British North America, 1775–1812*. Montreal: McGill-Queen's University Press, 1994.

Rivers, Isabel. "John Wesley as Editor and Publisher." In *The Cambridge Companion to John Wesley*, ed. Randy L. Maddox and Jason E. Vickers (Cambridge: Cambridge University Press, 2010), 150–1.

Roberts, Kyle. "Locating Popular Religion in the Evangelical Tract: The Roots and Routs of The Dairyman's Daughter." *Early American Studies* 4, no. 1 (2006): 233–70.

Semple, Neil. *The Lord's Dominion: The History of Canadian Methodism.* Montreal: McGill-Queen's University Press, 1996.

Shepherd, T.B. *Methodism and the Literature of the Eighteenth Century.* New York: Haskell House, 1966.

Sheppard, George. *Plunder, Profit, and Paroles: A Social History of the War of 1812 in Upper Canada.* Montreal: McGill-Queen's University Press, 1994.

Smith, Donald B. *Sacred Feathers: The Reverend Peter Jones (Kahkewaquonaby) & the Mississauga Indians.* Toronto: University of Toronto Press, 1987.

Smith, Karen. "Community Libraries." In *History of the Book in Canada,* vol. 1, *Beginnings to 1840,* edited by Patricia Lockhart Fleming, Gilles Gallichan, and Yvan Lamonde, 144–51. Toronto: University of Toronto Press, 2004.

Tolar Burton, Vicki. *Spiritual Literacy in John Wesley's Methodism: Reading, Writing, and Speaking to Believe.* Studies in Rhetoric and Religion 6. Waco, TX: Baylor University Press, 2008.

Tyson, John. "The Methodist National Anthem." In *Sing Them Over Again to Me: Hymns and Hymnbooks in America,* edited by Mark A. Noll and Edith Waldvogel Blumhofer, 20–42. Tuscaloosa, AL: University of Alabama Press, 2006.

Verrette, Michel. "The Spread of Literacy." In *History of the Book in Canada,* vol. 1, *Beginnings to 1840,* edited by Patricia Lockhart Fleming, Gilles Gallichan, and Yvan Lamonde, 165–72. Toronto: University of Toronto Press, 2004.

Vincent, Thomas Brewer, Sandra Alston, and Eli MacLaren. "Magazines in English." In *History of the Book in Canada,* vol. 1, *Beginnings to 1840,* edited by Patricia Lockhart Fleming, Gilles Gallichan, and Yvan Lamonde, 240–51. Toronto: University of Toronto Press, 2004.

Webb, Todd. "How the Canadian Methodist Became British: Unity, Schism, and Transatlantic Identity, 1827–54." In *Transatlantic Subjects: Ideas, Institutions, and Social Experience in Post-Revolutionary British North America,* edited by Nancy Christie, 159–98. Montreal: McGill-Queen's University Press, 2008.

– *Transatlantic Methodists: British Wesleyanism and the Formation of an Evangelical Culture in Nineteenth-Century Ontario and Quebec.* Montreal: McGill-Queen's University Press, 2014.

Westfall, William. *Two Worlds: The Protestant Culture of Nineteenth-Century Ontario.* McGill-Queen's Studies in the History of Religion 2. Montreal: McGill-Queen's University Press, 1989.

Wigger, John H. *Taking Heaven by Storm: Methodism and the Rise of Popular Christianity in America.* Urbana, IL: University of Illinois Press, 2001.

– *American Saint: Francis Asbury and the Methodists.* Oxford: Oxford University Press, 2009.

Wilson, J. Donald. "The Pre-Ryerson Years." In *Egerton Ryerson and His Times*, edited by Neil McDonald and Alf Chaiton, 19–42. Toronto: Macmillan, 1978.

Wilton, Carol. *Popular Politics and Political Culture in Upper Canada, 1800–1850*. Montreal: McGill-Queen's University Press, 2000.

Wyatt, Kyle. "Rejoicing in This Unpronounceable Name: Peter Jones's Authorial Identity." *Papers of the Bibliographical Society of Canada* 47, no. 2 (2009): 159.

Index

Studies in Book and Print Culture

General Editor: Leslie Howsam

Hazel Bell, *Indexers and Indexes in Fact and Fiction*
Heather Murray, *Come, bright Improvement! The Literary Societies of Nineteenth-Century Ontario*
Joseph A. Dane, *The Myth of Print Culture: Essays on Evidence, Textuality, and Bibliographical Method*
Christopher J. Knight, *Uncommon Readers: Denis Donoghue, Frank Kermode, George Steiner, and the Tradition of the Common Reader*
Eva Hemmungs Wirtén, *No Trespassing: Authorship, Intellectual Property Rights, and the Boundaries of Globalization*
William A. Johnson, *Bookrolls and Scribes in Oxyrhynchus*
Siân Echard and Stephen Partridge, eds, *The Book Unbound: Editing and Reading Medieval Manuscripts and Texts*
Bronwen Wilson, *The World in Venice: Print, the City, and Early Modern Identity*
Peter Stoicheff and Andrew Taylor, eds, *The Future of the Page*
Jennifer Phegley and Janet Badia, eds, *Reading Women: Literary Figures and Cultural Icons from the Victorian Age to the Present*
Elizabeth Sauer, *'Paper-contestations' and Textual Communities in England, 1640–1675*
Nick Mount, *When Canadian Literature Moved to New York*
Jonathan Earl Carlyon, *Andrés González de Barcia and the Creation of the Colonial Spanish American Library*
Leslie Howsam, *Old Books and New Histories: An Orientation to Studies in Book and Print Culture*
Deborah McGrady, *Controlling Readers: Guillaume de Machaut and His Late Medieval Audience*
David Finkelstein, ed., *Print Culture and the Blackwood Tradition*
Bart Beaty, *Unpopular Culture: Transforming the European Comic Book in the 1990s*
Elizabeth Driver, *Culinary Landmarks: A Bibliography of Canadian Cookbooks, 1825–1949*

Benjamin C. Withers, *The Illustrated Old English Hexateuch, Cotton Ms. Claudius B.iv: The Frontier of Seeing and Reading in Anglo-Saxon England*
Mary Ann Gillies, *The Professional Literary Agent in Britain, 1880–1920*
Willa Z. Silverman, *The New Bibliopolis: French Book-Collectors and the Culture of Print, 1880–1914*
Lisa Surwillo, *The Stages of Property: Copyrighting Theatre in Spain*
Dean Irvine, *Editing Modernity: Women and Little-Magazine Cultures in Canada, 1916–1956*
Janet Friskney, *New Canadian Library: The Ross-McClelland Years, 1952–1978*
Janice Cavell, *Tracing the Connected Narrative: Arctic Exploration in British Print Culture, 1818–1860*
Elspeth Jajdelska, *Silent Reading and the Birth of the Narrator*
Martyn Lyons, *Reading Culture and Writing Practices in Nineteenth-Century France*
Robert A. Davidson, *Jazz Age Barcelona*
Gail Edwards and Judith Saltman, *Picturing Canada: A History of Canadian Children's Illustrated Books and Publishing*
Miranda Remnek, ed., *The Space of the Book: Print Culture in the Russian Social Imagination*
Adam Reed, *Literature and Agency in English Fiction Reading: A Study of the Henry Williamson Society*
Bonnie Mak, *How the Page Matters*
Eli MacLaren, *Dominion and Agency: Copyright and the Structuring of the Canadian Book Trade, 1867–1918*
Ruth Panofsky, *The Literary Legacy of the Macmillan Company of Canada: Making Books and Mapping Culture*
Archie L. Dick, *The Hidden History of South Africa's Book and Reading Cultures*
Darcy Cullen, ed., *Editors, Scholars, and the Social Text*
James J. Connolly, Patrick Collier, Frank Felsenstein, Kenneth R. Hall, and Robert Hall, eds., *Print Culture Histories Beyond the Metropolis*
Kristine Kowalchuk, *Preserving on Paper: Seventeenth-Century Englishwomen's Receipt Books*
Ian Hesketh, *Victorian Jesus: J. R. Seeley, Religion, and the Cultural Significance of Anonymity*
Kirsten MacLeod, *American Little Magazines of the Fin de Siècle: Art, Protest, and Cultural Transformation*
Emily Francomano, *The Prison of Love: Romance, Translation and the Book in the Sixteenth Century*
Kirk Melnikoff, *Elizabethan Publishing and the Makings of Literary Culture*
Amy Bliss Marshall, *Magazines and the Making of Mass Culture in Japan*
Scott McLaren, *Pulpit, Press, and Politics: Methodists and the Market for Books in Upper Canada*

www.ingramcontent.com/pod-product-compliance
Lightning Source LLC
LaVergne TN
LVHW040150080826
844660LV00014B/908/J

* 9 7 8 1 4 4 2 6 4 9 2 3 1 *